Of the new crop of languages appearing on the Java Virtual Machine, Clojure might be the most compelling. Because of its time-honored roots in Lisp, compelling new features, and clever ways of mixing these features with existing Java libraries, it will expand the way you think about writing code. Stu has written a masterwork, making both new and old concepts blend together into an accessible and thought-provoking tour of this elegant language. Read the first chapter, and you will be hooked.

▶ **David Bock**
  Principal, CodeSherpas, Inc.

Stuart has charted the smoothest path yet to Clojure fluency with this well-organized and easy-to-read book. He has a knack for creating simple and effective examples that demonstrate the language's unique features and how they fit together.

▶ **Chris Houser**
  A primary Clojure contributor and clojure-contrib lib author

Not only a great reference for an exciting new language, this book establishes Clojure as a serious tool for working programmers.

▶ **Stuart Sierra**
  Author of several clojure-contrib libraries, including the test-is testing framework

Stu is passionate about finding better ways to develop software, and *Programming Clojure* shows it. This book shows rather than tells how and why Clojure can help you and, because of its tight integration with the Java platform, how you can leverage your investment in existing infrastructure and numerous Java APIs. I found the book extremely easy to read, with some of the most unique and interesting code examples in any technical book I've read.

▶ **Scott Leberknight**
  Chief architect, Near Infinity Corp.

As someone following Clojure's development closely before *Programming Clojure* was available, I was very impressed with how much I learned by reading it. Stuart's organized approach, excellent flow from introductory to more in-depth treatments, fine examples, and light spicing with humor conspire to make it both very informative and a real pleasure to read.

▶ **Stephen C. Gilardi**
Principal author of clojure.core/[require,use] and clojure.main

Clojure is a surprisingly mature and polished language, given its youth, and Stuart's book is a surprisingly mature and polished guide to such new and not yet widely charted territory. Any new language seeking to build adoption would be lucky to have such a resource so early.

▶ **Jerry Kuch**
Software architect, Purple Iguana, Inc.

Stu's approach restores the balance of programmer over language by providing both the blade to free us from Java's syntactic straitjacket and the Lisp-based chains to make the JVM do our bidding. Whether your favorite part is Stu's coverage of multimethods, his careful development of the Lancet build tool, or his alchemy-free discussion of macros, you will find that *Programming Clojure* has earned its place on the "close shelf" alongside Dybvig's *The Scheme Programming Language* and Seibel's *Practical Common Lisp*.

▶ **Jeremy J. Sydik**
Director of Research Technology Development, University of Nebraska-Lincoln Center for Instructional Innovation

In the land of multicore, functional programming, concepts are vital, and concurrent languages like Clojure are increasingly important. If you've avoided Lisp languages because of confusing syntax, take heart; Stu clearly and effectively explains this variant. Don't worry, parentheses don't bite!

▶ **Nathaniel T. Schutta**
Author, speaker, teacher

Programming Clojure

Programming Clojure

Stuart Halloway

The Pragmatic Bookshelf
Raleigh, North Carolina   Dallas, Texas

Many of the designations used by manufacturers and sellers to distinguish their products are claimed as trademarks. Where those designations appear in this book, and The Pragmatic Programmers, LLC was aware of a trademark claim, the designations have been printed in initial capital letters or in all capitals. The Pragmatic Starter Kit, The Pragmatic Programmer, Pragmatic Programming, Pragmatic Bookshelf and the linking *g* device are trademarks of The Pragmatic Programmers, LLC.

Every precaution was taken in the preparation of this book. However, the publisher assumes no responsibility for errors or omissions, or for damages that may result from the use of information (including program listings) contained herein.

Our Pragmatic courses, workshops, and other products can help you and your team create better software and have more fun. For more information, as well as the latest Pragmatic titles, please visit us at

http://www.pragprog.com

ISBN-10: 1-934356-33-6

ISBN-13: 978-1-934356-33-3

Printed on acid-free paper.

P2.0 printing, September 2009

Version: 2009-9-16

Contents

Foreword

We are drowning in complexity. Much of it is incidental—arising from the way we are solving problems, instead of the problems themselves. Object-oriented programming seems easy, but the programs it yields can often be complex webs of interconnected mutable objects. A single method call on a single object can cause a cascade of change throughout the object graph. Understanding what is going to happen when, how things got into the state they did, and how to get them back into that state in order to try to fix a bug are all very complex. Add concurrency to the mix, and it can quickly become unmanageable. We throw mock objects and test suites at our programs but too often fail to question our tools and programming models.

Functional programming offers an alternative. By emphasizing pure functions that take and return immutable values, it makes side effects the exception rather than the norm. This is only going to become more important as we face increasing concurrency in multicore architectures. Clojure is designed to make functional programming approachable and practical for commercial software developers. It recognizes the need for running on trusted infrastructure like the JVM and supporting existing investments made by customers in Java frameworks and libraries, as well as the immense practicality of doing so.

What is so thrilling about Stuart's book is the extent to which he "gets" Clojure, because the language is targeted to professional developers just like himself. He clearly has enough experience of the pain points Clojure addresses, as well as an appreciation of its pragmatic approach. This book is an enthusiastic tour of the key features of Clojure, well grounded in practical applications, with gentle introductions to what might be new concepts. I hope it inspires you to write software in Clojure that you can look back at and say, "Not only does this do the job, but it does so in a robust and simple way, and writing it was fun too!"

—Rich Hickey
  Creator of Clojure

Acknowledgments

Many people have contributed to what is good in this book. The problems and errors that remain are mine alone.

Thanks to my co-workers at Relevance for creating an atmosphere in which good ideas can grow and thrive. Clojure helps answer questions that working at Relevance has taught me to ask.

Thanks to Jay Zimmerman and all the speakers and attendees on the No Fluff, Just Stuff conference tour. I have sharpened my ideas about Clojure in conversations with you all over the United States—sometimes in the formal sessions but equally often in the hotel bar.

Thanks to the kind folks on the Clojure mailing list[1] for all their help and encouragement. Tom Ayerst, Meikel Brandmeyer, Bill Clementson, Brian Doyle, Mark Engelberg, Graham Fawcett, Steve Gilardi, Christophe Grand, Christian Vest Hansen, Rich Hickey, Mark Hoemmen, Shawn Hoover, Chris Houser, Parth Malwankar, J. McConnell, Achim Passen, Timothy Pratley, Randall Schulz, Stuart Sierra, Paul Stadig, Mark Volkmann, and many others helped with specific questions I had along the way.

Thanks to everyone at the Pragmatic Bookshelf. Thanks especially to my editor, Susannah Pfalzer, for good advice delivered on a very aggressive schedule. Thanks to Dave Thomas and Andy Hunt for creating a fun platform for writing technical books and for betting on the passions of their authors.

Thanks to all the people who posted suggestions on the book's errata page.[2] Special thanks to David Sletten for dozens of detailed, wide-ranging suggestions.

---

1. http://groups.google.com/group/clojure
2. http://www.pragprog.com/titles/shcloj/errata

Thanks to my many technical reviewers for all your comments. Craig Andera, Paul Barry, Aaron Bedra, Ola Bini, David Bock, Aaron Brooks, Tim Ewald, Andrey Fedorov, Steve Gilardi, Rich Hickey, Tom Hicks, Chris Houser, Scott Jaderholm, Scott Leberknight, Tim Riddell, Eric Rochester, Nate Schutta, Stuart Sierra, Brian Sletten, Paul Stadig, Travis Swicegood, Jeremy Sydik, and Joe Winter contributed numerous helpful suggestions.

Thanks to Rich Hickey for creating the excellent Clojure language and fostering a community around it.

Finally, thanks to my wife, Joey, and my daughters, Hattie, Harper, and Mabel Faire. You all make the sun rise.

Preface

Clojure is a dynamic programming language for the Java Virtual Machine (JVM), with a compelling combination of features:

- *Clojure is elegant.* Clojure's clean, careful design lets you write programs that get right to the essence of a problem, without a lot of clutter and ceremony.

- *Clojure is Lisp reloaded.* Clojure has the power inherent in Lisp but is not constrained by the history of Lisp.

- *Clojure is a functional language.* Data structures are immutable, and most functions are free from side effects. This makes it easier to write correct programs and to compose large programs from smaller ones.

- *Clojure simplifies concurrent programming.* Many languages build a concurrency model around locking, which is difficult to use correctly. Clojure provides several alternatives to locking: software transactional memory, agents, atoms, and dynamic variables.

- *Clojure embraces Java.* Calling from Clojure to Java is direct and fast, with no translation layer.

- *Unlike many popular dynamic languages, Clojure is fast.* Clojure is written to take advantage of the optimizations possible on modern JVMs.

Many other languages cover *some* of the features described in the previous list. My personal quest for a better JVM language included significant time spent with Ruby, Python, and JavaScript, plus less intensive exploration of Scala, Groovy, and Fan. These are all good languages, and they all simplify writing code on the Java platform.

But for me, Clojure stands out. The individual features listed earlier are powerful and interesting. Their clean synergy in Clojure is *compelling*.

We will cover all these features and more in Chapter 1, *Getting Started*, on page 1.

Who This Book Is For

Clojure is a powerful, general-purpose programming language. As such, this book is for experienced programmers looking for power and elegance. This book will be useful for anyone with experience in a modern programming language such as C#, Java, Python, or Ruby.

Clojure is built on top of the Java Virtual Machine, and it is *fast*. This book will be of particular interest to Java programmers who want the expressiveness of a dynamic language without compromising on performance.

Clojure is helping to redefine what features belong in a general-purpose language. If you program in Lisp, use a functional language such as Haskell, or write explicitly concurrent programs, you will enjoy Clojure. Clojure combines ideas from Lisp, functional programming, and concurrent programming and makes them more approachable to programmers seeing these ideas for the first time.

Clojure is part of a larger phenomenon. Languages such as Erlang, F#, Haskell, and Scala have garnered attention recently for their support of functional programming and/or their concurrency model. Enthusiasts of these languages will find much common ground with Clojure.

What Is in This Book

Chapter 1, *Getting Started*, on page 1, demonstrates Clojure's elegance as a general-purpose language, plus the functional style and concurrency model that make Clojure unique. It also walks you through installing Clojure and developing code interactively at the REPL.

Chapter 2, *Exploring Clojure*, on page 25, is a breadth-first overview of all of Clojure's core constructs. After this chapter, you will be able to read most day-to-day Clojure code.

Chapter 3, *Working with Java*, on page 59, shows you how to call Java from Clojure and call Clojure from Java. You will see how to take Clojure straight to the metal and get Java-level performance.

The next two chapters cover functional programming. Chapter 4, *Unifying Data with Sequences*, on page 91, shows how all data can be unified under the powerful sequence metaphor. Chapter 5, *Functional Programming*, on page 127, shows you how to write functional code in the same style used by the sequence library.

Chapter 6, *Concurrency*, on page 157, delves into Clojure's concurrency model. Clojure provides four powerful models for dealing with concurrency, plus all of the goodness of Java's concurrency libraries.

Chapter 7, *Macros*, on page 191, shows off Lisp's signature feature. Macros take advantage of the fact that Clojure code is data to provide metaprogramming abilities that are difficult or impossible in anything but a Lisp.

Chapter 8, *Multimethods*, on page 225, covers Clojure's answer to polymorphism. Polymorphism usually means "take the *class* of the *first* argument and dispatch a method based on that." Clojure's multimethods let you choose *any function* of *all* the arguments and dispatch based on that.

There is already a thriving Clojure community. Chapter 9, *Clojure in the Wild*, on page 247, introduces third-party libraries for automated testing, data access, and web development. You will see how to use these libraries to build Snippet, a database-backed web application for posting and reading code snippets.

At the end of most chapters there is an extended example demonstrating the ideas from that chapter in the context of a larger application: Lancet. Lancet[3] is a Clojure-based build system that works with Apache Ant. Starting from scratch, you will build a usable subset of Lancet by the end of the book.

Appendix A, on page 267, lists editor support options for Clojure, with links to setup instructions for each.

How to Read This Book

All readers should begin by reading the first two chapters in order. Pay particular attention to Section 1.1, *Why Clojure?*, on page 1, which provides an overview of Clojure's advantages.

---

3. http://github.com/stuarthalloway/lancet

Experiment continuously. Clojure provides an interactive environment where you can get immediate feedback; see Section 1.2, *Using the REPL*, on page 12 for more information.

After you read the first two chapters, skip around as you like. But read Chapter 4, *Unifying Data with Sequences*, on page 91 before you read Chapter 6, *Concurrency*, on page 157. These chapters lead you from Clojure's immutable data structures to a powerful model for writing correct concurrency programs.

As you make the move to longer code examples in the later chapters, make sure that you use an editor that does Clojure indentation for you. Appendix A, on page 267, will point you to common editor options.

For Functional Programmers

- Clojure's approach to FP strikes a balance between academic purity and the realities of execution on the current generation of JVMs. Read Chapter 5, *Functional Programming*, on page 127 carefully to understand how Clojure idioms differ from languages such as Haskell.

- The concurrency model of Clojure (Chapter 6, *Concurrency*, on page 157) provides several explicit ways to deal with side effects and state and will make FP appealing to a broader audience.

For Java/C# Programmers

- Read Chapter 2, *Exploring Clojure*, on page 25 carefully. Clojure has very little syntax (compared to Java), and we cover the ground rules fairly quickly.

- Pay close attention to macros in Chapter 7, *Macros*, on page 191. These are the most alien part of Clojure, when viewed from a Java or C# perspective.

For Lisp Programmers

- Some of Chapter 2, *Exploring Clojure*, on page 25 will be review, but read it anyway. Clojure preserves the key features of Lisp, but it breaks with Lisp tradition in several places, and they are covered here.

- Pay close attention to the lazy sequences in Chapter 5, *Functional Programming*, on page 127.

- Get an Emacs mode for Clojure that makes you happy before working through the code examples in later chapters.

For Perl/Python/Ruby Programmers

- Read Chapter 6, *Concurrency*, on page 157 carefully. Intraprocess concurrency is very important in Clojure.

- Embrace macros (Chapter 7, *Macros*, on page 191). But do not expect to easily translate metaprogramming idioms from your language into macros. Remember always that macros execute at read time, not runtime.

Notation Conventions

The following notation conventions are used throughout the book.

Literal code examples use the following font:

```
(+ 2 2)
```

The result of executing a code example is preceded by a ->:

```
(+ 2 2)
```
⇒   4

Where console output cannot easily be distinguished from code and results, it is preceded by a pipe character (|):

```
(println "hello")
| hello
```
⇒   nil

When introducing a Clojure form for the first time, I will show the grammar for the form like this:

```
(example-fn required-arg)
(example-fn optional-arg?)
(example-fn zero-or-more-arg*)
(example-fn one-or-more-arg+)
(example-fn & collection-of-variable-args)
```

The grammar is informal, using ?, *, +, and & to document different argument-passing styles, as shown previously.

Clojure code is organized into *libs* (libraries). Where examples in the book depend on a library that is not part of the Clojure core, I document that dependency with a use form:

```
(use '[lib-name :only (var-names+)])
```

This form of use brings in only the names in var-names, making each function's origin clear. For example, a commonly used function is str-join, from the clojure.contrib.str-utils library:

```
(use '[clojure.contrib.str-utils :only (str-join)])
(str-join "-" ["hello", "clojure"])
⇒   "hello-clojure"
```

Clojure returns nil from a successful call to use. For brevity, this is omitted from the example listings.

While reading the book, you will enter code in an interactive environment called the REPL. The REPL prompt looks like this:

```
user=>
```

The user before the prompt tells the namespace you are currently working in. For most of the book's examples, the current namespace is irrelevant. Where the namespace is irrelevant, I will use the following syntax for interaction with the REPL:

```
(+ 2 2)          ; input line without namespace prompt
⇒   4            ; return value
```

In those few instances where the current namespace is important, I will use this:

```
user=> (+ 2 2)   ; input line with namespace prompt
⇒   4            ; return value
```

Web Resources and Feedback

Programming Clojure's official home on the Web is the *Programming Clojure* home page[4] at the Pragmatic Bookshelf website. From there you can order electronic or paper copies of the book and download sample code. You can also offer feedback by submitting errata entries[5] or posting in the forum[6] for the book.

In addition to the book, I have written a number of articles about Clojure. These are all available under the "clojure" tag at the Relevance blog.[7]

---

4. http://www.pragprog.com/titles/shcloj/programming-clojure
5. http://www.pragprog.com/titles/shcloj/errata
6. http://forums.pragprog.com/forums/91
7. http://blog.thinkrelevance.com/tags/clojure

Downloading Sample Code

The sample code for the book is available from one of two locations:

- The *Programming Clojure* home page[8] links to the official copy of the source code and is updated to match each release of the book.

- The *Programming Clojure* git repository[9] is updated in real time. This is the latest, greatest code and may sometimes be *ahead* of the prose in the book.

Individual examples are in the examples directory, unless otherwise noted. The Lancet examples have their own separate lancet directory.

Throughout the book, listings begin with their filename, set apart from the actual code by a gray background. For example, the following listing comes from examples/preface.clj:

examples/preface.clj
```
(println "hello")
```

If you are reading the book in PDF form, you can click the little gray box preceding a code listing and download that listing directly.

With the sample code in hand, you are ready to get started. We will begin by meeting the combination of features that make Clojure unique.

---

8. http://www.pragprog.com/titles/shcloj
9. http://github.com/stuarthalloway/programming-clojure

Chapter 1

Getting Started

We will begin this chapter by briefly exploring the features that make Clojure compelling:

- Elegant, expressive code
- Lisp's powerful notion that code is data
- Easy, fast Java interoperability
- A sequence library that unifies all kinds of data
- Functional programming to encourage reusable, correct code
- Concurrency without the pain of manual lock management

This list of features acts as a road map for the rest of the book, so don't worry if you don't follow every little detail here. Each feature gets an entire chapter later.

Next, you'll dive in and build a small application. You'll also learn how to load and execute the larger examples we will use later in the book.

Finally, you will meet the Lancet sample application, a dependency-based build system that we will incrementally create over the course of the book.

1.1 Why Clojure?

Clojure feels like a general-purpose language beamed back from the near future. Its support for functional programming and software transactional memory is well beyond current practice and is well suited for multicore hardware.

At the same time, Clojure is well grounded in the past and the present. It brings together Lisp and the Java Virtual Machine. Lisp brings wisdom spanning most of the history of programming, and Java brings the robustness, extensive libraries, and tooling of the dominant platform available today.

Let's explore this powerful combination.

Clojure Is Elegant

Clojure is high signal, low noise. As a result, Clojure programs are short programs. Short programs are cheaper to build, cheaper to deploy, and cheaper to maintain.[1] This is particularly true when the programs are concise rather than merely terse. As an example, consider the following Java code, from the Apache Commons:

`snippets/isBlank.java`

```java
public class StringUtils {
  public static boolean isBlank(String str) {
    int strLen;
    if (str == null || (strLen = str.length()) == 0) {
      return true;
    }
    for (int i = 0; i < strLen; i++) {
        if ((Character.isWhitespace(str.charAt(i)) == false)) {
          return false;
        }
    }
    return true;
  }
}
```

The isBlank() method checks to see whether a string is *blank*: either empty or consisting of only whitespace. Here is a similar implementation in Clojure:

`examples/introduction.clj`

```clojure
(defn blank? [s] (every? #(Character/isWhitespace %) s))
```

The Clojure version is shorter. More important, it is *simpler*: it has no variables, no mutable state, and no branches. This is possible thanks to *higher-order functions*. A higher-order function is a function that takes functions as arguments and/or returns functions as results. The every?

---

1. *Software Estimation: Demystifying the Black Art* [McC06] is a great read and makes the case that smaller is cheaper.

function takes a function and a collection as its arguments and returns true if that function returns true for every item in the collection.

Because the Clojure version has no branches, it is easier to read and test. These benefits are magnified in larger programs. Also, while the code is concise, it is still readable. In fact, the Clojure program reads like a *definition* of blank: a string is blank if every character in it is whitespace. This is much better than the Commons method, which hides the definition of blank behind the implementation detail of loops and if statements.

As another example, consider defining a trivial Person class in Java:

snippets/Person.java
```java
public class Person {
        private String firstName;
        private String lastName;
        public Person(String firstName, String lastName) {
                this.firstName = firstName;
                this.lastName = lastName;
        }
        public String getFirstName() {
                return firstName;
        }
        public void setFirstName(String firstName) {
                this.firstName = firstName;
        }
        public String getLastName() {
                return lastName;
        }
        public void setLastName(String lastName) {
                this.lastName = lastName;
        }
}
```

In Clojure, you would define person with a single line:

```
(defstruct person :first-name :last-name)
```

defstruct and related functions are covered in Section 2.1, *Maps, Keywords, and Structs*, on page 32.

Other than being an order of magnitude shorter, the Clojure approach differs in that a Clojure person is *immutable*. Immutable data structures are naturally thread safe, and update capabilities can be layered in using Clojure's references, agents, and atoms, which are covered below in Chapter 6, *Concurrency*, on page 157. Because structures are immutable, Clojure also provides correct implementations of hashCode() and equals() automatically.

Clojure has a lot of elegance baked in, but if you find something missing, you can add it yourself, thanks to the power of Lisp.

Clojure Is Lisp Reloaded

Clojure is a Lisp. For decades, Lisp advocates have pointed out the advantages that Lisp has over, well, everything else. At the same time, Lisp's world domination plan seems to be proceeding slowly.

Like any other Lisp, Clojure faces two challenges:

- Clojure must succeed as a Lisp by persuading Lisp programmers that Clojure embraces the critical parts of Lisp.

- At the same time, Clojure needs to succeed *where past Lisps have failed* by winning support from the broader community of programmers.

Clojure meets these challenges by providing the metaprogramming capabilities of Lisp and at the same time embracing a set of syntax enhancements that make Clojure friendlier to non-Lisp programmers.

Why Lisp?

Lisps have a tiny language core, almost no syntax, and a powerful macro facility. With these features, you can bend Lisp to meet your design, instead of the other way around. By contrast, consider the following snippet of Java code:

```
public class Person {
  private String firstName;
  public String getFirstName() {
  // continues
```

In this code, getFirstName() is a method. Methods are polymorphic and can bend to meet your needs. But the interpretation of *every other word* in the example is *fixed by the language*. Sometimes you really need to change what these words mean. So for example, you might do the following:

- Redefine private to mean "private for production code but public for serialization and unit tests."

- Redefine class to automatically generate getters and setters for private fields, unless otherwise directed.

- Create a subclass of class that provides callback hooks for lifecycle events. For example, a lifecycle-aware class could fire an event whenever an instance of the class is created.

I have seen programs that needed all these features. Without them, programmers resort to repetitive, error-prone workarounds. Literally *millions* of lines of code have been written to work around missing features in programming languages.

In most languages, you would have to petition the language implementer to add the kinds of features mentioned earlier. In Clojure, you can add your own language features with *macros* (Chapter 7, *Macros*, on page 191). Clojure itself is built out of macros such as defstruct:

```
(defstruct person :first-name :last-name)
```

If you need different semantics, write your own macro. If you want a variant of structs with strong typing and configurable null-checking for all fields, you can create your own defrecord macro, to be used like this:

```
(defrecord
  person [String :first-name String :last-name]
  :allow-nulls false)
```

This ability to reprogram the language from within the language is the unique advantage of Lisp. You will see facets of this idea described in various ways:

- Lisp is homoiconic;[2] that is, Lisp code is just Lisp data. This makes it easy for programs to write other programs.
- The whole language is there, all the time. Paul Graham's essay "Revenge of the Nerds"[3] explains why this is so powerful.

Lisp syntax also eliminates rules for operator precedence and associativity. You will not find a table documenting operator precedence or associativity anywhere in this book. With fully parenthesized expressions, there is no possible ambiguity.

The downside of Lisp's simple, regular syntax, at least for beginners, is Lisp's fixation on parentheses and on lists as the core data type. Clojure offers an interesting combination of features that makes Lisp more approachable for non-Lispers.

---

2. http://en.wikipedia.org/wiki/Homoiconicity
3. http://www.paulgraham.com/icad.html

Lisp, with Fewer Parentheses

Clojure offers significant advantages for programmers coming to it from other Lisps:

- Clojure generalizes Lisp's physical list into an abstraction called a *sequence*. This preserves the power of lists, while extending that power to a variety of other data structures.

- Clojure's reliance on the JVM provides a standard library and a deployment platform with great reach.

- Clojure's approach to symbol resolution and syntax quoting makes it easier to write many common macros.

But many Clojure programmers will be new to Lisp, and they have probably heard bad things about all those parentheses. Clojure keeps the parentheses (and the power of Lisp!), but it improves on traditional Lisp syntax in several ways:

- Clojure provides a convenient literal syntax for a wide variety of data structures besides just lists: regular expressions, maps, sets, vectors, and metadata. These features make Clojure code less "listy" than most Lisps. For example, function parameters are specified in a vector: [] instead of a list: ().

  examples/introduction.clj
  ```
  (defn hello-world [username]
    (println (format "Hello, %s" username)))
  ```

  The vector makes the argument list jump out visually and makes Clojure function definitions easy to read.

- In Clojure, unlike most Lisps, commas are whitespace. Adding commas can make some data structures more readable. Consider vectors:

  ```
  ; make vectors look like arrays in other languages
  [1, 2, 3, 4]
  -> [1 2 3 4]
  ```

- Idiomatic Clojure does not nest parentheses more than necessary. Consider the cond macro, present in both Common Lisp and Clojure. cond evaluates a set of test/result pairs, returning the first result for which a test form yields true. Each test/result pair is grouped with parentheses, like so:

  ```
  ; Common Lisp cond
  (cond ((< x 10) "less")
        ((> x 10) "more"))
  ```

Clojure avoids the extra parentheses:

```
; Clojure cond
(cond (< x 10) "less"
      (> x 10) "more")
```

This is an aesthetic decision, and both approaches have their supporters. The important thing is that Clojure takes the opportunity to be less Lispy when it can do so without compromising Lisp's power.

Clojure is an excellent Lisp, both for Lisp experts and Lisp beginners.

Clojure Is a Functional Language

Clojure is a functional language, but not a pure functional language like Haskell. Functional languages have the following properties:

- Functions are *first-class objects*. That is, functions can be created at runtime, passed around, returned, and in general used like any other data type.

- Data is immutable.

- Functions are *pure*; that is, they have no side effects.

For many tasks, functional programs are easier to understand, less error-prone, and *much* easier to reuse. For example, the following short program searches a database of compositions for every composer who has written a composition named "Requiem":

```
(for [c compositions :when (= "Requiem" (:name c))] (:composer c))
⇒   ("W. A. Mozart" "Giuseppe Verdi")
```

The name for does not introduce a loop but a *list comprehension*. Read the earlier code as "For each c in compositions, where the name of c is "Requiem", yield the composer of c." List comprehension is covered more fully in Section 4.2, *Transforming Sequences*, on page 102.

This example has four desirable properties:

- It is *simple*; it has no loops, variables, or mutable state.

- It is *thread safe*; no locking is needed.

- It is *parallelizable*; you could farm individual steps out to multiple threads without changing the code for each step.

- It is *generic*; compositions could be a plain set or XML or a database result set.

Contrast functional programs with *imperative* programs, where explicit statements alter program state. Most object-oriented programs are written in an imperative style and have *none* of the advantages listed earlier; they are unnecessarily complex, not thread safe, not parallelizable, and difficult to generalize. (For a head-to-head comparison of functional and imperative styles, skip forward to Section 2.6, *Where's My for Loop?*, on page 50.)

People have known about the advantages of functional languages for a while now. And yet, pure functional languages like Haskell have not taken over the world, because developers find that not everything fits easily into the pure functional view.

There are four reasons that Clojure can attract more interest now than functional languages have in the past:

- Functional programming is more urgent today than ever before. Massively multicore hardware is right around the corner, and functional languages provide a clear approach for taking advantage of it. Functional programming is covered in Chapter 5, *Functional Programming*, on page 127.

- Purely functional languages can make it awkward to model state that really needs to change. Clojure provides a structured mechanism for working with changeable state via software transactional memory and refs (Section 6.2, *Refs and Software Transactional Memory*, on page 159), agents (Section 6.4, *Use Agents for Asynchronous Updates*, on page 167), atoms (Section 6.3, *Use Atoms for Uncoordinated, Synchronous Updates*, on page 166), and dynamic binding (Section 6.5, *Managing Per-Thread State with Vars*, on page 172).

- Many functional languages are statically typed. Clojure's dynamic typing makes it more accessible for programmers learning functional programming.

- Clojure's Java invocation approach is *not* functional. When you call Java, you enter the familiar, mutable world. This offers a comfortable haven for beginners learning functional programming and a pragmatic alternative to functional style when you need it. Java invocation is covered in Chapter 3, *Working with Java*, on page 59.

Clojure's approach to changing state enables concurrency without explicit locking and complements Clojure's functional core.

Clojure Simplifies Concurrent Programming

Clojure's support for functional programming makes it easy to write thread-safe code. Since immutable data structures cannot *ever* change, there is no danger of data corruption based on another thread's activity.

However, Clojure's support for concurrency goes beyond just functional programming. When you need references to mutable data, Clojure protects them via software transactional memory (STM). STM is a higher-level approach to thread safety than the locking mechanisms that Java provides. Rather than creating fragile, error-prone locking strategies, you can protect shared state with transactions. This is much more productive, because many programmers have a good understanding of transactions based on experience with databases.

For example, the following code creates a working, thread-safe, in-memory database of accounts:

```
(def accounts (ref #{}))
(defstruct account :id :balance)
```

The ref function creates a transactionally protected reference to the current state of the database. Updating is trivial. The following code adds a new account to the database:

```
(dosync (alter accounts conj (struct account "CLJ" 1000.00)))
```

The dosync causes the update to accounts to execute inside a transaction. This guarantees thread safety, and it is easier to use than locking. With transactions, you never have to worry about which objects to lock or in what order. The transactional approach will also perform better under some common usage scenarios, because (for example) readers will never block.

Although the example here is trivial, the technique is general, and it works on real-world-sized problems. See Chapter 6, *Concurrency*, on page 157 for more on concurrency and STM in Clojure.

Clojure Embraces the Java Virtual Machine

Clojure gives you clean, simple, direct access to Java. You can call any Java API directly:

```
(System/getProperties)
-> {java.runtime.name=Java(TM) SE Runtime Environment
    ... many more ...
```

Clojure adds a lot of syntactic sugar for calling Java. I won't get into the details here (see Section 3.1, *Calling Java*, on page 60), but notice that in the following code the Clojure version has both fewer dots *and fewer parentheses* than the Java version:

```
// Java
"hello".getClass().getProtectionDomain().getCodeSource()

; Clojure
(.. "hello" getClass getProtectionDomain getCodeSource)
```

Clojure provides simple functions for implementing Java interfaces and subclassing Java classes. Also, Clojure functions all implement Callable and Runnable. This makes it trivial to pass the following anonymous function to the constructor for a Java Thread.

```
(.start (new Thread (fn [] (println "Hello" (Thread/currentThread)))))
| Hello #<Thread Thread[Thread-0,5,main]>
```

The #<...> is Clojure's way of printing a Java instance. Thread is the class name of the instance, and Thread[Thread-0,5,main] is the instance's toString representation.

(Note that in the preceding example the new thread will run to completion, but its output may interleave in some strange way with the REPL prompt. This is not a problem with Clojure but simply the result of having more than one thread writing to an output stream.)

Because the Java invocation syntax in Clojure is clean and simple, it is idiomatic to use Java directly, rather than to hide Java behind Lispy wrappers.

Now that you have seen a few of the reasons to use Clojure, it is time to start writing some code.

1.2 Clojure Coding Quick Start

To run Clojure, you need two things:

- *A Java runtime.* Download[4] and install Java version 5 or greater. Java version 6 has significant performance improvements and better exception reporting, so prefer this if possible.

- *Clojure itself.* The book's sample code includes a version of Clojure that has been tested to work with all of the book's examples. While

---

4. http://java.sun.com/javase/downloads/index.jsp

you are working through the book, use the version of Clojure bundled with the book's sample code at lib/clojure.jar. After you read the book, you can follow the instructions in the sidebar on the next page to build an up-to-the-minute version of Clojure.

Instructions for downloading the sample code are on page xxi. Once you have downloaded the sample code, you can test your install by navigating to the directory where you placed the sample code and running a Clojure *read-eval-print loop* (REPL). The sample code includes REPL launch scripts that load Clojure, plus several other libraries that we will need later in the book.

On *nix/Mac the script is repl.sh:

```
cd /wherever/you/put/the/samples
bin/repl.sh
```

On Windows it is repl.bat:

```
cd \wherever\you\put\the\samples
bin\repl.bat
```

Another alternative for Windows users is to install Cygwin[5] and then follow the *nix instructions throughout the book.

When you run the appropriate REPL launch script, the REPL should prompt you with user=>:

```
Clojure
user=>
```

All scripts in the book should be launched from a console in the root directory of the sample code. Do *not* navigate into the bin directory, and do not click the scripts from a Windows environment.

In addition to Clojure, many of the samples in the book depend on the clojure-contrib library.[6] A few examples also require various Java JAR files. You do not have to worry about any of this, because the sample code includes all these files and the REPL launch scripts place them on the classpath.

Now you are ready for "Hello World."

---

5. http://www.cygwin.com
6. http://code.google.com/p/clojure-contrib

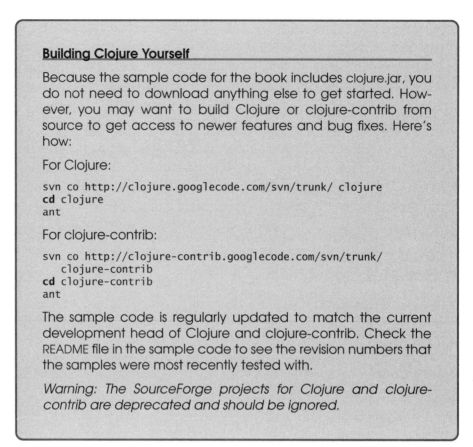

Building Clojure Yourself

Because the sample code for the book includes clojure.jar, you do not need to download anything else to get started. However, you may want to build Clojure or clojure-contrib from source to get access to newer features and bug fixes. Here's how:

For Clojure:

```
svn co http://clojure.googlecode.com/svn/trunk/ clojure
cd clojure
ant
```

For clojure-contrib:

```
svn co http://clojure-contrib.googlecode.com/svn/trunk/
    clojure-contrib
cd clojure-contrib
ant
```

The sample code is regularly updated to match the current development head of Clojure and clojure-contrib. Check the README file in the sample code to see the revision numbers that the samples were most recently tested with.

Warning: The SourceForge projects for Clojure and clojure-contrib are deprecated and should be ignored.

Using the REPL

To see how to use the REPL, let's create a few variants of "Hello World." First, type (println "hello world") at the REPL prompt:

```
user=> (println "hello world")
| hello world
-> nil
```

The second line, hello world, is the console output you requested. This third line, nil, is the return value of the call to println.

Next, encapsulate your "Hello World" into a function that can address a person by name:

```
user=> (defn hello [name] (str "Hello, " name))
    #'user/hello
```

Let's break this down:

- defn defines a function.
- hello is the function name.

- hello takes one argument, name.
- str is a function call that concatenates an arbitrary list of arguments into a string.
- defn, hello, name, and str are all *symbols*, which are names that refer to things. Legal symbols are defined in Section 2.1, *Symbols*, on page 29.

Look at the return value, #'user/hello. The prefix #' indicates that the function was stored in a Clojure *var*, and user is the *namespace* of the function. (The user namespace is the REPL default, like the default package in Java.) You do not need to worry about vars and namespaces yet; they are covered in Section 2.4, *Vars, Bindings, and Namespaces*, on page 40.

Now you can call hello, passing in your name:

```
user=> (hello "Stu")
```
⇒
```
    "Hello, Stu"
```

If you get your REPL into a state that confuses you, the simplest fix is to kill the REPL with [Ctrl]+[C] on Windows or [Ctrl]+[D] on *nix and then start another one.

Special Variables

The REPL includes several useful special variables. When you are working in the REPL, the results of evaluating the three most recent expressions are stored in the special variables *1, *2, and *3, respectively. This makes it easy to work iteratively. Say hello to a few different names:

```
user=> (hello "Stu")
```
⇒
```
    "Hello, Stu"
```

```
user=> (hello "Clojure")
```
⇒
```
    "Hello, Clojure"
```

Now, you can use the special variables to combine the results of your recent work:

```
(str *1 " and " *2)
```
⇒
```
    "Hello, Clojure and Hello, Stu"
```

If you make a mistake in the REPL, you will see a Java exception. The details are often omitted for brevity. For example, dividing by zero is a no-no:

```
user=> (/ 1 0)
```
⇒
```
    java.lang.ArithmeticException: Divide by zero
```

Here the problem is obvious, but sometimes the problem is more subtle and you want the detailed stack trace. The *e special variable holds the last exception. Because Clojure exceptions are Java exceptions, you can call Java methods such as printStackTrace():

```
user=> (.printStackTrace *e)
⇒    java.lang.ArithmeticException: Divide by zero
   |   at clojure.lang.Compiler.eval(Compiler.java:4094)
   |   at clojure.lang.Repl.main(Repl.java:87)
   | Caused by: java.lang.ArithmeticException: Divide by zero
   |   at clojure.lang.Numbers.divide(Numbers.java:142)
   |   at user.eval__2677.invoke(Unknown Source)
   |   at clojure.lang.Compiler.eval(Compiler.java:4083)
   |   ... 1 more
```

Java interop is covered in Chapter 3, *Working with Java*, on page 59.

If you have a block of code that is too large to conveniently type at the REPL, save the code into a file, and then load that file from the REPL. You can use an absolute path or a path relative to where you launched the REPL:

```
; save some work in temp.clj, and then ...
user=> (load-file "temp.clj")
```

The REPL is a terrific environment for trying ideas and getting immediate feedback. For best results, keep a REPL open at all times while reading this book.

Adding Shared State

The hello function of the previous section is *pure*; that is, it has no side effects. Pure functions are easy to develop, test, and understand, and you should prefer them for many tasks.

That said, most programs have some shared state and will use impure functions to manage that shared state. Let's extend hello to keep track of past visitors and offer a different greeting to people it has met before. First, you will need something to track the visitors. A set will do the trick:

```
#{}
⇒    #{}
```

The #{} is a literal for an empty set. Next, you will need conj:

```
(conj coll item)
```

conj is short for conjoin, and it builds a new collection with an item added. conj an element onto a set to see that a new set is created:

```
(conj #{} "Stu")
⇒    #{"Stu"}
```

Now that you can build new sets, you need some way to keep track of the *current* set of visitors. Clojure provides *references* (refs) for this purpose:

```
(ref initial-state)
```

To name your reference, you can use def:

```
(def symbol initial-value?)
```

def is like defn but more general. A def can define functions *or* data. Use ref to create a reference, and use def to bind this reference to the name visitors:

```
(def visitors (ref #{}))
⇒    #'user/visitors
```

In order to update a reference, you must use a function such as alter:

```
(alter r update-fn & args)
```

alter applies an update-fn to reference r, with optional args if necessary. Try to alter a visitor into visitors, using conj as the update function:

```
(alter visitors conj "Stu")
⇒    java.lang.IllegalStateException: No transaction running
```

As you can see, Clojure protects references. References must be updated in a transaction so that Clojure can do the hard work of dealing with multiple concurrent users of visitors:

To create a transaction, use dosync:

```
(dosync & exprs)
```

Use dosync to add a visitor within a transaction:

```
(dosync (alter visitors conj "Stu"))
⇒    #{"Stu"}
```

alter is one of several functions that can update a ref. Choosing the right update function requires care and is discussed in Section 6.2, *Refs and Software Transactional Memory*, on page 159.

At any time, you can peek inside the ref with deref or with the shorter @:

```
(deref visitors)
```
⇒   `#{"Stu"}`

```
@visitors
```
⇒   `#{"Stu"}`

Now you are ready to build the new, more elaborate version of hello:

examples/introduction.clj

```
Line 1  (defn hello
   -      "Writes hello message to *out*. Calls you by username.
   -       Knows if you have been here before."
   -      [username]
   5      (dosync
   -        (let [past-visitor (@visitors username)]
   -          (if past-visitor
   -            (str "Welcome back, " username)
   -            (do
   10             (alter visitors conj username)
   -              (str "Hello, " username)))))))
```

On line 6, @visitors returns the current value of the visitors reference. Sets are functions of their members, so (@visitors username) checks to see whether username is a member of the current value of visitors. The let then binds the result of this check to the name past-visitor.

On line 10, alter updates the visitors to include the name username.

Lines 8 and 11 return different strings based on whether the user was a visitor in the past.

You can verify that new visitors get one message the first time around:

```
(hello "Rich")
```
⇒   `"Hello, Rich"`

...and that they get a different message when they return again later:

```
(hello "Rich")
```
⇒   `"Welcome back, Rich"`

The use of references and transactions in the previous example offers a great benefit: the hello function is safe for multiple threads and processors. And although they may be retried, calls to dosync will not deadlock. Clojure transactions are described in more detail in Chapter 6, *Concurrency*, on page 157.

At this point, you should feel comfortable entering small bits of code at the REPL. Larger units of code aren't that different; you can load and run Clojure libraries from the REPL as well. Let's explore that next.

1.3 Exploring Clojure Libraries

Clojure code is packaged in *libraries*. Each Clojure library belongs to a *namespace*, which is analogous to a Java package. You can load a Clojure library with require:

```
(require quoted-namespace-symbol)
```

When you require a library named clojure.contrib.str-utils, Clojure looks for a file named clojure/contrib/str-utils.clj on the CLASSPATH. Try it:

```
user=> (require 'clojure.contrib.str-utils)
⇒    nil
```

The leading single quote (') is required, and it *quotes* the library name (quoting is covered in Section 2.2, *Reader Macros*, on page 35). The nil return indicates success and that you have the clojure-contrib library on your classpath. While you are at it, test that you can load the sample code for this chapter, examples.introduction:

```
user=> (require 'examples.introduction)
⇒    nil
```

The examples.introduction library includes an implementation of the Fibonacci numbers, which is the traditional "Hello World" program for functional languages. We will explore the Fibonacci numbers in more detail in Section 5.2, *How to Be Lazy*, on page 132. For now, just make sure that you can execute the sample function fibs. Enter the following line of code at the REPL to take the first ten Fibonacci numbers:

```
user=> (take 10 examples.introduction/fibs)
⇒    (0 1 1 2 3 5 8 13 21 34)
```

If you see the first ten Fibonacci numbers as listed here, you have successfully installed the book samples.

The book samples are all unit tested, with tests located in the examples/test and lancet/test directories. (Testing is covered in Section 9.1, *Automating Tests*, on page 248.) The tests for the samples themselves are not explicitly covered in the book, but you may find them useful for reference. You can run the unit tests yourself with bin/runtests.sh or bin\runtests.bat.

Don't Just Require, Use!

When you require a Clojure library, you must refer to items in the library with a namespace-qualified name. Instead of fibs, you must say examples.introduction/fibs. Make sure to launch a new REPL,[7] and then try it:

```
(require 'examples.introduction)
```
⇒   nil

```
(take 10 examples.introduction/fibs)
```
⇒   (0 1 1 2 3 5 8 13 21 34)

Fully qualified names get old quickly. You can refer a namespace, creating mappings for all its names in your current namespace:

```
(refer quoted-namespace-symbol)
```

Call refer on examples.introduction, and verify that you can then call fibs directly:

```
(refer 'examples.introduction)
```
⇒   nil

```
(take 10 fibs)
```
⇒   (0 1 1 2 3 5 8 13 21 34)

For convenience, the use function will require and refer a library in a single step:

```
(use quoted-namespace-symbol)
```

From a new REPL you should be able to do the following:

```
(use 'examples.introduction)
```
⇒   nil

```
(take 10 fibs)
```
⇒   (0 1 1 2 3 5 8 13 21 34)

As you are working through the book samples, you can call require or use with a :reload-all flag to force a library to reload:

```
(use :reload-all 'examples.introduction)
```
⇒   nil

The :reload-all flag is useful if you are making changes and want to see results without restarting the REPL.

---

7. Creating a new REPL will prevent name collisions between your previous work and the sample code functions of the same name. This is not a problem in real-world development, as you will see in Section 2.4, *Namespaces*, on page 44.

Finding Documentation

Often you can find the documentation you need right at the REPL. The most basic helper function is doc:

```
(doc name)
```

Use doc to print the documentation for str:

```
user=> (doc str)
-------------------------
clojure.core/str
([] [x] [x & ys])
  With no args, returns the empty string. With one arg x, returns
  x.toString().  (str nil) returns the empty string. With more than
  one arg, returns the concatenation of the str values of the args.
```

The first line of doc's output contains the fully qualified name of the function. The next line contains the possible argument lists, generated directly from the code. (Some common argument names and their uses are explained in the sidebar on the following page.) Finally, the remaining lines contain the function's *doc-string*, if the function definition included one.

You can add a doc-string to your own functions by placing it immediately after the function name:

examples/introduction.clj

```
(defn hello
  "Writes hello message to *out*. Calls you by username"
  [username]
  (println (str "Hello, " username)))
```

Sometimes you will not know the exact name you want documentation for. The find-doc function will search for anything whose doc output matches a regular expression or string you pass in:

```
(find-doc s)
```

Use find-doc to explore how Clojure does reduce:

```
user=> (find-doc "reduce")
-------------------------
clojure/areduce
([a idx ret init expr])
Macro
   ... details elided ...
-------------------------
clojure/reduce
([f coll] [f val coll])
   ... details elided ...
```

Conventions for Parameter Names

The documentation strings for reduce and areduce show several terse parameter names. Here are some parameter names and how they are normally used:

Parameter	Usage
a	A Java array
agt	An agent
coll	A collection
expr	An expression
f	A function
idx	Index
r	A ref
v	A vector
val	A value

These names may seem a little terse, but there is a good reason for them: the "good names" are often taken by Clojure functions! Naming a parameter that collides with a function name is legal but considered bad style: the parameter will shadow the function, which will be unavailable while the parameter is in scope. So, don't call your refs ref, your agents agent, or your counts count. Those names refer to functions.

---

reduce reduces Clojure collections and is covered in Section 4.2, *Transforming Sequences*, on page 102. areduce is for interoperation with Java arrays and is covered in Section 3.1, *Using Java Collections*, on page 63.

Much of Clojure is written in Clojure, and it is often instructive to read the source code. Using Chris Houser's repl-utils library, you can view the source of a Clojure function:

```
(clojure.contrib.repl-utils/source a-symbol)
```

Try viewing the source of the simple identity function:

```
(use 'clojure.contrib.repl-utils)
```

```
(source identity)
(defn identity
  "Returns its argument."
  [x] x)
```

Under the covers, Clojure is Java. You can use show to enumerate all the Java members (fields and methods) of any Java object:

```
(clojure.contrib.repl-utils/show obj)
```

Try showing the members of a java.util.HashMap:

```
(show java.util.HashMap)
===  public java.util.HashMap  ===
[ 0] <init> ()
[ 1] <init> (Map)
[ 2] <init> (int)
[ 3] <init> (int,float)
[ 4] clear : void ()
[ 5] clone : Object ()
[ 6] containsKey : boolean (Object)
[ 7] containsValue : boolean (Object)
[ 8] entrySet : Set ()
... elided for brevity ...
```

Because Clojure objects are Java objects, you can also show *any* Clojure form to see its underlying Java API. Try showing a Clojure set:

```
(show #{})
===  public clojure.lang.PersistentHashSet  ===
[ 0] static EMPTY : PersistentHashSet
[ 1] static applyToHelper : Object (IFn,ISeq)
[ 2] static create : PersistentHashSet (ISeq)
[ 3] static create : PersistentHashSet (List)
[ 4] static create : PersistentHashSet (Object[])
[ 5] add : boolean (Object)
[ 6] addAll : boolean (Collection)
[ 7] applyTo : Object (ISeq)
[ 8] call : Object ()
... elided for brevity ...
```

Of course, you can also use Java's Reflection API. You can use methods such as class, ancestors, and instance? to reflect against the underlying Java object model. You can tell, for example, that Clojure's collections are also Java collections:

```
(ancestors (class [1 2 3]))
⇒    #{java.util.List clojure.lang.IPersistentVector
     java.lang.Object java.util.Comparator
     java.io.Serializable java.lang.Iterable
     java.util.Collection clojure.lang.APersistentVector
     java.util.RandomAccess clojure.lang.IObj clojure.lang.AFn
     java.lang.Comparable clojure.lang.Obj clojure.lang.IFn}
```

Clojure's complete API is documented online at http://clojure.org/api. The right sidebar links to all functions and macros by name, and the left sidebar links to a set of overview articles on various Clojure features.

You can download a PDF version of the online documentation from the Clojure Google Group's file archive;[8] the filename is manual.pdf.

Now you have written a bit of Clojure code and can load and explore Clojure libraries. It is time to introduce the main sample application for the book: Lancet.

1.4 Introducing Lancet

Lancet is a more involved project that we will build together throughout the book. Lancet is a *dependency-based* build system. In a dependency-based system, you describe the dependencies between various *targets* (objectives). Then you can request performance of a particular target, and the system will determine what other targets also need to run, and in what order. Popular dependency-based build systems include Make,[9] Ant,[10] SCons,[11] and Rake.[12]

Lancet can function stand-alone, or it can invoke tasks from Ant. In fact, Lancet was inspired by a review of Ant's build syntax. Here is a simple Ant build script:

lancet/step_0/build.xml
```xml
<project name="example" default="compile">

        <property name="src" location="src"/>
        <property name="build" location="classes"/>

        <target name="init">
                <tstamp/>
                <mkdir dir="${build}"/>
        </target>

        <target name="compile" depends="init"
                description="Compile Java sources.">
                <javac srcdir="${src}"
                        destdir="${build}"/>
        </target>

</project>
```

---

8. http://groups.google.com/group/clojure/files
9. http://en.wikipedia.org/wiki/Make_(software)
10. http://ant.apache.org
11. http://www.scons.org
12. http://rake.rubyforge.org/

Ant's design can be summarized as follows:

- A build is composed of one or more distinct *targets*, such as init and compile.
- Targets are related by *dependencies*. In the previous sample, compile depends on init.
- By tracking dependency relationships, Ant can run only the targets that are needed and run each target only once per build.
- You can provide and override configuration settings by setting arbitrary *properties*, such as src and build in the example.
- The actual work of targets is performed by *tasks*, such as tstamp, mkdir, and javac.
- Ant build scripts are usually written in XML, as shown earlier, but the underlying implementation is typically Java.

At first glance, Lancet syntax looks like Ant syntax but Lispy instead of XMLish:

lancet/step_0/build.clj

```
(use 'lancet)
(use 'lancet.ant)

(def src "src")
(def build "classes")

(deftarget init
        (tstamp)
        (mkdir {:dir build}))

(deftarget compile
        "Compile Java sources"
        (init)
        (javac {:srcdir src :destdir build}))
```

The surface similarity belies some important differences:

- Lancet is pure Clojure code. Lancet uses no XML and does not have to convert between XML and Java.
- Because Lancet is Clojure code, the need for properties disappears. You can simply use Clojure vars such as src and build.
- Likewise, there is no need for tasks. Tasks are just functions.
- Targets such as init and compile are also just functions, with the special property that they run only once. deftarget defines a function with run-once semantics.

- Explicit dependencies are unnecessary. They fall out naturally when one target calls another, because compile calls init in the earlier example.

Lancet also provides direct access to Ant's most important feature: its large, tested library of tasks. Lancet can call Ant tasks such as tstamp, mkdir, and javac directly as Clojure functions.

Most of the abstractions in Ant exist not to build projects but to manage the impedance mismatch between XML and Java. Lancet avoids all that ceremony and distills the essence of a dependency-based system: functions that run only once, when needed.

At the end of most chapters, you will build a little bit of Lancet. By the end of the book, you will have a usable Clojure build system.

1.5 Wrapping Up

You have just gotten the whirlwind tour of Clojure. You have seen Clojure's expressive syntax, learned about Clojure's approach to Lisp, and seen how easy it is to call Java code from Clojure.

You have Clojure running in your own environment, and you have written short programs at the REPL to demonstrate functional programming and software transactional memory. You have seen what Lancet will look like, once you know how to build it. Now it is time to explore the entire language.

Chapter 2

Exploring Clojure

Clojure offers great power through functional style, concurrency support, and clean Java interop. But before you can appreciate all these features, you have to start with the language basics. In this chapter, you will take a quick tour of the Clojure language, including the following:

- Forms
- Reader macros
- Functions
- Bindings and namespaces
- Flow control
- Metadata

If your background is primarily in imperative languages, this tour may seem to be missing key language constructs, such as variables and **for** loops. Section 2.6, *Where's My for Loop?*, on page 50 will show you how you can *live better* without **for** loops and variables.

Clojure is very expressive, and this chapter covers many concepts quite quickly. Don't worry if you don't understand every detail; we will revisit these topics in more detail in later chapters. If possible, bring up a REPL, and follow along with the examples as you read.

2.1 Forms

Clojure is *homoiconic*, which is to say that Clojure code is composed of Clojure data. When you run a Clojure program, a part of Clojure called the *reader* reads the text of the program in chunks called *forms* and translates them into Clojure data structures. Clojure then compiles and executes the data structures.

Form	Example(s)	Primary Coverage
Boolean	true, false	Section 2.1, *Booleans and Nil*, on page 31
Character	\a	Section 2.1, *Strings and Characters*, on page 29
Keyword	:tag, :doc	Section 2.1, *Maps, Keywords, and Structs*, on page 32
List	(1 2 3), (println "foo")	Chapter 4, *Unifying Data with Sequences*, on page 91
Map	{:name "Bill", :age 42}	Section 2.1, *Maps, Keywords, and Structs*, on page 32
Nil	nil	Section 2.1, *Booleans and Nil*, on page 31
Number	1, 4.2	Section 2.1, *Using Numeric Types*
Set	#{:snap :crackle :pop}	Chapter 4, *Unifying Data with Sequences*, on page 91
String	"hello"	Section 2.1, *Strings and Characters*, on page 29
Symbol	user/foo, java.lang.String	Section 2.1, *Symbols*, on page 29
Vector	[1 2 3]	Chapter 4, *Unifying Data with Sequences*, on page 91

Figure 2.1: CLOJURE FORMS

The Clojure forms covered in this book are summarized in Figure 2.1. To see forms in action, let's start with some simple forms supporting numeric types.

Using Numeric Types

Numeric literals are forms. Numbers simply evaluate to themselves. If you enter a number, the REPL will give it back to you:

```
42
```
⇒
```
    42
```

A vector of numbers is another kind of form. Create a vector of the numbers 1, 2, and 3:

```
[1 2 3]
```
⇒
```
    [1 2 3]
```

A list is also a kind of form. A list is "just data," but it is also used to call functions. Create a list whose first item names a Clojure function, like the symbol +:

```
(+ 1 2)
```
⇒
```
    3
```

As you can see, Clojure evaluates the list as a function call. The style of placing the function first is called *prefix notation*,[1] as opposed to

---

1. More specifically, it's called Cambridge Polish notation.

the more familiar *infix notation* 1 + 2 = 3. Of course, prefix notation is perfectly familiar for functions whose names are words. For example, most programmers would correctly expect concat to come first in this expression:

```
(concat [1 2] [3 4])
```
⇒   (1 2 3 4)

Clojure is simply being consistent in treating mathematical operators like all other functions and placing them first.

A practical advantage of prefix notation is that you can easily extend it for arbitrary numbers of arguments:

```
(+ 1 2 3)
```
⇒   6

Even the degenerate case of no arguments works as you would expect, returning zero. This helps to eliminate fragile, special-case logic for boundary conditions:

```
(+)
```
⇒   0

Many mathematical and comparison operators have the names and semantics that you would expect from other programming languages. Addition, subtraction, multiplication, comparison, and equality all work as you would expect:

```
(- 10 5)
```
⇒   5

```
(* 3 10 10)
```
⇒   300

```
(> 5 2)
```
⇒   true

```
(>= 5 5)
```
⇒   true

```
(< 5 2)
```
⇒   false

```
(= 5 2)
```
⇒   false

Division may surprise you:

```
(/ 22 7)
```
⇒   22/7

As you can see, Clojure has a built-in Ratio type:

```
(class (/ 22 7))
```
⇒   clojure.lang.Ratio

If you actually want decimal division, use a floating-point literal for the dividend:

```
(/ 22.0 7)
```
⇒   3.142857142857143

If you want to stick to integers, you can get the integer quotient and remainder with quot and rem:

```
(quot 22 7)
```
⇒   3

```
(rem 22 7)
```
⇒   1

If you are doing arbitrary-precision math, append M to a number to create a BigDecimal literal:

```
(+ 1 (/ 0.00001 1000000000000000000))
```
⇒   1.0

```
(+ 1 (/ 0.00001M 1000000000000000000))
```
⇒   1.00000000000000000000001M

Clojure relies on Java's BigDecimal class for arbitrary-precision decimal numbers. See the online documentation[2] for details. BigDecimals provide arbitrary precision but at a price: BigDecimal math is significantly slower than Java's floating-point primitives.

Clojure's approach to arbitrary-sized integers is simple: just don't worry about it. Clojure will upgrade to BigInteger when you need it. Try creating some small and large integers, and then inspect their class:

```
(class (* 1000 1000 1000))
```
⇒   java.lang.Integer

```
(class (* 1000 1000 1000 1000 1000 1000 1000 1000))
```
⇒   java.math.BigInteger

Clojure relies on Java's BigInteger class for arbitrary-precision integers. See the online documentation at http://tinyurl.com/big-integer for more on BigInteger.

---

2. http://tinyurl.com/big-decimal

Symbols

Forms such as +, concat, and java.lang.String are called *symbols* and are used to name things. For example, + names the function that adds things together. Symbols name all sorts of things in Clojure:

- Functions like str and concat
- "Operators" like + and -, which are, after all, just functions
- Java classes like java.lang.String and java.util.Random
- Namespaces like clojure.core and Java packages like java.lang
- Data structures and references

Symbols cannot start with a number and can consist of alphanumeric characters, plus +, -, *, /, !, ?, ., and _. The list of legal symbol characters is a minimum set that Clojure promises to support. You should stick to these characters in your own code, but do not assume the list is exhaustive. Clojure may use other, undocumented characters in symbols that it employs internally and may add more legal symbol characters in the future. See Clojure's online documentation[3] for updates to the list of legal symbol characters.

Clojure treats / and . specially in order to support namespaces; see Section 2.4, *Namespaces*, on page 44 for details.

Strings and Characters

Strings are another kind of reader form. Clojure strings are Java strings. They are delimited by double quotes ("), and they can span multiple lines:

```
"This is a\nmultiline string"
    "This is a\nmultiline string"
```

```
"This is also
a multiline String"
    "This is also\na multiline String"
```

As you can see, the REPL always shows string literals with escaped newlines. If you actually print a multiline string, it will print on multiple lines:

```
(println "another\nmultiline\nstring")
| another
| multiline
| string
    nil
```

---

3. http://clojure.org/reader

Clojure does not wrap most of Java's string functions. Instead, you can call them directly using Clojure's Java interop forms:

```
(.toUpperCase "hello")
```
⇒   "HELLO"

The dot before toUpperCase tells Clojure to treat it as the name of a Java method instead of a Clojure function.

One string function that Clojure *does* wrap is toString. You do not need to call toString directly. Instead of calling toString, use Clojure's str function:

```
(str & args)
```

str differs from toString in two ways. It smashes together multiple arguments, and it skips nil without error:

```
(str 1 2 nil 3)
```
⇒   "123"

Clojure characters are Java characters. Their literal syntax is \{letter}, where letter can be a letter or the name of a character: backspace, form-feed, newline, return, space, or tab:

```
(str \h \e \y \space \y \o \u)
```
⇒   "hey you"

As is the case with strings, Clojure does not wrap Java's character functions. Instead, you can use a Java interop form such as Character/toUpperCase:

```
(Character/toUpperCase \s)
```
⇒   \S

The Java interop forms are covered in Section 3.1, *Calling Java*, on page 60. For more on Java's Character class, see the API documentation at http://tinyurl.com/java-character.

Strings are sequences of characters. When you call Clojure sequence functions on a string, you get a sequence of characters back. Imagine that you wanted to conceal a secret message by interleaving it with a second, innocuous message. You could use interleave to combine the two messages:

```
(interleave "Attack at midnight" "The purple elephant chortled")
```
⇒   (\A \T \t \h \t \e \a \space \c \p \k \u \space \r
     \a \p \t \l \space \e \m \space \i \e \d \l \n \e
     \i \p \g \h \h \a \t \n)

That works, but you probably want the resulting sequence as a string
for transmission. It is tempting to use str to pack the characters back
into a string, but that doesn't quite work:

```
(str (interleave "Attack at midnight" "The purple elephant chortled"))
```
⇒   "clojure.core$concat__3174$cat__3188$fn__3189@d4ea9f36"

The problem is that str works with a variable number of arguments, and
you are passing it a *single* argument that contains the argument list.
The solution is apply:

```
(apply f args* argseq)
```

apply takes a function f, some optional args, and a sequence of args
argseq. It then calls f, unrolling args and argseq into an argument list.
Use (apply str ...) to build a string from a sequence of characters:

```
(apply str (interleave "Attack at midnight"
                       "The purple elephant chortled"))
```
⇒   "ATthtea cpku raptl em iedlneipghhatn"

You can use (apply str ...) again to reveal the message:

```
(apply str (take-nth 2 "ATthtea cpku raptl em iedlneipghhatn"))
```
⇒   "Attack at midnight"

The call to (take-nth 2 ...) takes every second element of the sequence,
extracting the obfuscated message.

Booleans and Nil

Clojure's rules for booleans are easy to understand:

- true is true, and false is false.
- In addition to false, nil also evaluates to false when used in a boolean context.
- Other than false and nil, *everything else* evaluates to true in a boolean context.

Lisp programmers be warned: the empty list is not false in Clojure:

```
;         (if part)              (else part)
(if () "We are in Clojure!" "We are in Common Lisp!")
```
⇒   "We are in Clojure!"

C programmers be warned: zero is not false in Clojure, either:

```
;         (if part)      (else part)
(if 0 "Zero is true" "Zero is false")
```
⇒   "Zero is true"

A *predicate* is a function that returns either true or false. In Clojure, it is idiomatic to name predicates with a trailing question mark, for example true?, false?, nil?, and zero?:

```
(true? expr)
```

```
(false? expr)
```

```
(nil? expr)
```

```
(zero? expr)
```

true? tests whether a value is actually true, *not* whether the value evaluates to true in a boolean context. The only thing that is true? is true itself:

```
(true? true)
```
⇒   true

```
(true? "foo")
```
⇒   false

nil? and false? work the same way. Only nil is nil?, and only false is false?.

zero? works with any numeric type, returning true if it is zero:

```
(zero? 0.0)
```
⇒   true

```
(zero? (/ 22 7))
```
⇒   false

There are many more predicates in Clojure. To review them, enter (find-doc #"\?$") at the REPL.

Maps, Keywords, and Structs

A Clojure *map* is a collection of key/value pairs. Maps have a literal form surrounded by curly braces. You can use a map literal to create a lookup table for the inventors of programming languages:

```
(def inventors {"Lisp" "McCarthy" "Clojure" "Hickey"})
```
⇒   #'user/inventors

The value "McCarthy" is associated with the key "Lisp", and the value "Hickey" is associated with the key "Clojure".

If you find it easier to read, then you can use commas to delimit each key/value pair. Clojure doesn't care. It treats commas as whitespace:

```
(def inventors {"Lisp" "McCarthy", "Clojure" "Hickey"})
```
⇒   #'user/inventors

Maps are functions. If you pass a key to a map, it will return that key's value, or it will return nil if the key is not found:

```
(inventors "Lisp")
⇒    "McCarthy"
```

```
(inventors "Foo")
⇒    nil
```

You can also use the more verbose get function:

```
(get a-map key not-found-val?)
```

get allows you to specify a different return value for missing keys:

```
(get inventors "Lisp" "I dunno!")
⇒    "McCarthy"
```

```
(get inventors "Foo"  "I dunno!")
⇒    "I dunno!"
```

Because Clojure data structures are immutable and implement hash-Code correctly, *any Clojure data structure can be a key in a map.* That said, a very common key type is the Clojure keyword.

A *keyword* is like a symbol, except that keywords begin with a colon (:). Keywords resolve to themselves:

```
:foo
⇒    :foo
```

This is different from symbols, which want to refer *to* something:

```
foo
⇒    java.lang.Exception: Unable to resolve symbol: foo in this context
```

The fact that keywords resolve to themselves makes keywords useful as keys. You could redefine the inventors map using keywords as keys:

```
(def inventors {:Lisp "McCarthy" :Clojure "Hickey"})
⇒    #'user/inventors
```

Keywords are also functions. They take a map argument and look themselves up in the map. Having switched to keyword keys for the inventors, you can look up an inventor by calling the map or by calling a key:

```
(inventors :Clojure)
⇒    "Hickey"
```

```
(:Clojure inventors)
⇒    "Hickey"
```

This flexibility in ordering comes in handy when calling higher-order functions, such as the reference and agent APIs in Chapter 6, *Concurrency*, on page 157.

If several maps have keys in common, you can document (and enforce) this fact by creating a struct with defstruct:

```
(defstruct name & keys)
```

The keys are called the *basis* of the struct. Use defstruct to create a book struct:

```
(defstruct book :title :author)
```
⇒   `#'user/book`

Then, you can instantiate a struct with struct:

```
(struct name & vals)
```

Once you instantiate a struct, it behaves almost like any other map:

```
(def b (struct book "Anathem" "Neal Stephenson"))
```
⇒   `#'user/b`

```
b
```
⇒   `{:title "Anathem", :author "Neal Stephenson"}`

```
(:title b)
```
⇒   `"Anathem"`

The basis keys of a structure set an expectation, not a requirement. When you create a struct, you can omit values for some of the basis keys and even add values for keys not in the basis using the struct-map function:

```
(struct-map name & inits)
```

The inits are alternating keys and values. Try creating a book with additional values that are not part of the structure basis:

```
(struct-map book :copyright 2008 :title "Anathem")
```
⇒   `{:title "Anathem", :author nil, :copyright 2008}`

Stylistically, the advantage of a struct is that it documents the keys you expect. Internally, the struct stores its values in indexed slots, which results in more efficient key storage.

So far, you have seen numeric literals, lists, vectors, symbols, strings, characters, booleans, and nil. The remaining forms are covered later in the book, as they are needed. For your reference, Figure 2.1, on page 26, lists all the forms used in the book, a brief example of each, and a pointer to more complete coverage.

2.2 Reader Macros

Clojure forms are read by the *reader*, which converts text into Clojure data structures. In addition to the basic forms, the Clojure reader also recognizes a set of *reader macros*.[4] Reader macros are special reader behaviors triggered by prefix *macro characters*.

The most familiar reader macro is the comment. The macro character that triggers a comment is the semicolon (;), and the special reader behavior is "ignore everything else up to the end of this line."

Reader macros are abbreviations of longer list forms and are used to reduce clutter. You have already seen one of these. The quote character (') prevents evaluation:

'(1 2)

⇒   (1 2)

'(1 2) is equivalent to the longer (quote (1 2)):

(quote (1 2))

⇒   (1 2)

The other reader macros are covered later in the book. In the following table, you'll find a quick syntax overview and references to where each reader macro is covered.

Reader Macro	Example(s)	Primary Coverage
Anonymous function	#(.toUpperCase %)	Section 2.3, *Functions*, on the next page
Comment	; single-line comment	Section 2.2, *Reader Macros*
Deref	@form => (deref form)	Chapter 6, *Concurrency*, on page 157
Meta	^form => (meta form)	Section 2.7, *Metadata*, on page 54
Metadata	#^metadata form	Section 2.7, *Metadata*, on page 54
Quote	'form => (quote form)	Section 2.1, *Forms*, on page 25
Regex pattern	#"foo" => a java.util.regex.Pattern	Section 4.4, *Seq-ing Regular Expressions*, on page 108
Syntax-quote	`x	Section 7.3, *Making Macros Simpler*, on page 198
Unquote	~	Section 7.3, *Making Macros Simpler*, on page 198
Unquote-splicing	~@	Section 7.3, *Making Macros Simpler*, on page 198
Var-quote	#'x => (var x)	Chapter 6, *Concurrency*, on page 157

Clojure does not allow programs to define new reader macros. The rationale for this has been explained (and debated) on the Clojure mailing list.[5] If you come from a Lisp background, this may be frustrating. I feel your pain. But this compromise in flexibility gives Clojure a more stable core. Custom reader macros could make Clojure programs more difficult to read and less interoperable.

---

4. Reader macros are totally different from macros, which are discussed in Chapter 7, *Macros*, on page 191.

5. http://tinyurl.com/clojure-reader-macros

2.3 Functions

In Clojure, a function call is simply a list whose first element resolves to a function. For example, this call to str concatenates its arguments to create a string:

```
(str "hello" " " "world")
⇒    "hello world"
```

Function names are typically hyphenated, as in clear-agent-errors. If a function is a predicate, then by convention its name should end with a question mark. As an example, the following predicates test the type of their argument, and all end with a question mark:

```
(string? "hello")
⇒    true
```

```
(keyword? :hello)
⇒    true
```

```
(symbol? 'hello)
⇒    true
```

To define your own functions, use defn:

```
(defn name doc-string? attr-map? [params*] body)
```

The attr-map associates metadata with the function's var and is covered separately in Section 2.7, *Metadata*, on page 54. To demonstrate the other components of a function definition, create a greeting function that takes a name and returns a greeting preceded by "Hello":

examples/exploring.clj
```
(defn greeting
  "Returns a greeting of the form 'Hello, username.'"
  [username]
  (str "Hello, " username))
```

You can call greeting:

```
(greeting "world")
⇒    "Hello, world"
```

You can also consult the documentation for greeting:

```
user=> (doc greeting)
-------------------------
exploring/greeting
([username])
  Returns a greeting of the form 'Hello, username.'
```

What does greeting do if the caller omits username?

```
(greeting)
```
⇒
```
   java.lang.IllegalArgumentException: \
   Wrong number of args passed to: greeting (NO_SOURCE_FILE:0)
```

Clojure functions enforce their *arity*, that is, their expected number of arguments. If you call a function with an incorrect number of arguments, Clojure will throw an IllegalArgumentException. If you want to make greeting issue a generic greeting when the caller omits username, you can use this alternate form of defn, which takes multiple argument lists and method bodies:

```
(defn name doc-string? attr-map?
 ([params*] body)+ )
```

Different arities of the same function can call one another, so you can easily create a zero-argument greeting that delegates to the one-argument greeting, passing in a default username:

examples/exploring.clj

```
(defn greeting
  "Returns a greeting of the form 'Hello, username.'
   Default username is 'world'."
  ([] (greeting "world"))
  ([username] (str "Hello, " username)))
```

You can verify that the new greeting works as expected:

```
(greeting)
```
⇒
```
   "Hello, world"
```

You can create a function with variable arity by including an ampersand in the parameter list. Clojure will bind the name after the ampersand to a sequence of all the remaining parameters.

The following function allows two people to go on a date with a variable number of chaperones:

examples/exploring.clj

```
(defn date [person-1 person-2 & chaperones]
  (println person-1 "and" person-2
          "went out with" (count chaperones) "chaperones."))
```

```
(date "Romeo" "Juliet" "Friar Lawrence" "Nurse")
| Romeo and Juliet went out with 2 chaperones.
```

Variable arity is very useful in recursive definitions. See Chapter 5, *Functional Programming*, on page 127 for examples.

Writing function implementations differing by arity is useful. But if you come from an object-oriented background, you'll want *polymorphism*, that is, different implementations that are selected by *type*. Clojure can do this and a whole lot more. See Chapter 8, *Multimethods*, on page 225 for details.

defn is intended for defining functions at the top level. If you want to create a function from within another function, you should use an anonymous function form instead.

Anonymous Functions

In addition to named functions with defn, you can also create anonymous functions with fn. There are at least three reasons to create an anonymous function:

- The function is so brief and self-explanatory that giving it a name makes the code harder to read, not easier.

- The function is being used only from inside another function and needs a local name, not a top-level binding.

- The function is created inside another function for the purpose of closing over some data.

Filter functions are often brief and self-explanatory. For example, imagine that you want to create an index for a sequence of words, and you do not care about words shorter than three characters. You can write an indexable-word? function like this:

`examples/exploring.clj`

```
(defn indexable-word? [word]
  (> (count word) 2))
```

Then, you can use indexable-word? to extract the indexable words from a sentence:

```
(use '[clojure.contrib.str-utils :only (re-split)])
(filter indexable-word? (re-split #"\W+" "A fine day it is"))
-> ("fine" "day")
```

The call to re-split breaks the sentence into words, and then filter calls indexable-word? once for each word, returning those words for which indexable-word? returns true.

Anonymous functions let you do the same thing in a single line. The simplest anonymous fn form is the following:

```
(fn [params*] body)
```

With this form, you can plug the implementation of indexable-word? directly into the call to filter:

```
(filter (fn [w] (> (count w) 2)) (re-split #"\W+" "A fine day"))
```
⇒   ("fine" "day")

There is an even shorter syntax for anonymous functions, using implicit parameter names. The parameters are named %1, %2, and so on. You can also use % for the first parameter. This syntax looks like this:

```
#(body)
```

You can rewrite the call to filter with the shorter anonymous form:

```
(filter #(> (count %) 2) (re-split #"\W+" "A fine day it is"))
```
⇒   ("fine" "day")

A second motivation for anonymous functions is wanting a named function, but only inside the scope of another function. Continuing with the indexable-word? example, you could write this:

examples/exploring.clj

```
(defn indexable-words [text]
  (let [indexable-word? (fn [w] (> (count w) 2))]
    (filter indexable-word? (re-split #"\W+" text))))
```

The let binds the name indexable-word? to the same anonymous function you wrote earlier, this time inside the (lexical) scope of indexable-words. (let is covered in more detail under Section 2.4, *Vars, Bindings, and Namespaces*, on the next page.)

You can verify that indexable-words works as expected:

```
(indexable-words "a fine day it is")
```
⇒   ("fine" "day")

The combination of let and an anonymous function says the following to readers of your code: "The function indexable-word? is interesting enough to have a name but is relevant only inside indexable-words."

A third reason to use anonymous functions is when you create a function dynamically at runtime. Earlier, you implemented a simple greeting function. Extending this idea, you can create a make-greeter function that creates greeting functions. make-greeter will take a greeting-prefix and return a new function that composes greetings from the greeting-prefix and a name.

examples/exploring.clj

```
(defn make-greeter [greeting-prefix]
  (fn [username] (str greeting-prefix ", " username)))
```

It makes no sense to name the fn, because it is creating a *different* function each time make-greeter is called. However, you may want to name the results of specific calls to make-greeter. You can use def to name functions created by make-greeter:

```
(def hello-greeting (make-greeter "Hello"))
```
⇒   #'user/hello-greeting

```
(def aloha-greeting (make-greeter "Aloha"))
```
⇒   #'user/aloha-greeting

Now, you can call these functions, just like any other functions:

```
(hello-greeting "world")
```
⇒   "Hello, world"

```
(aloha-greeting "world")
```
⇒   "Aloha, world"

Moreover, there is no need to give each greeter a name. You can simply create a greeter and place it in the first (function) slot of a form:

```
((make-greeter "Howdy") "pardner")
```
⇒   "Howdy, pardner"

As you can see, the different greeter functions remember the value of greeting-prefix at the time they were created. More formally, the greeter functions are *closures* over the value of greeting-prefix.

When to Use Anonymous Functions

Anonymous functions have a terse syntax that is not always appropriate. You may actually prefer to be explicit and create named functions such as indexable-word?.

That is perfectly fine and will certainly be the right choice if indexable-word? needs to be called from more than one place.

Anonymous functions are an option, not a requirement. Use the anonymous forms only when you find that they make your code more readable. They take a little getting used to, so don't be surprised if you gradually use them more and more.

2.4 Vars, Bindings, and Namespaces

When you define an object with def or defn, that object is stored in a Clojure *var*. For example, the following def creates a var named user/foo:

```
(def foo 10)
```
⇒   #'user/foo

The symbol user/foo refers to a var that is *bound* to the value 10. If you ask Clojure to evaluate the symbol foo, it will return the value of the associated var:

foo
⇒   10

The initial value of a var is called its *root binding*. Sometimes it is useful to have thread-local bindings for a var; this is covered in Section 6.5, *Managing Per-Thread State with Vars*, on page 172.

You can refer to a var directly. The var special form returns a var itself, not the var's value:

```
(var a-symbol)
```

You can use var to return the var bound to user/foo:

(var foo)
⇒   #'user/foo

You will almost never see the var form directly in Clojure code. Instead, you will see the equivalent reader macro #', which also returns the var for a symbol:

#'foo
⇒   #'user/foo

Why would you want to refer to a var directly? Most of the time, you won't, and you can often simply ignore the distinction between symbols and vars.

But keep in the back of your mind that vars have many abilities other than just storing a value:

- The same var can be aliased into more than one namespace (Section 2.4, *Namespaces*, on page 44). This allows you to use convenient short names.

- Vars can have metadata (Section 2.7, *Metadata*, on page 54). Var metadata includes documentation (Section 1.3, *Finding Documentation*, on page 19), type hints for optimization (Section 3.2, *Adding Type Hints*, on page 72), and unit tests (Section 9.1, *Test with :test*, on page 248).

- Vars can be dynamically rebound on a per-thread basis (Section 6.5, *Managing Per-Thread State with Vars*, on page 172).

Bindings

Vars are bound to names, but there are other kinds of bindings as well. For example, in a function call, argument values bind to parameter names. In the following call, 10 binds to the name number inside the triple function:

```
(defn triple [number] (* 3 number))
```
⇒   `#'user/triple`

```
(triple 10)
```
⇒   `30`

A function's parameter bindings have a *lexical* scope: they are visible only inside the text of the function body. Functions are not the only way to create a lexical binding. The special form let does nothing other than create a set of lexical bindings:

```
(let [bindings*] exprs*)
```

The bindings are then in effect for exprs, and the value of the let is the value of the last expression in exprs.

Imagine that you want coordinates for the four corners of a square, given the bottom, left, and size. You can let the top and right coordinates, based on the values given:

examples/exploring.clj

```
(defn square-corners [bottom left size]
  (let [top (+ bottom size)
        right (+ left size)]
    [[bottom left] [top left] [top right] [bottom right]]))
```

The let binds top and right. This saves you the trouble of calculating top and right more than once. (Both are needed twice to generate the return value.) The let then returns its last form, which in this example becomes the return value of square-corners.

Destructuring

In many programming languages, you bind a variable to an *entire* collection when you need to access only *part* of the collection.

Imagine that you are working with a database of book authors. You track both first and last names, but some functions need to use only the first name:

examples/exploring.clj

```
(defn greet-author-1 [author]
  (println "Hello," (:first-name author)))
```

The greet-author-1 function works fine:

```
(greet-author-1 {:last-name "Vinge" :first-name "Vernor"})
| Hello, Vernor
```

Having to bind author is unsatisfying. You don't need the author; all you need is the first-name. Clojure solves this with *destructuring*. Any place that you bind names, you can nest a vector or a map in the binding to reach into a collection and bind only the part you want. Here is a variant of greet-author that binds only the first name:

examples/exploring.clj
```
(defn greet-author-2 [{fname :first-name}]
  (println "Hello," fname))
```

The binding form {fname :first-name} tells Clojure to bind fname to the :first-name of the function argument. greet-author-2 behaves just like greet-author-1:

```
(greet-author-2 {:last-name "Vinge" :first-name "Vernor"})
| Hello, Vernor
```

Just as you can use a map to destructure any associative collection, you can use a vector to destructure any sequential collection. For example, you could bind only the first two coordinates in a three-dimensional coordinate space:

```
(let [[x y] [1 2 3]]
  [x y])
    [1 2]
```

The expression [x y] destructures the vector [1 2 3], binding x to 1 and y to 2. Since no symbol lines up with the final element 3, it is not bound to anything.

Sometimes you want to skip elements at the start of a collection. Here's how you could bind only the z coordinate:

```
(let [[_ _ z] [1 2 3]]
  z)
    3
```

The underscore (_) is a legal symbol and is used idiomatically to indicate "I don't care about this binding." Binding proceeds from left to right, so the _ is actually bound twice:

```
; *not* idiomatic!
(let [[_ _ z] [1 2 3]]
  _)
    2
```

It is also possible to simultaneously bind both a collection and elements within the collection. Inside a destructuring expression, an :as clause gives you a binding for the entire enclosing structure. For example, you could capture the x and y coordinates individually, plus the entire collection as coords, in order to report the total number of dimensions:

```
(let [[x y :as coords] [1 2 3 4 5 6]]
  (str "x: " x ", y: " y ", total dimensions " (count coords)))
⇒  "x: 1, y: 2, total dimensions 6"
```

Try using destructuring to create an ellipsize function. ellipsize should take a string and return the first three words followed by ....

examples/exploring.clj
```
(use '[clojure.contrib.str-utils :only (re-split str-join)])
(defn ellipsize [words]
  (let [[w1 w2 w3] (re-split #"\s+" words)]
    (str-join " " [w1 w2 w3 "..."])))

(ellipsize "The quick brown fox jumps over the lazy dog.")
⇒  "The quick brown ..."
```

re-split splits the string around whitespace, and then the destructuring form [w1 w2 w3] grabs the first three words. The destructuring ignores any extra items, which is exactly what we want. Finally, str-join reassembles the three words, adding the ellipsis at the end.

Destructuring has several other features not shown here and is a mini-language in itself. The Snake game in Section 6.6, *A Clojure Snake*, on page 176 makes heavy use of destructuring. For a complete list of destructuring options, see the online documentation for let.[6]

Namespaces

Root bindings live in a namespace. You can see evidence of this when you start the Clojure REPL and create a binding:

```
user=> (def foo 10)
⇒  #'user/foo
```

The user=> prompt tells you that you are currently working in the user namespace.[7] You should treat user as a scratch namespace for exploratory development.

---

6. http://clojure.org/special_forms
7. Most of the REPL session listings in the book omit the REPL prompt for brevity. In this section, the REPL prompt will be included whenever the current namespace is important.

When Clojure resolves the name foo, it namespace-qualifies foo in the current namespace user. You can verify this by calling resolve:

```
(resolve sym)
```

resolve returns the var or class that a symbol will resolve to in the current namespace. Use resolve to explicitly resolve the symbol foo:

```
(resolve 'foo)
⇒   #'user/foo
```

You can switch namespaces, creating a new one if needed, with in-ns:

```
(in-ns name)
```

Try creating a myapp namespace:

```
user=> (in-ns 'myapp)
⇒   #<Namespace myapp>
myapp=>
```

Now you are in the myapp namespace, and anything you def or defn will belong to myapp.

When you create a new namespace with in-ns, the java.lang package is automatically available to you:

```
myapp=> String
⇒   java.lang.String
```

While you are learning Clojure, you should use the clojure.core namespace whenever you move to a new namespace, making Clojure's core functions available in the new namespace as well:

```
(clojure.core/use 'clojure.core)
⇒   nil
```

By default, class names outside java.lang must be fully qualified. You cannot just say File:

```
myapp=> File/separator
⇒   java.lang.Exception: No such namespace: File
```

Instead, you must specify the fully qualified java.io.File. Note that your file separator character may be different from that shown here:

```
myapp=> java.io.File/separator
⇒   "/"
```

If you do not want to use a fully qualified class name, you can map one or more class names from a Java package into the current namespace using import:

```
(import '(package Class+))
```

Once you import a class, you can use its short name:

```
(import '(java.io InputStream File))
⇒    nil
```

```
myapp=> File/separator
⇒    "/"
```

import is only for Java classes. If you want to use a Clojure var from another namespace, you must use its fully qualified name or map the name into the current namespace. For example, round lives in Mark Engelberg's clojure.contrib.math:

```
(require 'clojure.contrib.math)
(clojure.contrib.math/round 1.7)
⇒    2
```

```
(round 1.7)
⇒    java.lang.Exception:
     Unable to resolve symbol: round in this context
```

In order to map round into the current namespace, call use on round's namespace:

```
(use 'clojure.contrib.math)
⇒    nil
```

The simple form of use shown earlier causes the current namespace to refer to *all* public vars in clojure.contrib.math. This can be confusing, because it does not make explicit which names are being referred to. Be nice to future readers of your code, and pass the :only option to use, listing only the vars you need:

```
(use '[clojure.contrib.math :only (round)])
⇒    nil
```

Now you can call round without having to qualify its name:

```
(round 1.2)
⇒    1
```

If you make changes to library code in a file and want to make those changes available to a running program, add the :reload option to use:

```
(use :reload '[clojure.contrib.math :only (round)])
⇒    nil
```

I regularly :reload while working on code samples for this book. This chapter's examples are in the examples.exploring namespace. You can reload the examples at any time:

```
(use :reload 'examples.exploring)
```

If you want to also reload any namespaces that examples.exploring refers to, you can pass :reload-all:

```
(use :reload-all 'examples.exploring)
```

It is idiomatic to import Java classes and use namespaces at the top of a source file, using the ns macro:

```
(ns name & references)
```

The ns macro sets the current namespace (available as *ns*) to name, creating the namespace if necessary. The references can include :import, :require, and :use, which work like the similarly named functions to set up the namespace mappings in a single form at the top of a source file. For example, this call to ns appears at the top of the sample code for this chapter:

examples/exploring.clj

```
(ns examples.exploring
    (:use examples.utils clojure.contrib.str-utils)
    (:import (java.io File)))
```

Clojure's namespace functions can do quite a bit more than I have shown here.

You can reflectively traverse namespaces and add or remove mappings at any time. To find out more, issue this command at the REPL:

```
(find-doc "ns-")
```

Alternately, browse the documentation at http://clojure.org/namespaces.

2.5 Flow Control

Clojure has very few flow control forms. In this section, you will meet if, do, and loop/recur. As it turns out, this is almost all you will ever need.

Branch with if

Clojure's if evaluates its first argument. If the argument is logically true, it returns the result of evaluating its second argument:

examples/exploring.clj

```
(defn is-small? [number]
  (if (< number 100) "yes"))

(is-small? 50)
⇒   "yes"
```

If the first argument to if is logically false, it returns nil:

```
(is-small? 50000)
```
⇒   nil

If you want to define a result for the "else" part of if, add it as a third argument:

examples/exploring.clj

```
(defn is-small? [number]
  (if (< number 100) "yes" "no"))
```

```
(is-small? 50000)
```
⇒   "no"

The when and when-not control flow macros are built on top of if and are described in Section 7.2, *when and when-not*, on page 197.

Introduce Side Effects with do

Clojure's if allows only one form for each branch. What if you want to do more than one thing on a branch? For example, you might want to log that a certain branch was chosen. do takes any number of forms, evaluates them all, and returns the last.

You can use a do to print a logging statement from within an if:

examples/exploring.clj

```
(defn is-small? [number]
  (if (< number 100)
    "yes"
    (do
      (println "Saw a big number" number)
      "no")))
```

```
(is-small? 200)
| Saw a big number 200
```
⇒   "no"

This is an example of a *side effect*. The println doesn't contribute to the return value of is-small? at all. Instead, it reaches out into the world outside the function and actually *does something*.

Many programming languages mix pure functions and side effects in completely ad hoc fashion. Not Clojure. In Clojure, side effects are explicit and unusual. do is one way to say "side effects to follow." Since do ignores the return values of all its forms save the last, those forms must have side effects to be of any use at all.

Recur with loop/recur

The Swiss Army knife of flow control in Clojure is loop:

```
(loop [bindings *] exprs*)
```

The loop special form works like let, establishing bindings and then evaluating exprs. The difference is that loop sets a recursion point, which can then be targeted by the recur special form:

```
(recur exprs*)
```

recur binds new values for loop's bindings and returns control to the top of the loop. For example, the following loop/recur returns a countdown:

examples/exploring.clj

```
(loop [result [] x 5]
  (if (zero? x)
    result
    (recur (conj result x) (dec x))))
```

⇒ [5 4 3 2 1]

The first time through, loop binds result to an empty vector and binds x to 5. Since x is not zero, recur then rebinds the names x and result:

- result binds to the previous result conjoined with the previous x.

- x binds to the decrement of the previous x.

Control then returns to the top of the loop. Since x is again not zero, the loop continues, accumulating the result and decrementing x. Eventually, x reaches zero, and the if terminates the recurrence, returning result.

Instead of using a loop, you can use recur back to the top of a function. This makes it simple to write a function whose entire body acts as an implicit loop:

examples/exploring.clj

```
(defn countdown [result x]
  (if (zero? x)
    result
    (recur (conj result x) (dec x))))
```

(countdown [] 5)

⇒ [5 4 3 2 1]

recur is a powerful building block. But you may not use it very often, because many common recursions are provided by Clojure's sequence library.

For example, countdown could also be expressed as any of these:

```
(into [] (take 5 (iterate dec 5)))
```
⇒   [5 4 3 2 1]

```
(into [] (drop-last (reverse (range 6))))
```
⇒   [5 4 3 2 1]

```
(vec (reverse (rest (range 6))))
```
⇒   [5 4 3 2 1]

Do not expect these forms to make sense yet—just be aware that there are often alternatives to using recur directly. The sequence library functions used here are described in Section 4.2, *Using the Sequence Library*, on page 97. Clojure *will not* perform automatic tail-call optimization (TCO). However, it will optimize calls to recur. Chapter 5, *Functional Programming*, on page 127 defines TCO and explores recursion and TCO in detail.

At this point, you have seen quite a few language features but still no variables. Some things really do vary, and Chapter 6, *Concurrency*, on page 157 will show you how Clojure deals with changeable *references*. But most variables in traditional languages are unnecessary and downright dangerous. Let's see how Clojure gets rid of them.

2.6 Where's My for Loop?

Clojure has no for loop and no direct mutable variables.[8] So, how do you write all that code you are accustomed to writing with for loops?

Rather than create a hypothetical example, I decided to grab a piece of open source Java code (sort of) randomly, find a method with some for loops and variables, and port it to Clojure. I opened the Apache Commons project, which is very widely used. I selected the StringUtils class in Commons Lang, assuming that such a class would require little domain knowledge to understand. I then browsed for a method that had multiple for loops and local variables and found indexOfAny:

snippets/StringUtils.java

```java
// From Apache Commons Lang, http://commons.apache.org/lang/
public static int indexOfAny(String str, char[] searchChars) {
    if (isEmpty(str) || ArrayUtils.isEmpty(searchChars)) {
        return -1;
    }
}
```

---

8. Clojure provides *indirect* mutable references, but these must be explicitly called out in your code. See Chapter 6, *Concurrency*, on page 157 for details.

```
    for (int i = 0; i < str.length(); i++) {
        char ch = str.charAt(i);
        for (int j = 0; j < searchChars.length; j++) {
            if (searchChars[j] == ch) {
                return i;
            }
        }
    }
    return -1;
}
```

indexOfAny walks str and reports the index of the first char that matches any char in searchChars, returning -1 if no match is found. Here are some example results from the documentation for indexOfAny:

```
StringUtils.indexOfAny(null, *)                = -1
StringUtils.indexOfAny("", *)                  = -1
StringUtils.indexOfAny(*, null)                = -1
StringUtils.indexOfAny(*, [])                  = -1
StringUtils.indexOfAny("zzabyycdxx",['z','a']) =  0
StringUtils.indexOfAny("zzabyycdxx",['b','y']) =  3
StringUtils.indexOfAny("aba", ['z'])           = -1
```

There are two ifs, two fors, three possible points of return, and three mutable local variables in indexOfAny, and the method is fourteen lines long, as counted by David A. Wheeler's SLOCCount.[9]

Now let's build a Clojure index-of-any, step by step. If we just wanted to find the matches, we could use a Clojure filter. But we want to find the *index* of a match. So, we create indexed,[10] a function that takes a collection and returns an indexed collection:

examples/exploring.clj

```
(defn indexed [coll] (map vector (iterate inc 0) coll))
```

indexed returns a sequence of pairs of the form [idx elt]. The expression (iterate inc 0) produces the indexes, and the coll argument provides the elements. Try indexing a string:

```
(indexed "abcde")
⇒   ([0 \a] [1 \b] [2 \c] [3 \d] [4 \e])
```

Next, we want to find the indices of all the characters in the string that match the search set.

---

9.   http://www.dwheeler.com/sloccount/
10. The indexed function already exists as part of clojure-contrib, but I am reimplementing it here for fairness of comparison.

Create an index-filter function that is similar to Clojure's filter but that returns the indices instead of the matches themselves:

```
(defn index-filter [pred coll]
  (when pred
    (for [[idx elt] (indexed coll) :when (pred elt)] idx)))
```

Clojure's for is *not* a loop but a sequence comprehension (see Section 4.2, *Transforming Sequences*, on page 102). The index/element pairs of (indexed coll) are bound to the names idx and elt but only when (pred elt) is true. Finally, the comprehension yields the value of idx for each matching pair.

Clojure sets are functions that test membership in the set. So, you can pass a set of characters and a string to index-filter and get back the indices of all characters in the string that belong to the set. Try it with a few different strings and character sets:

```
(index-filter #{\a \b} "abcdbbb")
```
⇒
```
    (0 1 4 5 6)
```

```
(index-filter #{\a \b} "xyz")
```
⇒
```
    ()
```

At this point, we have accomplished *more* than the stated objective. index-filter returns the indices of all the matches, and we need only the first index. So, index-of-any simply takes the first result from index-filter:

```
(defn index-of-any [pred coll]
  (first (index-filter pred coll)))
```

Test that index-of-any works correctly with a few different inputs:

```
(index-of-any #{\z \a} "zzabyycdxx")
```
⇒
```
    0
```
```
(index-of-any #{\b \y} "zzabyycdxx")
```
⇒
```
    3
```

The Clojure version is simpler than the imperative version by every metric (see Figure 2.2, on the facing page). What accounts for the difference?

- The imperative indexOfAny must deal with several special cases: null or empty strings, a null or empty set of search characters, and the absence of a match. These special cases add branches and exits to the method. With a functional approach, most of these kinds of special cases just work without any explicit code.

Metric	LOC	Branches	Exits/Method	Variables
Imperative Version	14	4	3	3
Functional Version	6	1	1	0

Figure 2.2: RELATIVE COMPLEXITY OF IMPERATIVE AND FUNCTIONAL INDEXOFANY

- The imperative indexOfAny introduces local variables to traverse collections (both the string and the character set). By using higher-order functions such as map and sequence comprehensions such as for, the functional index-of-any avoids all need for variables.

Unnecessary complexity tends to snowball. For example, the special case branches in the imperative indexOfAny use the magic number -1 to indicate a nonmatch. Should the magic number be a symbolic constant? Whatever you think the right answer is, *the question itself disappears* in the functional version. While shorter and simpler, the functional index-of-any is also *vastly more general*:

- indexOfAny searches a string, while index-of-any can search any sequence.
- indexOfAny matches against a set of characters, while index-of-any can match against any predicate.
- indexOfAny returns the first match, while index-filter returns all the matches and can be further composed with other filters.

As an example of how much more general the functional index-of-any is, you could use code we just wrote to find the third occurrence of "heads" in a series of coin flips:

```
(nth (index-filter #{:h} [:t :t :h :t :h :t :t :t :h :h])
     2)
⇒  8
```

So, it turns out that writing index-of-any in a functional style, without loops or variables, is simpler, less error prone, and more general than the imperative indexOfAny.[11] On larger units of code, these advantages become even more telling.

---

11. It is worth mentioning that you could write a functional indexForAny in plain Java, although it would not be idiomatic. It may become more idiomatic when closures are added to the language. See http://functionaljava.org/ for more information.

2.7 Metadata

The Wikipedia entry on metadata[12] begins by saying that metadata is "data about data." That is true but not usably specific. In Clojure, metadata is data that is *orthogonal to the logical value of an object.* For example, a person's first and last names are plain old data. The fact that a person object can be serialized to XML has nothing to do with the person and is metadata. Likewise, the fact that a person object is dirty and needs to be flushed to the database is metadata.

You can add metadata to a collection or a symbol using the with-meta function:

```
(with-meta object metadata)
```

Create a simple data structure, then use with-meta to create another object with the same data but its own metadata:

```
(def stu {:name "Stu" :email "stu@thinkrelevance.com"})
(def serializable-stu (with-meta stu {:serializable true}))
```

Metadata makes no difference for operations that depend on an object's value, so stu and serializable-stu are equal:

```
(= stu serializable-stu)
```
⇒   true

The = tests for value equality, like Java's equals. To test reference equality, use identical?:

```
(identical? obj1 obj2)
```

You can prove that stu and serializable-stu are different objects by calling identical?:

```
(identical? stu serializable-stu)
```
⇒   false

identical? is equivalent to == in Java.

You can access metadata with the meta macro, verifying that serializable-stu has metadata and stu does not:

```
(meta stu)
```
⇒   nil

```
(meta serializable-stu)
```
⇒   {:serializable true}

---

12. http://en.wikipedia.org/wiki/Metadata

For convenience, you do not even have to spell out the meta function. You can use the reader macro ^ instead:

```
^stu
```
⇒
```
    nil
```

```
^serializable-stu
```
⇒
```
    {:serializable true}
```

When you create a new object based on an existing object, the existing object's metadata flows to the new object. For example, you could add some more information to serializable-stu. The assoc function returns a new map with additional key/value pairs added:

```
(assoc map k v & more-kvs)
```

Use assoc to create a new collection based on serializable-stu, but with a :state value added:

```
(def stu-with-address (assoc serializable-stu :state "NC"))
```
⇒
```
    {:name "Stu", :email "stu@thinkrelevance.com", :state "NC"}
```

stu-with-address has the new key/value pair, and it also takes on the metadata from serializable-stu:

```
^stu-with-address
```
⇒
```
    {:serializable true}
```

In addition to adding metadata to your own data structures, you can also pass metadata to the Clojure compiler using the reader metadata macro.

Reader Metadata

The Clojure language itself uses metadata in several places. For example, vars have a metadata map containing documentation, type information, and source information. Here is the metadata for the str var:

```
(meta #'str)
```
⇒
```
    {:ns #<Namespace clojure.core>,
     :name str,
     :file "core.clj",
     :line 313,
     :arglists ([] [x] [x & ys]),
     :tag java.lang.String,
     :doc "With no args, ... etc."}
```

Some common metadata keys and their uses are shown in Figure 2.3, on page 57.

Much of the metadata on a var is added automatically by the Clojure compiler. To add your own key/value pairs to a var, use the metadata reader macro:

```
#^metadata form
```

For example, you could create a simple shout function that upcases a string and then document that shout both expects and returns a string, using the :tag key:

```
; see also shorter form below
(defn #^{:tag String} shout [#^{:tag String} s] (.toUpperCase s))
⇒    #'user/shout
```

You can inspect shout's metadata to see that Clojure added the :tag:

```
^#'shout
{:ns #<Namespace user>,
 :name shout,
 :file "NO_SOURCE_FILE",
 :line 57,
 :arglists ([s]),
 :tag java.lang.String}
```

You provided the :tag, and Clojure provided the other keys. The :file value NO_SOURCE_FILE indicates that the code was entered at the REPL.

You can also pass a nonstring to shout and see that Clojure casts the argument to a String before calling toUpperCase():

```
(shout 1)
⇒    java.lang.ClassCastException: \
     java.lang.Integer cannot be cast to java.lang.String
```

Because :tag metadata is so common, you can also use the short-form #^Classname, which expands to #^{:tag Classname}. Using the shorter form, you can rewrite shout as follows:

```
(defn #^String shout [#^String s] (.toUpperCase s))
⇒    #'user/shout
```

If you find the metadata disruptive when you are reading the definition of a function, you can place the metadata last. Use a variant of defn that wraps one or more body forms in parentheses, followed by a metadata map:

```
(defn shout
  ([s] (.toUpperCase s))
  {:tag String})
```

Metadata Key	Used For
:arglists	Parameter info used by doc
:doc	Documentation used by doc
:file	Source file
:line	Source line number
:macro	True for macros
:name	Local name
:ns	Namespace
:tag	Expected argument or return type

Figure 2.3: COMMON METADATA KEYS

It is important to note that the metadata reader macro is *not the same* as with-meta. The metadata reader macro adds metadata for the compiler, and with-meta adds metadata for your own data:

```
(def #^{:testdata true} foo (with-meta [1 2 3] {:order :ascending}))
```
⇒   #'user/foo

When Clojure reads the previous form, the compiler adds :testdata to the metadata for the *var* foo:

```
(meta #'foo)
{:ns #<Namespace user>, :name foo, :file "NO_SOURCE_FILE",
 :line 6, :testdata true}
```

The with-meta adds :order to the *value* [1 2 3], which is then bound to foo:

```
(meta foo)
```
⇒   {:order :ascending}

As a general rule, use the metadata reader macro to add metadata to vars and parameters. Use with-meta to add metadata to data.[13]

2.8 Wrapping Up

This has been a long chapter. But think how much ground you have covered: you can instantiate basic literal types, define and call functions, manage namespaces, and read and write metadata. You can write purely functional code, and yet you can easily introduce side effects

---

13. As with any good rule, there are exceptions. Inside a macro definition you may need to use with-meta to add metadata to vars. See Section 7.5, *Making a Lancet DSL*, on page 213 for an example.

when you need to do so. You have also met Lisp concepts including reader macros, special forms, and destructuring.

The material here would take hundreds of pages to cover in most other languages. Is the Clojure way really that much simpler? Yes, in part. Half the credit for this chapter belongs to Clojure. Clojure's elegant design and abstraction choices make the language much easier to learn than most.

That said, the language may not *seem* so easy to learn right now. That's because we are taking advantage of Clojure's power to move much faster than most programming language books.

So, the other half of the credit for this chapter belongs to you, the reader. Clojure will give back what you put in, and then some. Take the time you need to feel comfortable with the chapter's examples and with using the REPL.

In the next chapter, we will see how Clojure interoperates seamlessly with Java libraries.

Chapter 3

Working with Java

Clojure's Java support is both powerful and lean. It's powerful, in that it brings the expressiveness of Lisp syntax, plus some syntactic sugar tailored to Java. It's lean, in that it can get right to the metal. Clojure code compiles to bytecode and does not have to go through any special translation layer on the way to Java.

Clojure embraces Java and its libraries. Idiomatic Clojure code calls Java libraries directly and does not try to wrap everything under the sun to look like Lisp. This surprises many new Clojure developers but is very pragmatic. Where Java isn't broken, Clojure doesn't fix it.

In this chapter, you will see how Clojure access to Java is convenient, elegant, and fast:

- Calling Java is simple and direct. Clojure provides syntax extensions for accessing anything you could reach from Java code: classes, instances, constructors, methods, and fields. Although you will typically call Java code directly, you can also wrap Java APIs and use them in a more functional style.

- Clojure is *fast*, unlike many other dynamic languages on the JVM. You can use custom support for primitives and arrays, plus type hints, to cause Clojure's compiler to generate the same code that a Java compiler would generate.

- Java code can call Clojure code, too. Clojure can generate Java classes on the fly. On a one-off basis, you can use proxy, or you can generate and save classes with gen-class.

- Clojure's exception handling is easy to use. Better yet, explicit exception handling is rarely necessary. Clojure's exception primitives are the same as Java's. However, Clojure does not require you to deal with checked exceptions and makes it easy to clean up resources using the with-open idiom.

At the end of the chapter, you will use Clojure's Java invocation features to integrate Lancet with Ant projects and tasks.

3.1 Calling Java

Clojure provides simple, direct syntax for calling Java code: creating objects, invoking methods, and accessing static methods and fields. In addition, Clojure provides syntactic sugar that makes calling Java from Clojure more concise than calling Java from Java!

Not all types in Java are created equal: the primitives and arrays work differently. Where Java has special cases, Clojure gives you direct access to these as well. Finally, Clojure provides a set of convenience functions for common tasks that would be unwieldy in Java.

Accessing Constructors, Methods, and Fields

The first step in many Java interop scenarios is creating a Java object. Clojure provides the new special form for this purpose:

```
(new classname)
```

Try creating a new Random:

```
(new java.util.Random)
```
⇒   java.util.Random@4f1ada

The REPL simply prints out the new Random instance by calling its toString() method. To use a Random, you will need to save it away somewhere. For now, simply use def to save the Random into a Clojure Var:

```
(def rnd (new java.util.Random))
```
⇒   #'user/rnd

Now you can call methods on rnd using Clojure's dot (.) special form:

```
(. class-or-instance member-symbol & args)
(. class-or-instance (member-symbol & args))
```

The . can call methods. For example, the following code calls the no-argument version of nextInt():

```
(. rnd nextInt)
```
⇒   -791474443

Random also has a nextInt() that takes an argument. You can call that version by simply adding the argument to the list:

```
(. rnd nextInt 10)
```
⇒   8

In the previous call, the . form is being used to access an instance method. But . works with all kinds of class members: fields as well as methods, and statics as well as instances. Here you can see the . used to get the value of pi:

```
(. Math PI)
```
⇒   3.141592653589793

Notice that Math is not fully qualified. It doesn't have to be, because Clojure imports java.lang automatically. To avoid typing java.util.Random everywhere, you could explicitly import it:

```
(import [& import-lists])
; import-list => (package-symbol & class-name-symbols)
```

import takes a variable number of lists, with the first part of each list being a package name and the rest being names to import from that package. The following import allows unqualified access to Random, Locale, and MessageFormat:

```
(import '(java.util Random Locale)
        '(java.text MessageFormat))
```
⇒   java.text.MessageFormat

```
Random
```
⇒   java.util.Random

```
Locale
```
⇒   java.util.Locale

```
MessageFormat
```
⇒   java.text.MessageFormat

At this point, you have almost everything you need to call Java from Clojure. You can do the following:

- Import class names

- Create instances

- Access fields

- Invoke methods

However, there isn't anything particularly exciting about the syntax. It is just "Java with different parentheses." In the next section, you will see how Clojure provides syntactic sugar to ease Java interop.

Syntactic Sugar

Most of the Java forms shown in the previous section have a shorter form. Instead of new, you can use the Classname. form. (Note the dot after Classname.) The following are equivalent:

```
(new Random)
(Random.)
```

For static fields, the short form is Classname/membername. The following are equivalent:

```
(. Math PI)
Math/PI
```

For static methods, you can use (Classname/membername):

```
(System/currentTimeMillis)
```
⇒   1226260030788

Another short form is .methodOrFieldName, and it comes *first* in the form. The following calls are equivalent:

```
(. rnd nextInt)
(.nextInt rnd)
```

The Java APIs often introduce several layers of indirection between you and where you want to be. For example, to find out the URL for the source code of a particular object, you need to chain through the following objects: the class, the protection domain, the code source, and finally the location. The prefix-dot notation gets ugly fast:

```
(.getLocation
 (.getCodeSource (.getProtectionDomain (.getClass '(1 2)))))
```
⇒   #<URL file:/Users/stuart/repos/clojure/clojure.jar>

Clojure's .. macro cleans this up:

```
(.. class-or-instance form & forms)
```

The .. chains together multiple member accesses by making each result the this object for the next member access in the chain. Looking up an object's code URL becomes the following:

```
(.. '(1 2) getClass getProtectionDomain getCodeSource getLocation)
```
⇒
```
    #<URL file:/Users/stuart/repos/clojure/clojure.jar>
```

The .. reads left to right, like Java, not inside out, like Lisp. For longer expressions, it is shorter than the pure-Java equivalent in both characters and number of parentheses.

The .. macro is great if the result of each operation is an input to the next. Sometimes you don't care about the results of method calls and simply want to make several calls on the same object. The doto macro makes it easy to make several calls on the same object:

```
(doto class-or-inst & member-access-forms)
```

As the "do" in doto suggests, you can use doto to cause side effects in the mutable Java world. For example, use doto to set multiple system properties:

```
(doto (System/getProperties)
  (.setProperty "name" "Stuart")
  (.setProperty "favoriteColor" "blue"))
```

Clojure's syntactic sugar makes code that calls Java shorter and easier to read. In idiomatic Clojure, prefer the sugared versions shown here:

Java	Clojure	Sugared
new Widget("red")	(new Widget "red")	(Widget. "red")
Math.PI	(. Math PI)	Math/PI
System.currentTimeMillis()	(. System currentTimeMillis)	(System/currentTimeMillis)
rnd.nextInt()	(. rnd nextInt)	(.nextInt rnd)
person.getAddress().getZipCode()	(. (. person getAddress) getZipCode)	(.. person getAddress getZipCode)

Using Java Collections

Clojure's collections supplant the Java collections for most purposes. Clojure's collections are concurrency-safe, have good performance characteristics, and implement the appropriate Java collection interfaces. So, you should generally prefer Clojure's own collections when you are working in Clojure and even pass them back into Java when convenient.

If you do choose to use the Java collections, nothing in Clojure will stop you. From Clojure's perspective, the Java collections are classes like any other, and all the various Java interop forms will work. But the Java collections are designed for lock-based concurrency. They will not provide the concurrency guarantees that Clojure collections do and will not work well with Clojure's software transactional memory.

One place where you *will* need to deal with Java collections is the special case of Java arrays. In Java, arrays have their own syntax and their own bytecode instructions. Java arrays do not implement any Java interface. Clojure collections cannot masquerade as arrays. (Java collections can't either!) The Java platform makes arrays a special case in every way, so Clojure does too.

Clojure provides make-array to create Java arrays:

```
(make-array class length)
(make-array class dim & more-dims)
```

make-array takes a class and a variable number of array dimensions. For a one-dimensional array of strings, you might say this:

```
(make-array String 5)
```
⇒   #<String[] [Ljava.lang.String;@45a270b2>

The odd output is courtesy of Java's implementation of toString() for arrays: [Ljava.lang.String is the JVM specification's encoding for "one-dimensional array of strings." That's not very useful at the REPL, so you can use Clojure's seq to wrap any Java array as a Clojure sequence so that the REPL can print the individual array entries:

```
(seq (make-array String 5))
```
⇒   (nil nil nil nil nil)

Clojure also includes a family of functions with names such as int-array for creating arrays of Java primitives. You can issue the following command at the REPL to review the documentation for these and other array functions:

```
(find-doc "-array")
```

Clojure provides a set of low-level operations on Java arrays, including aset, aget, and alength:

```
(aset java-array index value)
(aset java-array index-dim1 index-dim2 ... value)
```

```
(aget java-array index)
(aget java-array index-dim1 index-dim2 ...)
```

```
(alength java-array)
```

Use make-array to create an array, and then experiment with using aset, aget, and alength to work with the array:

```
(defn painstakingly-create-array []
  (let [arr (make-array String 5)]
    (aset arr 0 "Painstaking")
    (aset arr 1 "to")
    (aset arr 2 "fill")
    (aset arr 3 "in")
    (aset arr 4 "arrays")
    arr))

(aget (painstakingly-create-array) 0)
```
⇒   `"Painstaking"`

```
(alength (painstakingly-create-array))
```
⇒   `5`

Most of the time, you will find it simpler to use higher-level functions such as to-array, which creates an array directly from any collection:

```
(to-array sequence)
```

to-array always creates an Object array:

```
(to-array ["Easier" "array" "creation"])
```
⇒   `#<Object[] [Ljava.lang.Object;@1639f9e3>`

to-array is also useful for calling Java methods that take a variable argument list, such as String/format:

```
; example. prefer clojure.core/format
(String/format "Training Week: %s Mileage: %d"
  (to-array [2 26]))
```
⇒   `"Training Week: 2 Mileage: 26"`

In fact, String/format is used so frequently that it has a Clojure wrapper, format, which is described in Section 3.1, *Convenience Functions*, on the next page. to-array's cousin into-array can create an array with a more specific type than Object.

```
(into-array type? seq)
```

You can pass an explicit type as an optional first argument to into-array:

```
(into-array String ["Easier", "array", "creation"])
```
⇒   `#<String[] [Ljava.lang.String;@391ecf28>`

If you omit the type argument, into-array will guess the type based on the first item in the sequence:

```
(into-array ["Easier" "array" "creation"])
```
⇒   `#<String[] [Ljava.lang.String;@76bfd849>`

As you can see, the array contains Strings, not Objects.

If you want to transform every element of a Java array without converting to a Clojure sequence, you can use amap:

```
(amap a idx ret expr)
```

amap will create a clone of the array a, binding that clone to the name you specify in ret. It will then execute expr once for each element in a, with idx bound to the index of the element. Finally, amap returns the cloned array.

You could use amap to uppercase every string in an array of strings:

```
(def strings (into-array ["some" "strings" "here"]))
```
⇒   #'user/strings

```
(seq (amap strings idx _ (.toUpperCase (aget strings idx))))
```
⇒   ("SOME" "STRINGS" "HERE")

The ret parameter is set to _ to indicate that it is not needed in the map expression, and the wrapping seq is simply for convenience in printing the result at the REPL.

Similar to amap is areduce:

```
(areduce a idx ret init expr)
```

Where amap produces a new array, areduce produces *anything you want*. The ret is initially set to init and later set to the return value of each subsequent invocation of expr. areduce is normally used to write functions that "tally up" a collection in some way. For example, the following call finds the length of the longest string in the strings array:

```
(areduce strings idx ret 0 (max ret (.length (aget strings idx))))
```
⇒   7

amap and areduce are special-purpose macros for interoperating with Java arrays. Most of the time, you should prefer the more general (and more convenient) sequence functions map and reduce, covered in Section 4.2, *Transforming Sequences*, on page 102.

Convenience Functions

Clojure provides several convenience functions for working with Java code. For example, consider the mismatch between Clojure functions and Java methods. In Clojure, you often pass functions as arguments to other functions. This will not work with Java methods.

Try passing .toUpperCase to map in order to upcase a vector of strings:

```
(map .toUpperCase ["a" "short" "message"])
```
⇒   java.lang.Exception:\
    Unable to resolve symbol: .toUpperCase in this context

The problem is that toUpperCase() is a Java method, not a Clojure function. This member-as-function idiom is a common one, so Clojure provides the "member function" memfn macro to wrap methods for you:

```
(map (memfn toUpperCase) ["a" "short" "message"])
```
⇒   ("A" "SHORT" "MESSAGE")

As a preferred alternative to memfn,[1] you can use an anonymous function to wrap a method call:

```
(map #(.toUpperCase %) ["a" "short" "message"])
```
⇒   ("A" "SHORT" "MESSAGE")

Another common idiom is checking whether an object is an instance of a certain class. Clojure provides the instance? function for this purpose:

```
(instance? Integer 10)
```
⇒   true

```
(instance? Comparable 10)
```
⇒   true

```
(instance? String 10)
```
⇒   false

Java provides a string format method. Because the message signature for Java's format is slightly inconvenient to call in Clojure and because string formatting is so common, Clojure provides a wrapper:

```
(format fmt-string & args)
```

You use format like this:

```
(format "%s ran %d miles today" "Stu" 8)
```
⇒   "Stu ran 8 miles today"

The %s and %d format specifiers shown earlier barely scratch the surface. Complete documentation of the format specifiers is located in the Javadoc for the Formatter class.[2]

---

1.   memfn predates anonymous function support. Most Clojure programmers now prefer anonymous functions.

2.   http://java.sun.com/j2se/1.5.0/docs/api/java/util/Formatter.html

If you need to read data from existing JavaBeans, you can convert them to Clojure maps for convenience. Use Clojure's bean function to wrap a JavaBean in an immutable Clojure map:

```
(bean java-bean)
```

For example, the following code will return the properties of your JVM's default MessageDigest instance for the Secure Hash Algorithm (SHA):

```
(import '(java.security MessageDigest))
```
⇒   nil

```
(bean (MessageDigest/getInstance "SHA"))
```
⇒   {:provider #<Sun SUN version 1.6>,
      :digestLength 20, :algorithm "SHA",
      :class java.security.MessageDigest$Delegate}

Once you have converted a JavaBean into a Clojure map, you can use any of Clojure's map functions. For example, you can use a keyword as a function to extract a particular field:

```
(:digestLength (bean (MessageDigest/getInstance "SHA")))
```
⇒   20

Beans have never been easier to use.

3.2 Optimizing for Performance

In Clojure, it is idiomatic to call Java using the techniques described in Section 3.1, *Calling Java*, on page 60. The resulting code will be fast enough for 90 percent of scenarios. When you need to, though, you can make localized changes to boost performance. These changes will not change how outside callers invoke your code, so you are free to make your code work and *then* make it fast.

Using Primitives for Performance

In the preceding sections, function parameters carry no type information. Clojure simply does the right thing. Depending on your perspective, this is either a strength or a weakness. It's a strength, because your code is clean and simple and can take advantage of duck typing. But it's also a weakness, because a reader of the code cannot be certain of data types and because doing the right thing carries some performance overhead.

Why Duck Typing?

With duck typing, an object's type is the sum of *what it can do* (methods), rather than the sum of *what it is* (the inheritance hierarchy). In other words, it is more important to quack() and fly() than it is to insist that you implement the Duck interface.

Duck typing has two major benefits:

- Duck-typed code is easier to test. Since the rules of "what can go here" are relaxed, it is easier to isolate code under test from irrelevant dependencies.

- Duck-typed code is easier to reuse. Reuse is more granular, at the method level instead of the interface level. So, it is more likely that new objects can be plugged in directly, without refactoring or wrapping.

If you think about it, the "easier to test" argument is just a special case of the "easier to reuse" argument. Using code inside a test harness is itself a kind of reuse.

Idiomatic Clojure takes advantage of duck typing, but it is not mandatory. You can add type information for performance or documentation purposes, as discussed in Section 3.2, *Adding Type Hints*, on page 72.

Consider a function that calculates the sum of the numbers from 1 to n:

examples/interop.clj

```
; performance demo only, don't write code like this
(defn sum-to [n]
  (loop [i 1 sum 0]
    (if (<= i n)
      (recur (inc i) (+ i sum))
      sum)))
```

You can verify that this function works with a small input value:

```
(sum-to 10)
```
⇒
```
   55
```

Let's see how sum-to performs. To time an operation, you can use the time function.

When benchmarking, you'll tend to want to take several measurements so that you can eliminate startup overhead plus any outliers; therefore, you can call time from inside a dotimes macro:

```
(dotimes bindings & body)
;  bindings => name n
```

dotimes will execute its body repeatedly, with name bound to integers from zero to n-1. Using dotimes, you can collect five timings of sum-to as follows:

```
(dotimes [_ 5] (time (sum-to 10000)))
"Elapsed time: 0.778 msecs"
"Elapsed time: 0.559 msecs"
"Elapsed time: 0.633 msecs"
"Elapsed time: 0.548 msecs"
"Elapsed time: 0.647 msecs"
```

To speed things up, you can ask Clojure to treat n, i, and sum as ints:

examples/interop.clj
```
(defn integer-sum-to [n]
  (let [n (int n)]
    (loop [i (int 1) sum (int 0)]
      (if (<= i n)
        (recur (inc i) (+ i sum))
        sum))))
```

The integer-sum-to is indeed faster:

```
(dotimes [_ 5] (time (integer-sum-to 10000)))
"Elapsed time: 0.207 msecs"
"Elapsed time: 0.073 msecs"
"Elapsed time: 0.072 msecs"
"Elapsed time: 0.071 msecs"
"Elapsed time: 0.071 msecs"
```

Clojure's convenient math operators (+, -, and so on) make sure their results do not overflow. Maybe you can get an even faster function by using the unchecked version of +, unchecked-add:

examples/interop.clj
```
(defn unchecked-sum-to [n]
  (let [n (int n)]
    (loop [i (int 1) sum (int 0)]
      (if (<= i n)
        (recur (inc i) (unchecked-add i sum))
        sum))))
```

The unchecked-sum-to is faster still:

```
(dotimes [_ 5] (time (unchecked-sum-to 10000)))
"Elapsed time: 0.081 msecs"
"Elapsed time: 0.036 msecs"
"Elapsed time: 0.035 msecs"
"Elapsed time: 0.034 msecs"
"Elapsed time: 0.035 msecs"
```

Prefer accuracy first, and then optimize for speed only where necessary. sum-to is accurate but slow:

```
(sum-to 100000)
```
⇒
```
    5000050000
```

integer-sum-to will throw an exception on overflow. This is bad, but the problem is easily detected:

```
(integer-sum-to 100000)
```
⇒
```
    java.lang.ArithmeticException: integer overflow
```

unchecked-sum-to will fail silently on overflow. In a program setting, it can quietly but catastrophically corrupt data:

```
(unchecked-sum-to 100000)
```
⇒
```
    705082704 ; WRONG!!
```

Given the competing concerns of correctness and performance, you should normally prefer simple, undecorated code such as the original sum-to. If profiling identifies a bottleneck, you can force Clojure to use a primitive type in just the places that need it.

The sum-to example is deliberately simple in order to demonstrate the various options for integer math in Clojure. In a real Clojure program, it would be more expressive to implement sum-to using reduce. Summing a sequence is the same as summing the first two items, adding that result to the next item, and so on. That is exactly the loop that (reduce + ...) provides. With reduce, you can rewrite sum-to as a one-liner:

```
(defn better-sum-to [n]
  (reduce + (range 1 (inc n))))
```

The example also demonstrates an even more general point: *pick the right algorithm to begin with*. The sum of numbers from 1 to n can be calculated directly as follows:

```
(defn best-sum-to [n]
  (/ (* n (inc n)) 2))
```

Even without performance hints, this is faster than implementations based on repeated addition:

```
(dotimes [_ 5] (time (best-sum-to 10000)))
"Elapsed time: 0.037 msecs"
"Elapsed time: 0.018 msecs"
"Elapsed time: 0.0050 msecs"
"Elapsed time: 0.0040 msecs"
"Elapsed time: 0.0050 msecs"
```

Performance is a tricky subject. Don't write ugly code in search of speed. Start by choosing appropriate algorithms and getting your code to simply work correctly. If you have performance issues, profile to identify the problems. Then, introduce only as much complexity as you need to solve those problems.

Adding Type Hints

Clojure supports adding type hints to function parameters, let bindings, variable names, and expressions. These type hints serve three purposes:

- Optimizing critical performance paths
- Documenting the required type
- Enforcing the required type at runtime

For example, consider the following function, which returns information about a Java class:

examples/interop.clj

```
(defn describe-class [c]
  {:name (.getName c)
   :final (java.lang.reflect.Modifier/isFinal (.getModifiers c))})
```

You can ask Clojure how much type information it can infer, by setting the special variable *warn-on-reflection* to true:

```
(set! *warn-on-reflection* true)
⇒    true
```

The exclamation point on the end of set! is an idiomatic indication that set! changes mutable state. set! is described in detail in Section 6.5, *Working with Java Callback APIs*, on page 175.

With *warn-on-reflection* set to true, compiling describe-class will produce the following warnings:

```
Reflection warning, line: 87
 - reference to field getName can't be resolved.
```

```
Reflection warning, line: 88
  - reference to field getModifiers can't be resolved.
```

These warnings indicate that Clojure has no way to know the type of c. You can provide a type hint to fix this, using the metadata syntax #^Class:

examples/interop.clj

```
(defn describe-class [#^Class c]
  {:name (.getName c)
   :final (java.lang.reflect.Modifier/isFinal (.getModifiers c))})
```

With the type hint in place, the reflection warnings will disappear. The compiled Clojure code will be exactly the same as compiled Java code. Further, attempts to call describe-class with something other than a Class will fail with a ClassCastException:

```
(describe-class StringBuffer)
    {:name "java.lang.StringBuffer", :final true}
```

```
(describe-class "foo")
    java.lang.ClassCastException: \
    java.lang.String cannot be cast to java.lang.Class
```

If your ClassCastException provides a less helpful error message, it is because you are using a version of Java prior to Java 6. Improved error reporting is one of many good reasons to run your Clojure code on Java 6 or later.

When you provide a type hint, Clojure will insert an appropriate class cast in order to avoid making slow, reflective calls to Java methods. But if your function does not actually call any Java methods on a hinted object, then Clojure will *not* insert a cast. Consider this wants-a-string function:

```
(defn wants-a-string [#^String s] (println s))
    #'user/wants-a-string
```

You might expect that wants-a-string would complain about nonstring arguments. In fact, it will be perfectly happy:

```
(wants-a-string "foo")
| foo
```

```
(wants-a-string 0)
| 0
```

Clojure can tell that wants-a-string never actually uses its argument *as* a string (println will happily try to print any kind of argument). Since no string methods need to be called, Clojure does not attempt to cast s to a string.

When you need speed, type hints will let Clojure code compile down to the same code Java will produce. But you won't need type hints that often. Make your code *right* first, and then worry about making it fast.

3.3 Creating and Compiling Java Classes in Clojure

Clojure's objects all implement reasonable Java interfaces:

- Clojure's data structures implement interfaces from the Java Collections API.
- Clojure's functions implement Runnable and Callable.

In addition to these generic interfaces, you will occasionally need domain-specific interfaces. Often this comes in the form of callback handlers for event-driven APIs such as Swing or some XML parsers. Clojure can easily generate one-off proxies or classes on disk when needed, using a fraction of the lines of code necessary in Java.

Creating Java Proxies

To interoperate with Java, you will often need to implement Java interfaces. A good example is parsing XML with a Simple API for XML (SAX) parser. To get ready for this example, go ahead and import the following classes. We'll need them all before we are done:

```
(import '(org.xml.sax InputSource)
  '(org.xml.sax.helpers DefaultHandler)
  '(java.io StringReader)
  '(javax.xml.parsers SAXParserFactory))
```

To use a SAX parser, you need to implement a callback mechanism. The easiest way is often to extend the DefaultHandler class. In Clojure, you can extend a class with the proxy function:

```
(proxy class-and-interfaces super-cons-args & fns)
```

As a simple example, use proxy to create a DefaultHandler that prints the details of all calls to startElement:

examples/interop.clj

```
(def print-element-handler
    (proxy [DefaultHandler] []
      (startElement
        [uri local qname atts]
        (println (format "Saw element: %s" qname)))))
```

proxy generates an instance of a proxy class. The first argument to proxy is [DefaultHandler], a vector of the superclass and superinterfaces. The second argument, [], is a vector of arguments to the base class constructor. In this case, no arguments are needed.

After the proxy setup comes the implementation code for zero or more proxy methods. The proxy shown earlier has one method. Its name is startElement, and it takes four arguments and prints the name of the qname arg.

Now all you need is a parser to pass the handler to. This requires plowing through a pile of Java factory methods and constructors. For a simple exploration at the REPL, you can create a function that parses XML in a string:

```
(defn demo-sax-parse [source handler]
  (.. SAXParserFactory newInstance newSAXParser
      (parse (InputSource. (StringReader. source))
        handler)))
```

Now the parse is easy:

```
(demo-sax-parse "<foo>
<bar>Body of bar</bar>
</foo>" print-element-handler)
| Saw element: foo
| Saw element: bar
```

The previous example demonstrates the mechanics of creating a Clojure proxy to deal with Java's XML interfaces. You can take a similar approach to implementing your own custom Java interfaces. But if all you are doing is XML processing, clojure-contrib already has terrific XML support and can work with any SAX-compatible Java parser. See the clojure.contrib.lazy-xml library for details.

The proxy mechanism is completely general and can be used to generate any kind of Java object you want, on the fly. Sometimes the objects are so simple you can fit the entire object in a single line. The following code creates a new thread and then creates a new dynamic subclass of Runnable to run on the new thread:

```
(.start (Thread.
         (proxy [Runnable] [] (run [] (println "I ran!")))))
```

In Java, you must provide an implementation of every method on every interface you implement. In Clojure, you can leave them out:

```
(proxy [Callable] []) ; proxy with no methods (??)
```

If you omit a method implementation, Clojure provides a default implementation that throws an UnsupportedOperationException:

```
(.call (proxy [Callable] []))
```
⇒   `java.lang.UnsupportedOperationException: call`

The default implementation does not make much sense for interfaces with only one method, such as Runnable and Callable, but it can be handy when you are implementing larger interfaces and don't care about some of the methods.

So far in this section, you have seen how to use proxy to create implementations of Java interfaces. This is very powerful when you need it, but often Clojure is already there on your behalf. For example, functions automatically implement Runnable and Callable:

```
; normal usage: call an anonymous function
(#(println "foo"))
```
⇒   `foo`

```
; call through Runnable's run
(.run #(println "foo"))
```
⇒   `foo`

```
; call through Callable's call
(.call #(println "foo"))
```
⇒   `foo`

This makes it very easy to pass Clojure functions to other threads:

examples/interop.clj
```
(dotimes [i 5]
  (.start
   (Thread.
    (fn []
      (Thread/sleep (rand 500))
      (println (format "Finished %d on %s" i (Thread/currentThread)))))))
```

For one-off tasks such as XML and thread callbacks, Clojure's proxies are quick and easy to use. If you need a longer-lived class, you can generate new named classes from Clojure as well.

Compiling to Disk

The clojure proxy method is very powerful, but sometimes you want actual class files that you can save to disk. For example, you might want a Java main class that you can launch or an applet or a class to be deployed into a Java container.

In this section, we will build a stand-alone Java application in Clojure. The application will be named tasklist, and it will implement a simplified version of the ant -p command. tasklist will load an Ant build script and extract the names of all the tasks defined in the file.

The sample code for the book includes a prebuilt tasklist and an example Ant build script for testing at snippets/example-build.xml. To see how the completed tasklist should work, call the prebuilt version from the command line as follows:

On Windows:

```
bin\tasklist.bat snippets\example-build.xml
[init compile-java compile-clojure clojure jar all clean]
```

On *nix:

```
bin/tasklist.sh snippets/example-build.xml
[init compile-java compile-clojure clojure jar all clean]
```

The example build file is Clojure's own build file, and the tasks listed are tasks you can call when building Clojure from source.

Now, let's build our own implementation of tasklist, starting with the code in reader/tasklist.clj:

`reader/tasklist.clj`

```
Line 1   (ns reader.tasklist
     2     (:gen-class
     3       :extends org.xml.sax.helpers.DefaultHandler
     4       :state state
     5       :init init)
     6     (:use [clojure.contrib.duck-streams :only (reader)])
     7     (:import [java.io File]
     8              [org.xml.sax InputSource]
     9              [org.xml.sax.helpers DefaultHandler]
    10              [javax.xml.parsers SAXParserFactory]))
```

The :use and :import clauses are nothing new; they simply bring in the libraries and classes we will need. The interesting part is the :gen-class form beginning on line 2. This will cause Clojure to generate a Java class named reader.tasklist.

The :extends clause on line 3 specifies that the generated class will extend DefaultHandler. We do not need to implement any interfaces, but if you did, you could do this with an :implements clause.

Clojure-generated Java classes isolate their state in a single state structure. The :state clause on line 4 specifies that the state structure will be named state.

The :init clause on line 5 specifies the class's *initialization function*. The initialization function returns the base-class constructor arguments required by Java, plus the initial state structure used by Clojure.

When Clojure generates the reader.tasklist class, it will create the methods for you. These methods will then delegate to functions that you provide. Each method delegates to a function of the same name, prefixed with a hyphen (-). Add a -main function to reader.tasklist that prints the task list for each command-line argument.

examples/tasklist.clj

```
(defn -main [& args]
  (doseq [arg args]
    (println (task-list arg))))
```

Next, create the task-list function called by -main. (Place task-list before -main in your source file so that the definition of -main can see task-list.) task-list should create handler, an instance of your class, and then use the handler to parse the file. Finally, task-list should return the state of the handler.

examples/tasklist.clj

```
Line 1  (defn task-list [arg]
     2    (let [handler (new examples.tasklist)]
     3      (.. SAXParserFactory newInstance newSAXParser
     4          (parse (InputSource. (reader (File. arg)))
     5                 handler))
     6      @(.state handler)))
```

Line 2 shows the name of the prebuilt examples.tasklist. For your implementation, rename this to reader.tasklist instead. The body of the function is boilerplate code to launch a Java SAX parser with the handler as a callback.

Finally, on line 6, the task-list function returns the handler's accumulated state. The state field is named state because that is what we requested in :gen-class. As you will see in a moment, you will store the state in a Clojure atom. (You do not need to worry about the details of atoms now; we will cover them in detail in Section 6.3, *Use Atoms for Uncoordinated, Synchronous Updates*, on page 166.) The reader macro @ dereferences the atom, returning the atom's contents.

Next, implement a handler for the init method. Do not forget the prefix hyphen. The init method should return a vector of two items: the constructor arguments needed by the Java base class constructor and the initial state of the object.

```
examples/tasklist.clj
```

```
(defn -init []
  [[] (atom [])])
```

Since DefaultHandler has a no-argument constructor, the first part of init's return value is simply an empty vector. The second part creates an atom to store the handler's state.

Finally, implement a handler for startElement. You want to extract the names of targets from the build file. The XML will look like this:

```
snippets/example-build.xml
```

```
<target name="compile-java" depends="init"
        description="Compile Java sources.">
```

So, you will want to look for elements whose name is target and then extract those elements' name attributes.

Back in Section 3.3, *Creating Java Proxies*, on page 74, you implemented a proxy startElement that took four arguments. Generating a class is a little different from generating a proxy. In addition to the normal method arguments, you will add an explicit this argument to the beginning of the argument list. this is the Java identity of the object, and you can use it to access the object's state. The startElement handler should look like this:

```
examples/tasklist.clj
```

```
Line 1  (defn -startElement
     2    [this uri local qname atts]
     3    (when (= qname "target")
     4      (swap! (.state this) conj (.getValue atts "name"))))
```

When the qname is target, -startElement updates the state of this object by conjoining the name value to the end of the vector.

Now you are ready to compile your class. Clojure provides a compile function:

```
(compile lib)
```

Like any compiler, compile is finicky about the environment it runs in:

- The library you want to compile must be reachable from the classpath. For the reader.tasklist library, that means the file reader/tasklist.clj must be on the classpath.

- Classes will compile to the *compile-path* directory, which must *also* be on the classpath. By default, *compile-path* is set to the classes directory relative to where you launched Clojure.

The sample code for the book is organized with everything in the right place. If you launched the book REPL from the sample root directory by typing bin/repl.sh or bin\repl.bat, you should be able to compile your library with the following:

```
(compile 'reader.tasklist)
```

If you are having trouble, compare your code to the solution in examples/tasklist.clj.

After you compile your class, you can run it as a stand-alone Java application. You will need to have your classes on the classpath, plus clojure.jar and clojure-contrib.jar. The sample code includes scripts bin/reader-tasklist.sh and bin\reader-tasklist.bat that have everything in the proper place. So, for example, on Windows:

```
bin\reader-tasklist.bat snippets\example-build.xml
[init compile-java compile-clojure clojure jar all clean]
```

The tasklist class that you just created is a plain old Java class, consisting of constructors, fields, and methods. But the process of writing the class is quite different in Clojure. Aside from the syntax, Clojure's approach of a single state object encourages you to pay special attention to state and minimize its use.

A second difference, not visible in the source code, is the highly dynamic nature of the classes generated by Clojure. If you look in the classes/reader directory, you might expect to find a single tasklist.class. In fact, you will find *six* classes:

```
: ls -1
tasklist$_init__433.class
tasklist$_main__439.class
tasklist$_startElement__436.class
tasklist$task_list__430.class
tasklist.class
tasklist__init.class
```

There is one classfile for the class itself, plus one class file for each function or method in the class. In addition, the classfile with __init in its name is special. It executes any top-level code from the library the first time the class is loaded.

This modularity allows you to replace individual functions within a class at runtime. This is much more granular than reloading the entire class and may be useful in some situations. On the other hand, the extra level of indirection imposes a slight performance penalty on method invocation.

Where interop is concerned, these differences pale in comparison to the similarities with "normal" Java classes. The Java classfile format is the lingua franca for interop on the JVM. Clojure's generated classfiles are plain old Java classes. They can go anywhere Java classes can go and can live in any Java system. They can even be used by other JVM languages such as JRuby and Scala.

Clojure class generation has a number of features not shown here:

- There is a command-line compiler for use from build tools. See the build files for Clojure and clojure-contrib for examples of its use.

- Almost everything is configurable. You can change the generated class name or the prefix used when mapping from class method names to Clojure function names.

- There is a gen-interface that parallels gen-class.

For more information on these features, see the Compilation section of the Clojure website.[3]

Next, we will look at how Clojure programs deal with exceptions.

3.4 Exception Handling

In Java code, exception handling crops up for three reasons:

- Wrapping checked exceptions (see the sidebar on the following page if you are unfamiliar with checked exceptions)

- Using a **finally** block to clean up nonmemory resources such as file and network handles

- Responding to the problem: ignoring the exception, retrying the operation, converting the exception to a nonexceptional result, and so on

In Clojure, things are similar but simpler. The try and throw special forms give you all the capabilities of Java's **try, catch, finally,** and **throw.**

---

3. http://clojure.org/compilation

> ### Checked Exceptions
>
> Java's checked exceptions must be explicitly caught or rethrown from every method where they can occur. This seemed like a good idea at first: checked exceptions could use the type system to rigorously document error handling, with compiler enforcement. Most Java programmers now consider checked exceptions a failed experiment, because their costs in code bloat and maintainability outweigh their advantages. For more on the history of checked exceptions, see Rod Waldhoff's article* and the accompanying links.
>
> ---
>
> *. http://tinyurl.com/checked-exceptions-mistake

But you should not have to use them very often, because of the following reasons:

- You do not have to deal with checked exceptions in Clojure.

- You can use macros such as with-open to encapsulate resource cleanup.

Let's see what this looks like in practice.

Keeping Exception Handling Simple

Java programs often wrap checked exceptions at abstraction boundaries. A good example is Apache Ant, which tends to wrap low-level exceptions (such as I/O exceptions) with an Ant-level build exception:

```
// Ant-like code (simplified for clarity)
try {
  newManifest = new Manifest(r);
} catch (IOException e) {
  throw new BuildException(...);
}
```

In Clojure, you are not forced to deal with checked exceptions. You do not have to catch them or declare that you throw them. So, the previous code would translate to the following:

```
(Manifest. r)
```

The absence of exception wrappers makes idiomatic Clojure code easier to read, write, and maintain than idiomatic Java. That said, nothing prevents you from explicitly catching, wrapping, and rethrowing exceptions in Clojure. It simply is not required. You *should* catch exceptions when you plan to respond to them in a meaningful way.

Cleaning Up Resources

Garbage collection will clean up resources in memory. If you use resources that live outside of garbage-collected memory, such as file handles, you need to make sure that you clean them up, even in the event of an exception. In Java, this is normally handled in a **finally** block.

If the resource you need to free follows the convention of having a close method, you can use Clojure's with-open macro:

```
(with-open [name init-form] & body)
```

Internally, with-open creates a try block, sets name to the result of init-form, and then runs the forms in body. Most important, with-open always closes the object bound to name in a finally block.

A good example of with-open is the spit function in clojure-contrib:

```
(clojure.contrib.duck-streams/spit file content)
```

spit simply writes a string to file. Try it:

```
(use '[clojure.contrib.duck-streams :only (spit)])
(spit "hello.out" "hello, world")
   nil
```

You should now find a file at hello.out with contents hello, world.

The implementation of spit is simple:

```
; from clojure-contrib
(defn spit [f content]
  (with-open [#^PrintWriter w (writer f)]
  (.print w content)))
```

spit creates a PrintWriter on f, which can be just about anything that is writable: a file, a URL, a URI, or any of Java's various writers or output streams. It then prints content to the writer. Finally, with-open guarantees that the writer is closed at the end of spit.

If you need to do something other than close in a finally block, the Clojure try form looks like this:

```
(try expr* catch-clause* finally-clause?)
; catch-clause -> (catch classname name expr*)
; finally-clause -> (finally expr*)
```

It can be used thusly:

```
(try
 (throw (Exception. "something failed"))
 (finally
  (println "we get to clean up")))
| we get to clean up
⇒    java.lang.Exception: something failed
```

The previous fragment also demonstrates Clojure's throw form, which simply throws whatever exception is passed to it.

Responding to an Exception

The most interesting case is when an exception handler attempts to respond to the problem in a catch block. As a simple example, consider writing a function to test whether a particular class is available at runtime:

examples/interop.clj

```
; not caller-friendly
(defn class-available? [class-name]
  (Class/forName class-name))
```

This approach is not very caller-friendly. The caller simply wants a yes/no answer but instead gets an exception:

```
(class-available? "borg.util.Assimilate")
⇒    java.lang.ClassNotFoundException: borg.util.Assimilate
```

A friendlier approach uses a catch block to return false:

examples/interop.clj

```
(defn class-available? [class-name]
  (try
   (Class/forName class-name) true
   (catch ClassNotFoundException _ false)))
```

The caller experience is much better now:

```
(class-available? "borg.util.Assimilate")
⇒    false
```

```
(class-available? "java.lang.String")
⇒    true
```

Clojure gives you everything you need to throw and catch exceptions and to cleanly release resources. At the same time, Clojure keeps exceptions in their place. They are important but not so important that your mainline code is dominated by the exceptional.

You have seen how easy it is to access Java from Clojure. Now let's put that to a real test by adding Ant support to Lancet.

3.5 Adding Ant Projects and Tasks to Lancet

Ant ships with dozens of built-in tasks, plus there are hundreds of third-party tasks. There is no need to reinvent this wheel, so Lancet will call Ant tasks directly.

Lancet requires two Ant JAR files: ant.jar and ant-launcher.jar. The sample code for the book includes these files in the lib directory, and they are added to the classpath automatically when you launch the REPL with bin/repl.sh or bin\repl.bat.

To test that Ant is on your classpath, make sure you can instantiate an Ant Mkdir task. Assign it to a var named mkdir-task:

```
(def mkdir-task (org.apache.tools.ant.taskdefs.Mkdir.))
⇒    #'user/mkdir-task
```

If the variable assigns correctly, Ant is on your classpath.

If instantiating a task is that easy, maybe you are almost done. Reflect against Mkdir's method names to see whether you can spot the one that runs the task. You can use Java reflection to go from an instance to a class to methods to method names, like so:

```
(map #(.getName %) (.getMethods (class mkdir-task)))
⇒    ...lots of names here...
```

One of the method names is execute. That sounds pretty good, so let's try it:

```
(.execute mkdir-task)
| dir attribute is required
```

That doesn't seem to have worked, but the error message is a good pointer. Ant attributes, aka Java properties, are usually set with methods named like setXXX(), so try calling setDir to set the dir attribute of mkdir-task:

```
(.setDir mkdir-task "sample-dir")
⇒    java.lang.ClassCastException
```

It appears that the dir attribute is not a string.

To see what type dir expects, reflect against the methods again, this time filtering down to just methods whose name is setDir:

```
(filter #(= "setDir" (.getName %))
 (.getMethods (class mkdir-task)))
⇒    (#<Method public void ... Mkdir.setDir(java.io.File)>)
```

As you can see from setDir's signature, it expects a File, so give it one:

```
(.setDir mkdir-task (java.io.File. "sample-dir"))
⇒    nil
```

Now, you should be able to execute the mkdir-task and create a directory:

```
(.execute mkdir-task)
| Created dir: /lancet/examples/sample-dir
```

Invoking tasks successfully is a good start. However, Lancet needs a few more things from Ant. By reading the Ant source code and experimenting with various tasks, I discovered that Lancet would also need to use Ant's Project class. Lancet does not need Ant's project metaphor, but it does need various APIs that Ant hangs on a Project instance, including the logger.

Create a Project object at the REPL, and bind it to project:

```
(def project (org.apache.tools.ant.Project.))
⇒    #'user/project
```

The project object will want a logger. Ant's NoBannerLogger is a good choice, because it omits unnecessary information about empty targets. Create a NoBannerLogger bound to logger:

```
(def logger (org.apache.tools.ant.NoBannerLogger.))
⇒    #'user/logger
```

There are several steps to configure these objects and connect them. The logger needs a log level, output stream, and error stream. The project needs to initialize and add the logger as a build listener. You could call all of these methods one at a time, like this:

```
(.setOutputPrintStream logger System/out)
⇒    nil
```

```
(.setErrorPrintStream logger System/err)
⇒    nil

; etc.
```

A more readable approach is to use doto to group the configuration calls for each object. Use the following code to create an Ant project:

lancet/step_1_repl.clj

```
Line 1 (def
-       #^{:doc "Dummy ant project to keep Ant tasks happy"}
-       ant-project
-       (let [proj (org.apache.tools.ant.Project.)
5             logger (org.apache.tools.ant.NoBannerLogger.)]
-         (doto logger
-           (.setMessageOutputLevel org.apache.tools.ant.Project/MSG_INFO)
-           (.setOutputPrintStream System/out)
-           (.setErrorPrintStream System/err))
10        (doto proj
-           (.init)
-           (.addBuildListener logger))))
```

- Line 2 creates a documentation string. Since ant-project is a var, you create the documentation string directly in metadata. (Most documentation strings are attached to functions, where defn provides a layer of abstraction above the metadata.)
- Line 3 names the var. ant-project will be shared through an entire Lancet process, unless some need arises for a specific project instance.
- Line 4 binds new Project and NoBannerLogger instances to proj and logger.
- Starting on line 6, a doto form configures the logger.
- Starting on line 10, a doto form initializes the proj and sets its logger.
- The proj on line 10 becomes the return value of the doto and the let and binds to ant-project.

If the definition of ant-project executes correctly, you will then have an instance of Project that you can access at the REPL:

```
ant-project
⇒ #<org.apache.tools.ant.Project@637550b3>
```

As you can see, the REPL representation of a Project does not tell you much. When you are interactively testing a Java object such as an Ant Project from Clojure, the bean function provides a quick way to peek inside the object:

```
(bean ant-project)
⇒ ... 100s of lines follow! ...
```

Unfortunately, the insides of an Ant project are pretty big. You can use keys to get the ant-project's property names:

```
(keys (bean ant-project))
```
⇒
```
    (:userProperties :references :class :filters :defaultInputStream\
     :name :description :properties :taskDefinitions :buildListeners\
     :dataTypeDefinitions :inputHandler :coreLoader :baseDir\
     :globalFilterSet :keepGoingMode :defaultTarget :targets :executor)
```

Once you know the keys, you can use them to poke around further inside the bean. Your project should have a logger as a build listener, so use the :buildListeners key to verify that the listener was installed correctly:

```
(:buildListeners (bean ant-project))
```
⇒
```
    #=(java.util.Vector. [#<org. ... .NoBannerLogger@3583a303>])
```

There is the logger, right where you put it. Clojure's easy, reflective access to Java makes it a good language for exploring existing Java code.

Now that you have an Ant project handy at the REPL, let's revisit how Lancet should create Ant tasks. Earlier you created a mkdir-task directly:

```
(def mkdir-task (org.apache.tools.ant.taskdefs.Mkdir.))
```
⇒
```
    #'user/mkdir-task
```

Project provides a better way to create tasks, with the createTask method. One advantage of this approach is that you do not need to know the class name of a task; you need to know only its short name as it would appear in an Ant build script. Use your ant-project to create an echo-task:

```
(def echo-task (.createTask ant-project "echo"))
```
⇒
```
    #'user/echo-task
```

The Ant echo task takes a message attribute. Call setMessage to set a message, and execute the task to verify its behavior:

```
(.setMessage echo-task "hello ant")
```
⇒
```
    nil
```

```
(.execute echo-task)
  [echo] hello ant
```

Well-behaved tasks need a few more things. All tasks have an init method that Ant calls internally. You have been lucky so far, because mkdir and echo do not use init. But Lancet will need to call init on all tasks. Also, tasks maintain a reference to their projects.

Create an instantiate-task function that correctly performs all these steps:

`lancet/step_1_repl.clj`

```
(defn instantiate-task [project name]
  (let [task (.createTask project name)]
    (doto task
      (.init)
      (.setProject project))))
```

Create and execute a task to make sure that instantiate-task works as you expect:

```
(def echo-task (instantiate-task ant-project "echo"))
⇒    #'user/echo-task

(.setMessage echo-task "echo from instantiate-task")
⇒    nil

(.execute echo-task)
     [echo] echo from instantiate-task
```

There is one slight problem with instantiate-task. If you try to create a task using a name that doesn't exist, ant-project does not throw an exception. It just returns nil, which leads to a confusing error message:

```
(instantiate-task ant-project "sisyphus")
⇒    java.lang.NullPointerException
```

Create a safe-instantiate-task that adds a nil check, throwing an IllegalArgumentException if a task name does not exist:

`lancet/step_1_repl.clj`

```
(use '[clojure.contrib.except :only (throw-if)])
(defn safe-instantiate-task [project name]
  (let [task (.createTask project name)]
    (throw-if (nil? task)
              IllegalArgumentException (str "No task named " name))
    (doto task
      (.init)
      (.setProject project))))
```

Now the error message is much better:

```
(safe-instantiate-task ant-project "sisyphus")
⇒    java.lang.IllegalArgumentException: No task named sisyphus
```

The completed code for this section is listed in Section 3.5, *Lancet Step 1: Ant Projects and Tasks*, on the next page. In this section, you have given Lancet the ability to call Ant tasks. You have plumbed in an Ant project object, and you have wrapped correct initialization of tasks and projects in helper functions.

In later chapters you will make these functions so much easier to use that Lancet crosses the boundary from an API to a domain-specific language.

Lancet Step 1: Ant Projects and Tasks

`lancet/step_1_complete.clj`

```
(ns lancet.step-1-complete
    (:use clojure.contrib.except))

(def
 #^{:doc "Dummy ant project to keep Ant tasks happy"}
 ant-project
 (let [proj (org.apache.tools.ant.Project.)
       logger (org.apache.tools.ant.NoBannerLogger.)]
   (doto logger
     (.setMessageOutputLevel org.apache.tools.ant.Project/MSG_INFO)
     (.setOutputPrintStream System/out)
     (.setErrorPrintStream System/err))
   (doto proj
     (.init)
     (.addBuildListener logger))))

(defn instantiate-task [project name]
  (let [task (.createTask project name)]
    (throw-if (nil? task)
              IllegalArgumentException (str "No task named " name))
    (doto task
      (.init)
      (.setProject project))))
```

3.6 Wrapping Up

Clojure code can call directly into Java and can implement Java classes and interfaces where necessary. Do not be afraid to drop to Java when you need it. Clojure is pragmatic and does not aspire to wrap or replace Java code that already works.

One part of Java that you will use rarely is the Collections API. Clojure provides a powerful, functional, thread-safe alternative to Java collections: the sequence library. In the next chapter, you will meet Clojure's ubiquitous sequences.

Chapter 4

Unifying Data with Sequences

Programs manipulate data. At the lowest level, programs work with structures such as strings, lists, vectors, maps, sets, and trees. At a higher level, these same data structure abstractions crop up again and again. For example:

- XML data is a tree.
- Database result sets can be viewed as lists or vectors.
- Directory hierarchies are trees.
- Files are often viewed as one big string or as a vector of lines.

In Clojure, all these data structures can be accessed through a single abstraction: the sequence (or *seq*). A seq (pronounced "seek") is a *logical* list. It's logical because Clojure does not tie sequences to *implementation details* of a list such as a Lisp cons cell (see the sidebar on page 93 for the history of cons). Instead, the seq is an abstraction that can be used everywhere.

Collections that can be viewed as seqs are called *seq-able* (pronounced "SEEK-a-bull"). In this chapter, you will meet a variety of seq-able collections:

- All Clojure collections
- All Java collections
- Java arrays and strings
- Regular expression matches
- Directory structures
- I/O streams
- XML trees

You will also meet the sequence library, a set of functions that can work with any seq-able. Because so many things are sequences, the sequence library is much more powerful and general than the collection APIs in most languages. The sequence library includes functions to create, filter, and transform data. These functions act as the Collections API for Clojure, and they also replace many of the loops you would write in an imperative language.

In this chapter, you will become a power user of Clojure sequences. You will see how to use a common set of very expressive functions with an incredibly wide range of data types. Then, in the next chapter (Chapter 5, *Functional Programming*, on page 127), you will learn the functional style in which the sequence library is written.

Finally, you will use the sequence API to traverse Java's property reflection and create a property-setting mechanism for Lancet to use when creating Ant tasks.

4.1 Everything Is a Sequence

Every aggregate data structure in Clojure can be viewed as a sequence. A sequence has three core capabilities:

- You can get the first item in a sequence:

```
(first aseq)
```

first returns nil if its argument is empty or nil.

- You can get everything after the first item, in other words, the rest of a sequence:

```
(rest aseq)
```

rest returns an empty seq (not nil) if there are no more items.

- You can construct a new sequence by adding an item to the front of an existing sequence. This is called consing:

```
(cons elem aseq)
```

Under the hood, these three capabilities are declared in a Java interface clojure.lang.ISeq. (Keep this in mind when reading about Clojure, because the name ISeq is often used interchangeably with seq.)

The seq function will return a seq on any seq-able collection:

```
(seq coll)
```

The Origin of Cons

Clojure's sequence is an abstraction based on Lisp's concrete lists. In the original implementation of Lisp, the three fundamental list operations were named car, cdr, and cons. car and cdr are acronyms that refer to implementation details of Lisp on the original IBM 704 platform. Many Lisps, including Clojure, replace these esoteric names with the more meaningful names first and rest.

The third function, cons, is short for construct. Lisp programmers use cons as a noun, verb, and adjective. You use cons to create a data structure called a *cons cell*, or just a *cons* for short.

Most Lisps, including Clojure, retain the original cons name, since "construct" is a pretty good mnemonic for what cons does. It also helps remind you that sequences are immutable. For convenience, you might say that cons adds an element to a sequence, but it is more accurate to say that cons *constructs* a new sequence, which is like the original sequence but with one element added.

---

seq will return nil if its coll is empty or nil. The next function will return the seq of items after the first:

```
(next aseq)
```

(next aseq) is equivalent to (seq (rest aseq)).

If you have a Lisp background, you expect to find that the seq functions work for lists:

```
(first '(1 2 3))
```
⇒
```
   1
```

```
(rest '(1 2 3))
```
⇒
```
   (2 3)
```

```
(cons 0 '(1 2 3))
```
⇒
```
   (0 1 2 3)
```

In Clojure, the same functions will work for other data structures as well. You can treat vectors as seqs:

```
(first [1 2 3])
```
⇒
```
   1
```

```
(rest [1 2 3])
⇒   (2 3)
```

```
(cons 0 [1 2 3])
⇒   (0 1 2 3)
```

When you apply rest or cons to a vector, the result is a seq, not a vector. In the REPL, seqs print just like lists, as you can see in the earlier output. You can check the actual returned type by taking its class:

```
(class (rest [1 2 3]))
⇒   clojure.lang.APersistentVector$Seq
```

The $Seq at the end of the class name is Java's way of mangling nested class names. Seqs that you produce from a specific collection type are often implemented as a Seq class nested inside the original collection class (APersistentVector in this example).

The generality of seqs is very powerful, but sometimes you want to produce a specific implementation type. This is covered in Section 4.5, *Calling Structure-Specific Functions*, on page 113.

You can treat maps as seqs, if you think of a key/value pair as an item in the sequence:

```
(first {:fname "Stu" :lname "Halloway"})
⇒   [:fname "Stu"]
```

```
(rest {:fname "Stu" :lname "Halloway"})
⇒   ([:lname "Halloway"])
```

```
(cons [:mname "Dabbs"] {:fname "Stu" :lname "Halloway"})
⇒   ([:mname "Dabbs"] [:lname "Halloway"] [:fname "Stu"])
```

You can also treat sets as seqs:

```
(first #{:the :quick :brown :fox})
⇒   :brown
```

```
(rest #{:the :quick :brown :fox})
⇒   (:the :fox :quick)
```

```
(cons :jumped #{:the :quick :brown :fox})
⇒   (:jumped :brown :the :fox :quick)
```

Maps and sets have a stable traversal order, but that order depends on implementation details, and you should not rely on it. Elements of a set will not necessarily come back in the order that you put them in:

```
#{:the :quick :brown :fox}
⇒   #{:fox :the :brown :quick}
```

If you want a reliable order, you can use this:

```
(sorted-set & elements)
```

sorted-set will sort the values by their natural sort order:

```
(sorted-set :the :quick :brown :fox)
```
⇒   `#{:brown :fox :quick :the}`

Likewise, key/value pairs in maps won't necessarily come back in the order you put them in:

```
{:a 1 :b 2 :c 3}
```
⇒   `{:a 1, :c 3, :b 2}`

You can create a sorted map with sorted-map:

```
(sorted-map & elements)
```

sorted-maps won't come back in the order you put them in either, but they *will* come back sorted by key:

```
(sorted-map :c 3 :b 2 :a 1)
```
⇒   `{:a 1, :b 2, :c 3}`

In addition to the core capabilities of seq, two other capabilities are worth meeting immediately: conj and into.

```
(conj coll element & elements)
```

```
(into to-coll from-coll)
```

conj adds one or more elements to a collection, and into adds all the items in one collection to another. Both conj and into add items at an efficient insertion spot for the underlying data structure. For lists, conj and into add to the front:

```
(conj '(1 2 3) :a)
```
⇒   `(:a 1 2 3)`

```
(into '(1 2 3) '(:a :b :c))
```
⇒   `(:c :b :a 1 2 3)`

For vectors, conj and into add elements to the back:

```
(conj [1 2 3] :a)
```
⇒   `[1 2 3 :a]`

```
(into [1 2 3] [:a :b :c])
```
⇒   `[1 2 3 :a :b :c]`

Because conj (and related functions) do the efficient thing for the underlying data structure, you can often write code that is both efficient and completely decoupled from a specific underlying implementation.

> **Joe Asks...**
>
> #### Why Do Functions on Vectors Return Lists?
>
> When you try examples at the REPL, the results of rest and cons appear to be lists, even when the inputs are vectors, maps, or sets. Does this mean that Clojure is converting everything to a list internally? No! The sequence functions always return a seq, regardless of their inputs. You can verify this by checking the Java type of the returned objects:
>
> ```
> (class '(1 2 3))
>     clojure.lang.PersistentList
>
> (class (rest [1 2 3]))
>     clojure.lang.APersistentVector$Seq
> ```
>
> As you can see, the result of (rest [1 2 3]) is some kind of Seq, not a List. So, why does the result appear to be a list?
>
> The answer lies in the REPL. When you ask the REPL to display a sequence, all it knows is that it has a sequence. It does not know what kind of collection the sequence was built from. So, the REPL prints all sequences the same way: it walks the entire sequence, printing it as a list.

The Clojure sequence library is particularly suited for large (or even infinite) sequences. Most Clojure sequences are *lazy*: they generate elements only when they are actually needed. Thus, Clojure's sequence functions can process sequences too large to fit in memory.

Clojure sequences are *immutable*: they never change. This makes it easier to reason about programs and means that Clojure sequences are safe for concurrent access. It does, however, create a small problem for human language. English-language descriptions flow much more smoothly when describing mutable things. Consider the following two descriptions for a hypothetical sequence function triple.

- triple triples each element of a sequence.

- triple takes a sequence and returns a new sequence with each element of the original sequence tripled.

The latter version is specific and accurate. The former is much easier to read, but it might lead to the mistaken impression that a sequence is actually changing. Don't be fooled: *sequences never change*. If you see the phrase "foo changes x," mentally substitute "foo returns a changed copy of x."

4.2 Using the Sequence Library

The Clojure sequence library provides a rich set of functionality that can work with any sequence. If you come from an object-oriented background where nouns rule, the sequence library is truly "Revenge of the Verbs."[1] The functions provide a rich backbone of functionality that can take advantage of any data structure that obeys the basic first/rest/cons contract.

The following functions are grouped into four broad categories:

- Functions that create sequences
- Functions that filter sequences
- Sequence predicates
- Functions that transform sequences

These divisions are somewhat arbitrary. Since sequences are immutable, *most* of the sequence functions create new sequences. Some of the sequence functions both filter and transform. Nevertheless, these divisions provide a rough road map through a large library.

Creating Sequences

In addition to the sequence literals, Clojure provides a number of functions that create sequences. range produces a sequence from a start to an end, incrementing by step each time.

```
(range start? end step?)
```

Ranges include their start, but not their end. If you do not specify them, start defaults to zero, and step defaults to 1. Try creating some ranges at the REPL:

```
(range 10)
```
⇒
```
    (0 1 2 3 4 5 6 7 8 9)
```

```
(range 10 20)
```
⇒
```
    (10 11 12 13 14 15 16 17 18 19)
```

---

1. Steve Yegge's "Execution in the Kingdom of Nouns" (http://tinyurl.com/the-kingdom-of-nouns) argues that object-oriented programming has pushed nouns into an unrealistically dominant position and that it is time for a change.

```
(range 1 25 2)
```
⇒   (1 3 5 7 9 11 13 15 17 19 21 23)

The repeat function repeats an element x n times:

```
(repeat n x)
```

Try to repeat some items from the REPL:

```
(repeat 5 1)
```
⇒   (1 1 1 1 1)

```
(repeat 10 "x")
```
⇒   ("x" "x" "x" "x" "x" "x" "x" "x" "x" "x")

Both range and repeat represent ideas that can be extended infinitely. You can think of iterate as the infinite extension of range:

```
(iterate f x)
```

iterate begins with a value x and continues forever, applying a function f to each value to calculate the next.

If you begin with 1 and iterate with inc, you can generate the whole numbers:

```
(take 10 (iterate inc 1))
```
⇒   (1 2 3 4 5 6 7 8 9 10)

Since the sequence is infinite, you need another new function to help you view the sequence from the REPL.

```
(take n sequence)
```

take returns a lazy sequence of the first n items from a collection and provides one way to create a finite view onto an infinite collection.

The whole numbers are a pretty useful sequence to have around, so let's defn them for future use:

```
(defn whole-numbers [] (iterate inc 1))
```
⇒   #'user/whole-numbers

When called with a single argument, repeat returns a lazy, infinite sequence:

```
(repeat x)
```

Try repeating some elements at the REPL. Don't forget to wrap the result in a take:

```
(take 20 (repeat 1))
```
⇒   (1 1 1 1 1 1 1 1 1 1 1 1 1 1 1 1 1 1 1 1)

The cycle function takes a collection and cycles it infinitely:

```
(cycle coll)
```

Try cycling some collections at the REPL:

```
(take 10 (cycle (range 3)))
```
⇒   (0 1 2 0 1 2 0 1 2 0)

The interleave function takes multiple collections and produces a new collection that interleaves values from each collection until one of the collections is exhausted.

```
(interleave & colls)
```

When one of the collections is exhausted, the interleave stops. So, you can mix finite and infinite collections:

```
(interleave (whole-numbers) ["A" "B" "C" "D" "E"])
```
⇒   (1 "A" 2 "B" 3 "C" 4 "D" 5 "E")

Closely related to interleave is interpose, which returns a sequence with each of the elements of the input collection separated by a separator:

```
(interpose separator coll)
```

You can use interpose to build delimited strings:

```
(interpose "," ["apples" "bananas" "grapes"])
```
⇒   ("apples" "," "bananas" "," "grapes")

interpose works nicely with (apply str ...) to produce output strings:

```
(apply str (interpose \, ["apples" "bananas" "grapes"]))
```
⇒   "apples,bananas,grapes"

The (apply str ...) idiom is common enough that clojure-contrib wraps it as str-join:

```
(str-join separator sequence)
```

Use str-join to comma-delimit a list of words:

```
(use '[clojure.contrib.str-utils :only (str-join)])
(str-join \, ["apples" "bananas" "grapes"])
```
⇒   "apples,bananas,grapes"

For each collection type in Clojure, there is a function that takes an arbitrary number of arguments and creates a collection of that type:

```
(list & elements)
```

```
(vector & elements)
```

```
(hash-set & elements)
```

```
(hash-map key-1 val-1 ...)
```

hash-set has a cousin set that works a little differently: set expects a collection as its first argument:

```
(set [1 2 3])
```
⇒   `#{1 2 3}`

hash-set takes a variable list of arguments:

```
(hash-set 1 2 3)
```
⇒   `#{1 2 3}`

vector also has a cousin, vec, that takes a single collection argument instead of a variable argument list:

```
(vec (range 3))
```
⇒   `[0 1 2]`

Now that you have the basics of creating sequences, you can use other Clojure functions to filter and transform them.

Filtering Sequences

Clojure provides a number of functions that filter a sequence, returning a subsequence of the original sequence. The most basic of these is filter:

```
(filter pred coll)
```

filter takes a predicate and a collection and returns a sequence of objects for which the filter returns true (when interpreted in a boolean context). You can filter the whole-numbers from the previous section to get the odd numbers or the even numbers:

```
(take 10 (filter even? (whole-numbers)))
```
⇒   `(2 4 6 8 10 12 14 16 18 20)`

```
(take 10 (filter odd? (whole-numbers)))
```
⇒   `(1 3 5 7 9 11 13 15 17 19)`

You can take from a sequence while a predicate remains true with take-while:

```
(take-while pred coll)
```

For example, to take all the characters in a string up to the first vowel, use this:

```
(take-while (complement #{\a\e\i\o\u}) "the-quick-brown-fox")
```
⇒   `(\t \h)`

There are a couple of interesting things happening here:

- Sets also act as functions. So, you can read #{\a\e\i\o\u} either as "the set of vowels" or as "the function that tests to see whether its argument is vowel."

- complement reverses the behavior of another function. The previous complemented function tests to see whether its argument is *not* a vowel.

The opposite of take-while is drop-while:

```
(drop-while pred coll)
```

drop-while drops elements from the beginning of a sequence while a predicate is true and then returns the rest. You could drop-while to drop all leading nonvowels from a string:

```
(drop-while (complement #{\a\e\i\o\u}) "the-quick-brown-fox")
```
⇒
```
    (\e \- \q \u \i \c \k \- \b \r \o \w \n \- \f \o \x)
```

split-at and split-with will split a collection into two collections:

```
(split-at index coll)
```

```
(split-with pred coll)
```

split-at takes an index, and split-with takes a predicate:

```
(split-at 5 (range 10))
```
⇒
```
    [(0 1 2 3 4) (5 6 7 8 9)]
```

```
(split-with #(<= % 10) (range 0 20 2))
```
⇒
```
    [(0 2 4 6 8 10) (12 14 16 18)]
```

All the take-, split-, and drop- functions return lazy sequences, of course.

Sequence Predicates

Filter functions take a predicate and return a sequence. Closely related are the sequence predicates. A sequence predicate asks how some other predicate applies to every item in a sequence. For example, the every? predicate asks whether some other predicate is true for every element of a sequence.

```
(every? pred coll)
```

```
(every? odd? [1 3 5])
```
⇒
```
    true
```

```
(every? odd? [1 3 5 8])
```
⇒
```
    false
```

A lower bar is set by some:

```
(some pred coll)
```

some returns the first nonfalse value for its predicate or returns nil if no element matched:

```
(some even? [1 2 3])
```
⇒   true

```
(some even? [1 3 5])
```
⇒   nil

Notice that some does not end with a question mark. some is not a predicate, although it is often used like one. some returns the *actual value* of the first match instead of true. The distinction is invisible when you pair some with even?, since even? is itself a predicate. To see a non-true match, try using some with identity to find the first non-nil value in a sequence:

```
(some identity [nil false 1 nil 2])
```
⇒   1

The behavior of the other predicates is obvious from their names:

```
(not-every? pred coll)
```

```
(not-any? pred coll)
```

Not every whole number is even:

```
(not-every? even? (whole-numbers))
```
⇒   true

But it would be a lie to claim that not any whole number is even:

```
(not-any? even? (whole-numbers))
```
⇒   false

Note that I picked questions to which I already knew the answer. In general, you have to be careful when applying predicates to infinite collections. They might run forever.

Transforming Sequences

Transformation functions transform the values in the sequence. The simplest transformation is map:

```
(map f coll)
```

map takes a source collection coll and a function f, and it returns a new sequence by invoking f on each element in the coll. You could use map to wrap every element in a collection with an HTML tag.

```
(map #(format "<p>%s</p>" %) ["the" "quick" "brown" "fox"])
```
⇒   `("<p>the</p>" "<p>quick</p>" "<p>brown</p>" "<p>fox</p>")`

map can also take more than one collection argument. f must then be a function of multiple arguments. map will call f with one argument from each collection, stopping whenever the smallest collection is exhausted:

```
(map #(format "<%s>%s</%s>" %1 %2 %1)
     ["h1" "h2" "h3" "h1"] ["the" "quick" "brown" "fox"])
```
⇒   `("<h1>the</h1>" "<h2>quick</h2>" "<h3>brown</h3>"`
     `"<h1>fox</h1>")`

Another common transformation is reduce:

```
(reduce f coll)
```

f is a function of two arguments. reduce applies f on the first two elements in coll, then applies f to the result and the third element, and so on. reduce is useful for functions that "total up" a sequence in some way. You can use reduce to add items:

```
(reduce + (range 1 11))
```
⇒   `55`

or to multiply them:

```
(reduce * (range 1 11))
```
⇒   `3628800`

You can sort a collection with sort or sort-by:

```
(sort comp? coll)
```

```
(sort-by a-fn comp? coll)
```

sort sorts a collection by the natural order of its elements, where sort-by sorts a sequence by the result of calling a-fn on each element:

```
(sort [42 1 7 11])
```
⇒   `(1 7 11 42)`

```
(sort-by #(.toString %) [42 1 7 11])
```
⇒   `(1 11 42 7)`

If you do not want to sort by natural order, you can specify an optional comparison function comp for either sort or sort-by:

```
(sort > [42 1 7 11])
```
⇒   `(42 11 7 1)`

```
(sort-by :grade > [{:grade 83} {:grade 90} {:grade 77}])
```
⇒   `({:grade 90} {:grade 83} {:grade 77})`

The granddaddy of all filters and transformations is the *list comprehension*. A list comprehension creates a list based on an existing list, using set notation. In other words, a comprehension states the properties that the result list must satisfy. In general, a list comprehension will consist of the following:

- Input list(s)
- Placeholder variables[2] for elements in the input lists
- Predicates on the elements
- An output form that produces output from the elements of the input lists that satisfy the predicates

Of course, Clojure generalizes the notion of list comprehension to *sequence* comprehension. Clojure comprehensions use the for macro[3]:

```
(for [binding-form coll-expr filter-expr? ...] expr)
```

for takes a vector of binding-form/coll-exprs, plus an optional filter-expr, and then yields a sequence of exprs.

List comprehension is more general than functions such as map and filter and can in fact emulate most of the filtering and transformation functions described earlier. You can rewrite the previous map example as a list comprehension:

```
(for [word ["the" "quick" "brown" "fox"]]
  (format "<p>%s</p>" word))
```
⇒   ("<p>the</p>" "<p>quick</p>" "<p>brown</p>" "<p>fox</p>")

This reads almost like English: "For [each] word in [a sequence of words] format [according to format instructions]."

Comprehensions can emulate filter using a :when clause. You can pass even? to :when to filter the even numbers:

```
(take 10 (for [n (whole-numbers) :when (even? n)] n))
```
⇒   (2 4 6 8 10 12 14 16 18 20)

A :while clause continues the evaluation only while its expression holds true:

```
(for [n (whole-numbers) :while (even? n)] n)
```
⇒   ()

---

2. "Variables" in the mathematical sense, not the imperative programming sense. You won't be able to vary them. I humbly apologize for this overloading of the English language.
3. The list comprehension for has nothing to do with the for loop found in imperative languages.

The real power of for comes when you work with more than one binding expression. For example, you can express all possible positions on a chessboard in algebraic notation by binding both rank and file:

```
(for [file "ABCDEFGH" rank (range 1 9)] (format "%c%d" file rank))
```
⇒   ("A1" "A2" ... elided ... "H7" ""H8")

Clojure iterates over the rightmost binding expression in a sequence comprehension first and then works its way left. Because rank is listed to the right of file in the binding form, rank iterates faster. If you want files to iterate faster, you can reverse the binding order and list rank first:

```
(for [rank (range 1 9) file "ABCDEFGH"] (format "%c%d" file rank))
```
⇒   ("A1" "B1" ... elided ... "G8" "H8")

In many languages, transformations, filters, and comprehensions do their work immediately. Do not assume this in Clojure. Most sequence functions do not traverse elements until you actually try to use them.

4.3 Lazy and Infinite Sequences

Most Clojure sequences are *lazy*; in other words, elements are not calculated until they are needed. Using lazy sequences has many benefits:

- You can postpone expensive computations that may not in fact be needed.
- You can work with huge data sets that do not fit into memory.
- You can delay I/O until it is absolutely needed.

Consider the following expression:

```
(use '[clojure.contrib.lazy-seqs :only (primes)])
(def ordinals-and-primes (map vector (iterate inc 1) primes))
```
⇒   #'user/ordinals-and-primes

ordinals-and-primes includes pairs like [5, 11] (eleven is the fifth prime number). Both ordinals and primes are infinite, but ordinals-and-primes fits into memory just fine, because it is lazy. Just take what you need from it:

```
(take 5 (drop 1000 ordinals-and-primes))
```
⇒   ([1001 7927] [1002 7933] [1003 7937] [1004 7949] [1005 7951])

When should you prefer lazy sequences? Most of the time. Most sequence functions return lazy sequences, so you pay only for what you use. More important, lazy sequences do not require any special effort on your part. In the previous example, iterate, primes, and map return lazy sequences, so ordinals-and-primes gets laziness "for free."

Lazy sequences are critical to functional programming in Clojure. Section 5.2, *How to Be Lazy*, on page 132 explores creating and using lazy sequences in much greater detail.

Forcing Sequences

When you are viewing a large sequence from the REPL, you may want to use take to prevent the REPL from evaluating the entire sequence. In other contexts, you may have the opposite problem. You have created a lazy sequence, and you want to force the sequence to evaluate fully.

The problem usually arises when the code generating the sequence has side effects. Consider the following sequence, which embeds side effects via println:

```
(def x (for [i (range 1 3)] (do (println i) i)))
⇒    #'user/x
```

Newcomers to Clojure are surprised that the previous code prints nothing. Since the definition of x does not actually use the elements, Clojure does not evaluate the comprehension to get them. You can force evaluation with doall:

```
(doall coll)
```

doall forces Clojure to walk the elements of a sequence and returns the elements as a result:

```
(doall x)
| 1
| 2
⇒    (1 2)
```

You can also use dorun:

```
(dorun coll)
```

dorun walks the elements of a sequence without keeping past elements in memory. As a result, dorun can walk collections too large to fit in memory.

```
(def x (for [i (range 1 3)] (do (println i) i)))
⇒    #'user/x

(dorun x)
| 1
| 2
⇒    nil
```

The nil return value is a telltale reminder that dorun does not hold a reference to the entire sequence.

The dorun and doall functions help you deal with side effects, while most of the rest of Clojure discourages side effects. You should use these functions rarely. (The Clojure core calls each of these functions only once in about 4,000 lines of code.)

4.4 Clojure Makes Java Seq-able

The seq abstraction of first/rest applies to anything that there can be more than one of. In the Java world, that includes the following:

- The Collections API

- Regular expressions

- File system traversal

- XML processing

- Relational database results

Clojure wraps these Java APIs, making the sequence library available for almost everything you do.

Seq-ing Java Collections

If you try to apply the sequence functions to Java collections, you will find that they behave as sequences. Collections that can act as sequences are called *seq-able*. For example, arrays are seq-able:

```
; String.getBytes returns a byte array
(first (.getBytes "hello"))
```
⇒   104

```
(rest (.getBytes "hello"))
```
⇒   (101 108 108 111)

```
(cons (int \h) (.getBytes "ello"))
```
⇒   (104 101 108 108 111)

Hashtables and Maps are also seq-able:

```
; System.getProperties returns a Hashtable
(first (System/getProperties))
```
⇒   java.runtime.name=Java(TM) SE Runtime Environment

```
(rest (System/getProperties))
```
⇒   (sun.boot.library.path=/System/Library/... etc. ...

Remember that the sequence wrappers are immutable, even when the underlying Java collection is mutable. So, you cannot update the system properties by consing a new item onto (System/getProperties). cons will return a new sequence; the existing properties are unchanged. (See Section 3.1, *Syntactic Sugar*, on page 62 for an example using doto to update Java system properties.)

Since strings are sequences of characters, they also are seq-able:

```
(first "Hello")
```
⇒   \H

```
(rest "Hello")
```
⇒   (\e \l \l \o)

```
(cons \H "ello")
```
⇒   (\H \e \l \l \o)

Clojure will automatically wrap collections in sequences, but it will not automatically rewrap them back to their original type. With most collection types this behavior is intuitive, but with strings you will often want to convert the result to a string. Consider reversing a string. Clojure provides reverse:

```
; probably not what you want
(reverse "hello")
```
⇒   (\o \l \l \e \h)

To convert a sequence back to a string, use (apply str seq):

```
(apply str (reverse "hello"))
```
⇒   "olleh"

The Java collections are seq-able, but for most scenarios they do not offer advantages over Clojure's built in collections. Prefer the Java collections only in interop scenarios where you are working with legacy Java APIs.

Seq-ing Regular Expressions

Clojure's regular expressions use the java.util.regex library under the hood. At the lowest level, this exposes the mutable nature of Java's Matcher. You can use re-matcher to create a Matcher for a regular expression and a string and then loop on re-find to iterate over the matches.

```
(re-matcher regexp string)
```

examples/sequences.clj

```
; don't do this!
(let [m (re-matcher #"\w+" "the quick brown fox")]
```

```
(loop [match (re-find m)]
  (when match
    (println match)
    (recur (re-find m)))))
```
```
| the
| quick
| brown
| fox
⇒   nil
```

Much better is to use the higher-level re-seq.

`(re-seq regexp string)`

re-seq exposes an immutable seq over the matches. This gives you the power of all of Clojure's sequence functions. Try these expressions at the REPL:

```
(re-seq #"\w+" "the quick brown fox")
⇒   ("the" "quick" "brown" "fox")
```
```
(sort (re-seq #"\w+" "the quick brown fox"))
⇒   ("brown" "fox" "quick" "the")
```
```
(drop 2 (re-seq #"\w+" "the quick brown fox"))
⇒   ("brown" "fox")
```
```
(map #(.toUpperCase %) (re-seq #"\w+" "the quick brown fox"))
⇒   ("THE" "QUICK" "BROWN" "FOX")
```

re-seq is a great example of how good abstractions reduce code bloat. Regular expression matches are not a special kind of thing, requiring special methods to deal with them. They are sequences, just like everything else. Thanks to the large number of sequence functions, you get more functionality *for free* than you would likely end up with after a misguided foray into writing regexp-specific functions.

Seq-ing the File System

You can seq over the file system. For starters, you can call java.io.File directly:

```
(import '(java.io File))
(.listFiles (File. "."))
⇒   [Ljava.io.File;@1f70f15e
```

The [Ljava.io.File... is Java's toString() representation for an array of Files. Sequence functions would call seq on this automatically, but the REPL doesn't.

So, seq it yourself:

```
(seq (.listFiles (File. ".")) )
⇒    (#<./concurrency> #<./sequences> ...)
```

If the default print format for files does not suit you, you could map them to a string form with getName:

```
; overkill
(map #(.getName %) (seq (.listFiles (File. "."))))
⇒    ("concurrency" "sequences" ...)
```

Once you decide to use a function like map, calling seq is redundant. Sequence library functions call seq for you, so you don't have to. The previous code simplifies to this:

```
(map #(.getName %) (.listFiles (File. ".")))
⇒    ("concurrency" "sequences" ...)
```

Often, you want to recursively traverse the entire directory tree. Clojure provides a depth-first walk via file-seq. If you file-seq from the sample code directory for this book, you will see a lot of files:

```
(count (file-seq (File. ".")))
⇒    104 ; the final number will be larger!
```

What if you want to see only the files that have been changed recently? Write a predicate recently-modified? that checks to see whether File was touched in the last half hour:

examples/sequences.clj

```
(defn minutes-to-millis [mins] (* mins 1000 60))

(defn recently-modified? [file]
  (> (.lastModified file)
     (- (System/currentTimeMillis) (minutes-to-millis 30))))
```

Give it a try:

```
(filter recently-modified? (file-seq (File. ".")))
⇒    (./sequences ./sequences/sequences.clj)
```

Since I am working on the sequences examples as I write this, only they show as changed recently. Your results will vary from those shown here.

Seq-ing a Stream

You can seq over the lines of any Java Reader using line-seq. To get a Reader, you can use clojure-contrib's duck-streams library. The duck-streams library provides a reader function that returns a reader on a stream, file, URL, or URI.

```
(use '[clojure.contrib.duck-streams :only (reader)])
; leaves reader open...
(take 2 (line-seq (reader "examples/utils.clj")))
```
⇒   ("(ns utils)" "")

Since readers can represent non-memory resources that need to be
closed, you should wrap reader creation in a with-open. Create an expression that uses the sequence function count to count the number of
lines in a file and uses with-open to correctly close the reader:

```
(with-open [rdr (reader "book/utils.clj")]
  (count (line-seq rdr)))
```
⇒   25

To make the example a little more useful, add a filter to count only
nonblank lines:

```
(with-open [rdr (reader "book/utils.clj")]
  (count (filter #(re-find #"\S" %) (line-seq rdr))))
```
⇒   22

Using seqs on both the file system and on the contents of individual
files, you can quickly create interesting utilities. Create a program that
defines these three predicates:

- non-blank? detects nonblank lines.

- non-svn? detects files that are not Subversion metadata.

- clojure-source? detects Clojure source code files.

Then, create a clojure-loc function that counts the lines of Clojure code
in a directory tree, using a combination of sequence functions along the
way: reduce, for, count, and filter.

examples/sequences.clj

```
(use '[clojure.contrib.duck-streams :only (reader)])
(defn non-blank? [line] (if (re-find #"\S" line) true false))

(defn non-svn? [file] (not (.contains (.toString file) ".svn")))

(defn clojure-source? [file] (.endsWith (.toString file) ".clj"))

(defn clojure-loc [base-file]
  (reduce
    +
    (for [file (file-seq base-file)
          :when (and (clojure-source? file) (non-svn? file))]
      (with-open [rdr (reader file)]
        (count (filter non-blank? (line-seq rdr)))))))
```

Now, you can use clojure-loc to find out how much Clojure code is in
Clojure itself:

```
(clojure-loc (java.io.File. "/Users/stuart/repos/clojure"))
```
⇒   5804

Those few thousand lines pack quite a punch, because parts such as
the sequence library can be recombined in so many ways. Your code
can be this powerful, too. The clojure-loc function is very task-specific,
but because it is built out of sequence functions and simple predicates,
you can easily tweak it to very different tasks.

Seq-ing XML

Clojure can seq over XML data. The examples that follow use this XML:

examples/sequences/compositions.xml

```
<compositions>
  <composition composer="J. S. Bach">
    <name>The Art of the Fugue</name>
  </composition>
  <composition composer="J. S. Bach">
    <name>Musical Offering</name>
  </composition>
  <composition composer="W. A. Mozart">
    <name>Requiem</name>
  </composition>
</compositions>
```

The function clojure.xml.parse parses an XML file/stream/URI, returning
the tree of data as a Clojure map, with nested vectors for descendants:

```
(use '[clojure.xml :only (parse)])
(parse (java.io.File. "examples/sequences/compositions.xml"))
```
⇒   {:tag :compositions,
       :attrs nil,
       :content [{:tag :composition, ... etc. ...

You can manipulate this map directly, or you can use the xml-seq function to view the tree as a seq:

```
(xml-seq root)
```

The following example uses a list comprehension over an xml-seq to
extract just the composers:

examples/sequences.clj

```
(for [x (xml-seq
          (parse (java.io.File. "examples/sequences/compositions.xml")))
        :when (= :composition (:tag x))]
  (:composer (:attrs x)))
```

⇒   ("J. S. Bach" "J. S. Bach" "W. A. Mozart")

The previous code demonstrates the generality of seqs, but it only scratches the surface of Clojure's XML support. If you plan to do significant XML processing with Clojure, check out the lazy-xml and zip-filter/xml libraries in clojure-contrib.

4.5 Calling Structure-Specific Functions

Clojure's sequence functions allow you to write very general code. Sometimes you will want to be more specific and take advantage of the characteristics of a specific data structure. Clojure includes functions that specifically target lists, vectors, maps, structs, and sets.

We will take a quick tour of some of these structure-specific functions next. For a complete list of structure-specific functions in Clojure, see the Data Structures section of the Clojure website.[4]

Functions on Lists

Clojure supports the traditional names peek and pop for retrieving the first element of a list and the remainder, respectively:

```
(peek coll)
```

```
(pop coll)
```

Give a simple list a peek and pop:

```
(peek '(1 2 3))
```
⇒   1

```
(pop '(1 2 3))
```
⇒   (2 3)

peek is the same as first, but pop is *not* the same as rest. pop will throw an exception if the sequence is empty:

```
(rest ())
```
⇒   ()

```
(pop ())
```
⇒   java.lang.IllegalStateException: Can't pop empty list

---

4. http://clojure.org/data_structures

Functions on Vectors

Vectors also support peek and pop, but they deal with the element at
the end of the vector:

```
(peek [1 2 3])
```
⇒   3

```
(pop [1 2 3])
```
⇒   [1 2]

get returns the value at an index or returns nil if the index is outside
the vector:

```
(get [:a :b :c] 1)
```
⇒   :b

```
(get [:a :b :c] 5)
```
⇒   nil

Vectors are themselves functions. They take an index argument and
return a value, or they throw an exception if the index is out of bounds:

```
([:a :b :c] 1)
```
⇒   :b

```
([:a :b :c] 5)
```
⇒   java.lang.ArrayIndexOutOfBoundsException: 5

assoc associates a new value with a particular index:

```
(assoc [0 1 2 3 4] 2 :two)
```
⇒   [0 1 :two 3 4]

subvec returns a subvector of a vector:

```
(subvec avec start end?)
```

If end is not specified, it defaults to the end of the vector:

```
(subvec [1 2 3 4 5] 3)
```
⇒   [4 5]

```
(subvec [1 2 3 4 5] 1 3)
```
⇒   [2 3]

Of course, you could simulate subvec with a combination of drop and
take:

```
(take 2 (drop 1 [1 2 3 4 5]))
```
⇒   (2 3)

The difference is that take and drop are general and can work with any
sequence. On the other hand, subvec is *much* faster for vectors. When-

ever a structure-specific function like subvec duplicates functionality already available in the sequence library, it is probably there for performance. The documentation string for functions like subvec includes performance characteristics.

Functions on Maps

Clojure provides several functions for reading the keys and values in a map. keys returns a sequence of the keys, and vals returns a sequence of the values:

```
(keys map)
```

```
(vals map)
```

Try taking keys and values from a simple map:

```
(keys {:sundance "spaniel", :darwin "beagle"})
```
⇒   (:sundance :darwin)

```
(vals {:sundance "spaniel", :darwin "beagle"})
```
⇒   ("spaniel" "beagle")

get returns the value for a key or returns nil.

```
(get map key value-if-not-found?)
```

Use your REPL to test that get behaves as expected for keys both present and missing:

```
(get {:sundance "spaniel", :darwin "beagle"} :darwin)
```
⇒   "beagle"

```
(get {:sundance "spaniel", :darwin "beagle"} :snoopy)
```
⇒   nil

There is an approach even simpler than get. Maps are functions of their keys. So, you can leave out the get entirely, putting the map in function position at the beginning of a form:

```
({:sundance "spaniel", :darwin "beagle"} :darwin)
```
⇒   "beagle"

```
({:sundance "spaniel", :darwin "beagle"} :snoopy)
```
⇒   nil

Keywords are also functions. They take a collection as an argument and look themselves up in the collection. Since :darwin and :sundance are keywords, the earlier forms can be written with their elements in reverse order.

```
(:darwin {:sundance "spaniel", :darwin "beagle"} )
```
⇒   "beagle"

```
(:snoopy {:sundance "spaniel", :darwin "beagle"} )
```
⇒   nil

If you look up a key in a map and get nil back, you cannot tell whether the key was missing from the map or present with a value of nil. The contains? function solves this problem by testing for the mere presence of a key.

```
(contains? map key)
```

Create a map where nil is a legal value:

```
(def score {:stu nil :joey 100})
```

:stu is present, but if you see the nil value, you might not think so:

```
(:stu score)
```
⇒   nil

If you use contains?, you can verify that :stu is in the game, although presumably not doing very well:

```
(contains? score :stu)
```
⇒   true

Another approach is to call get, passing in an optional third argument that will be returned if the key is not found:

```
(get score :stu :score-not-found)
```
⇒   nil

```
(get score :aaron :score-not-found)
```
⇒   :score-not-found

The default return value of :score-not-found makes it possible to distinguish that :aaron is not in the map, while :stu is present with a value of nil.

If nil is a legal value in map, use contains? or the three-argument form of get to test the presence of a key.

Clojure also provides several functions for building new maps:

- assoc returns a map with a key/value pair added.

- dissoc returns a map with a key removed.

- select-keys returns a map, keeping only the keys passed in.

- merge combines maps. If multiple maps contain a key, the right-most map wins.

To test these functions, create some song data:

examples/sequences.clj

```
(def song {:name "Agnus Dei"
           :artist "Krzysztof Penderecki"
           :album "Polish Requiem"
           :genre "Classical"})
```

Next, create various modified versions of the song collection:

```
(assoc song :kind "MPEG Audio File")
```
⇒
```
    {:name "Agnus Dei", :album "Polish Requiem",
     :kind "MPEG Audio File", :genre "Classical",
     :artist "Krzysztof Penderecki"}
```

```
(dissoc song :genre)
```
⇒
```
    {:name "Agnus Dei", :album "Polish Requiem",
     :artist "Krzysztof Penderecki"}
```

```
(select-keys song [:name :artist])
```
⇒
```
    {:name "Agnus Dei", :artist "Krzysztof Penderecki"}
```

```
(merge song {:size 8118166, :time 507245})
```
⇒
```
    {:name "Agnus Dei", :album "Polish Requiem",
     :genre "Classical", :size 8118166,
     :artist "Krzysztof Penderecki", :time 507245}
```

Remember that song itself never changes. Each of the functions shown previously returns a new collection.

The most interesting map construction function is merge-with.

```
(merge-with merge-fn & maps)
```

merge-with is like merge, except that when two or more maps have the same key, you can specify your own function for combining the values under the key. You can use merge-with and concat to build a sequence of values under each key:

```
(merge-with
 concat
  {:rubble ["Barney"], :flintstone ["Fred"]}
  {:rubble ["Betty"], :flintstone ["Wilma"]}
  {:rubble ["Bam-Bam"], :flintstone ["Pebbles"]})
```
⇒
```
    {:rubble ("Barney" "Betty" "Bam-Bam"),
     :flintstone ("Fred" "Wilma" "Pebbles")}
```

Starting with three distinct collections of family members keyed by last name, the previous code combines them into a single collection keyed by last name.

Functions on Sets

In addition to the set functions in the clojure namespace, Clojure provides a group of functions in the clojure.set namespace. To use these functions with unqualified names, call (use 'clojure.set) from the REPL. For the following examples, you will also need the following vars:

`examples/sequences.clj`

```
(def languages #{"java" "c" "d" "clojure"})
(def letters #{"a" "b" "c" "d" "e"})
(def beverages #{"java" "chai" "pop"})
```

The first group of clojure.set functions perform operations from set theory:

- union returns the set of all elements present in either input set.

- intersection returns the set of all elements present in *both* input sets.

- difference returns the set of all elements present in the first input set, minus those in the second.

- select returns the set of all elements matching a predicate.

Write an expression that finds the union of all languages and beverages:

```
(union languages beverages)
```
⇒   `#{"java" "c" "d" "clojure" "chai" "pop"}`

Next, try the languages that are not also beverages:

```
(difference languages beverages)
```
⇒   `#{"c" "d" "clojure"}`

If you enjoy terrible puns, you will like the fact that some things are both languages *and* beverages:

```
(intersection languages beverages)
```
⇒   `#{"java"}`

A surprising number of languages cannot afford a name larger than a single character:

```
(select #(= 1 (.length %)) languages)
```
⇒   `#{"c" "d"}`

Relational Algebra	Database	Clojure Type System
Relation	Table	Anything set-like
Tuple	Row	Anything map-like

Figure 4.1: CORRESPONDENCES BETWEEN RELATIONAL ALGEBRA, DATABASES, AND THE CLOJURE TYPE SYSTEM

Set union and difference are part of set theory, but they are also part of *relational algebra*, which is the basis for query languages such as SQL. The relational algebra consists of six primitive operators: set union and set difference (described earlier), plus rename, selection, projection, and cross product.

You can understand the relational primitives by following the analogy with relational databases (see Figure 4.1). The following examples work against an in-memory database of musical compositions. Load the database before continuing:

`examples/sequences.clj`

```clojure
(def compositions
  #{{:name "The Art of the Fugue" :composer "J. S. Bach"}
    {:name "Musical Offering" :composer "J. S. Bach"}
    {:name "Requiem" :composer "Giuseppe Verdi"}
    {:name "Requiem" :composer "W. A. Mozart"}})
(def composers
  #{{:composer "J. S. Bach" :country "Germany"}
    {:composer "W. A. Mozart" :country "Austria"}
    {:composer "Giuseppe Verdi" :country "Italy"}})
(def nations
  #{{:nation "Germany" :language "German"}
    {:nation "Austria" :language "German"}
    {:nation "Italy" :language "Italian"}})
```

The rename function renames keys ("database columns"), based on a map from original names to new names.

```clojure
(rename relation rename-map)
```

Rename the compositions to use a title key instead of name:

```clojure
(rename compositions {:name :title})
⇒  #{{:title "Requiem", :composer "Giuseppe Verdi"}
     {:title "Musical Offering", :composer "J.S. Bach"}
     {:title "Requiem", :composer "W. A. Mozart"}
     {:title "The Art of the Fugue", :composer "J.S. Bach"}}
```

The select function returns maps for which a predicate is true and is analogous to the WHERE portion of a SQL SELECT:

```
(select pred relation)
```

Write a select expression that finds all the compositions whose title is "Requiem":

```
(select #(= (:name %) "Requiem") compositions)
⇒   #{{:name "Requiem", :composer "W. A. Mozart"}
     {:name "Requiem", :composer "Giuseppe Verdi"}}
```

The project function returns only the portions of the maps that match a set of keys.

```
(project relation keys)
```

project is similar to a SQL SELECT that specifies a subset of columns. Write a projection that returns only the name of the compositions:

```
(project compositions [:name])
⇒   #{{:name "Musical Offering"}
     {:name "Requiem"}
     {:name "The Art of the Fugue"}}
```

The final relational primitive, which is a cross product, is the foundation for the various kinds of joins in relational databases. The cross product returns every possible combination of rows in the different tables. You can do this easily enough in Clojure with a list comprehension:

```
(for [m compositions c composers] (concat m c))
⇒   ... 4 x 3 = 12 rows ...
```

Although the cross product is theoretically interesting, you will typically want some subset of the full cross product. For example, you might want to join sets based on shared keys:

```
(join relation-1 relation-2 keymap?)
```

You can join the composition names and composers on the shared key :composer:

```
(join compositions composers)
⇒   #{{:name "Requiem", :country "Austria",
      :composer "W. A. Mozart"}
     {:name "Musical Offering", :country "Germany",
      :composer "J. S. Bach"}
     {:name "Requiem", :country "Italy",
      :composer "Giuseppe Verdi"}
     {:name "The Art of the Fugue", :country "Germany",
      :composer "J. S. Bach"}}
```

If the key names in the two relations do not match, you can pass a keymap that maps the key names in relation-1 to their corresponding keys in relation-2. For example, you can join composers, which use :country, to nations, which use :nation. For example:

```
(join composers nations {:country :nation})
```
⇒
```
    #{{:language "German", :nation "Austria",
        :composer "W. A. Mozart", :country "Austria"}
      {:language "German", :nation "Germany",
        :composer "J. S. Bach", :country "Germany"}
      {:language "Italian", :nation "Italy",
        :composer "Giuseppe Verdi", :country "Italy"}}
```

You can combine the relational primitives. Perhaps you want to know the set of all countries that are home to the composer of a requiem. You can use select to find all the requiems, join them with their composers, and project to narrow the results to just the country names:

```
(project
  (join
    (select #(= (:name %) "Requiem") compositions)
    composers)
  [:country])
```
⇒
```
    #{{:country "Italy"} {:country "Austria"}}
```

The analogy between Clojure's relational algebra and a relational database is instructive. Remember, though, that Clojure's relational algebra is a general-purpose tool. You can use it on any kind of set-relational data. And while you are using it, you also have the entire power of Clojure and Java at your disposal. Next, let's use the sequence library to improve Lancet's support for properties on Ant tasks.

4.6 Adding Properties to Lancet Tasks

This section continues the example begun in Section 3.5, *Adding Ant Projects and Tasks to Lancet*, on page 85. You will need to start with the completed code from that previous section, which you can get from Section 3.5, *Lancet Step 1: Ant Projects and Tasks*, on page 90.

In step 1, you created an instantiate-task function to automate the instantiation and setup of Ant tasks. One thing that instantiate-task does *not* yet do is set any properties on an Ant task. You have to call setters in a separate step, such as calling setMessage:

```
(def echo-task (instantiate-task ant-project "echo"))
```
⇒
```
    #'user/echo-task
```

```
(.setMessage echo-task "some message")
⇒    nil
```

In this section, you will improve instantiate-task to take an additional argument, a map of properties. That way, you can create a new task in a single form:

```
; TODO: enable this signature
(instantiate-task ant-project "echo" {:message "hello"})
```

To handle properties in a generic way, you will need to reflect against the available properties of a Java object. Java provides this information via a reflective helper class called the Introspector. From the REPL, import the Introspector, and use it to getBeanInfo on the Echo class:

```
(import '(java.beans Introspector))
(Introspector/getBeanInfo (class echo-task))
⇒    #<java.beans.GenericBeanInfo@d506900>
```

So far so good. The GenericBeanInfo instance has a getPropertyDescriptors that will return property information for every available property. Using the *1 special variable, dig into the previous result, and pull out the property descriptors:

```
(.getPropertyDescriptors *1)
⇒    #<[Ljava.beans.PropertyDescriptor;@4c3b55a5>
```

The [L prefix is the Java toString() form for an array, so now you have something seq-able to work with. You are going to use this object several times, so stuff it into a var named prop-descs:

```
(def prop-descs *1)
⇒    #'user/prop-descs
```

Now you have all of the sequence library at your disposal to explore the sequence. Use count to find out how many properties an echo task has:

```
(count prop-descs)
⇒    13
```

Use first and bean to examine the first property descriptor in more detail:

```
; output reformatted and elided
(bean (first prop-descs))
⇒    {:class #=java.beans.PropertyDescriptor,
       :writeMethod        ...,
       :name               ...,
       :displayName        ...,
       :constrained        ...,
       :propertyEditorClass ...,
       :readMethod         ...,
       :preferred          ...,
```

```
:expert          ...,
:hidden          ...,
:propertyType    ...,
:bound           ...,
:shortDescription ...}
```

Most of the bean properties are rarely used, and in this section Lancet will need only name (to find a property) and writeMethod (to set it).

Using the Introspector API, plus the sequence library's filter function, you can write a property-descriptor function that takes a Java instance and a property name and returns a property descriptor:

lancet/step_2_repl.clj

```
(import '(java.beans Introspector))
(defn property-descriptor [inst prop-name]
  (first
    (filter #(= (name prop-name) (.getName %))
            (.getPropertyDescriptors
              (Introspector/getBeanInfo (class inst))))))
```

I prefer to use keywords for names, so the call to (name prop-name) converts a prop-name keyword to a string, which is what Java will expect. The filter finds only those property descriptors whose name matches prop-name. There can be only one such property, since Java objects cannot have two properties with the same name. Test property-descriptor against echo's message property:

```
(bean (property-descriptor echo-task :message))
```
⇒
```
    {:class #=java.beans.PropertyDescriptor,
     :writeMethod #<public void Echo.setMessage(java.lang.String)>,
     :name "message",
     ... lots of other properties ...}
```

With property-descriptor in place, it is easy work to create a set-property! function that sets a property to a new value:

lancet/step_2_repl.clj

```
Line 1  (use '[clojure.contrib.except :only (throw-if)])
2  (defn set-property! [inst prop value]
3    (let [pd (property-descriptor inst prop)]
4      (throw-if (nil? pd) (str "No such property " prop))
5      (.invoke (.getWriteMethod pd) inst (into-array [value])))))
```

Line 3 binds pd to a property descriptor, calling the property-descriptor you wrote previously. Line 4 provides a helpful error message if the property does not exist.

Line 5 invokes the write method for the property. Because Java's method invoke requires a Java array, not a Clojure sequence, you use into-array to perform a conversion.

Test that you can actually set echo-task's message property:

```
(set-property! echo-task :message "a new message!")
```
⇒   nil

```
(.execute echo-task)
|   [echo] a new message!
```
⇒   nil

Now you can build a set-properties! that takes a map of property name/ property value pairs and invokes set-property! once for each pair. But hold on for just a second. All this talk of invocation sounds very much like the mutable, imperative world of Java, not the immutable, functional world of Clojure. That is because you are interoperating with Ant, which is a mutable, imperative Java API, full of side effects.

Clojure forms that deal with side effects are often prefixed with do, and in fact there is a do-family macro made to order for this situation: doseq:

(doseq bindings & body)

doseq repeatedly executes its body, with the same bindings and filtering as a list comprehension. Using doseq, implement set-properties! thusly:

lancet/step_2_repl.clj
```
(defn set-properties! [inst prop-map]
  (doseq [[k v] prop-map] (set-property! inst k v)))
```

Notice how destructuring simplifies this function definition by allowing you to destructure each key/value pair directly into bindings k and v.

Test set-properties!, using your old friend echo-task:

```
(set-properties! echo-task {:message "yet another message"})
```
⇒   nil

```
(.execute echo-task)
|   [echo] yet another message
```
⇒   nil

With set-properties! in place, you are now ready to enhance the instantiate-task function you wrote in Section 3.5, *Adding Ant Projects and Tasks to Lancet*, on page 85.

Create a new version of instantiate-task that takes an additional props argument and uses it to set the task's properties:

`lancet/step_2_repl.clj`

```
(defn instantiate-task [project name props]
  (let [task (.createTask project name)]
    (throw-if (nil? task) (str "No task named " name))
    (doto task
      (.init)
      (.setProject project)
      (set-properties! props))
    task))
```

To test instantiate-task, create a new var echo-with-msg that binds to a fully configured echo, and verify that it executes correctly:

```
(def echo-with-msg
  (instantiate-task ant-project "echo" {:message "hello"}))
⇒   #'user/echo-with-msg
```

```
(.execute echo-with-msg)
| [echo] hello
⇒   nil
```

The completed code for this section is listed at the very end of the chapter. Note that many of the functions you built in this section are not Ant-specific. property-descriptor, set-property!, and set-properties! are generic and can work with any Java object model. There are plenty of Java libraries other than Ant suffering from tedious XML configuration. Using the generic code you have written here, be an open source hero and give a Java library a Clojure DSL that is easier to use.

Lancet Step 2: Setting Properties

`lancet/step_2_complete.clj`

```
(ns lancet.step-2-complete
    (:use clojure.contrib.except)
    (:import (java.beans Introspector)))

(def
 #^{:doc "Dummy ant project to keep Ant tasks happy"}
 ant-project
 (let [proj (org.apache.tools.ant.Project.)
       logger (org.apache.tools.ant.NoBannerLogger.)]
   (doto logger
     (.setMessageOutputLevel org.apache.tools.ant.Project/MSG_INFO)
     (.setOutputPrintStream System/out)
     (.setErrorPrintStream System/err))
```

```
          (doto proj
            (.init)
            (.addBuildListener logger)))))

      (defn property-descriptor [inst prop-name]
        (first
          (filter #(= (name prop-name) (.getName %))
                  (.getPropertyDescriptors
                    (Introspector/getBeanInfo (class inst))))))))

      (defn set-property! [inst prop value]
        (let [pd (property-descriptor inst prop)]
          (throw-if (nil? pd) (str "No such property " prop))
          (.invoke (.getWriteMethod pd) inst (into-array [value]))))

      (defn set-properties! [inst prop-map]
        (doseq [[k v] prop-map] (set-property! inst k v)))

      (defn instantiate-task [project name props]
        (let [task (.createTask project name)]
          (throw-if (nil? task) (str "No task named " name))
          (doto task
            (.init)
            (.setProject project)
            (set-properties! props))
          task))
```

4.7 Wrapping Up

Clojure unifies all kinds of collections under a single abstraction, the sequence. After more than a decade dominated by object-oriented programming, Clojure's sequence library is the "Revenge of the Verbs."

Clojure's sequences are implemented using functional programming techniques: immutable data, recursive definition, and lazy realization. In the next chapter, you will see how to use these techniques directly, further expanding the power of Clojure.

Chapter 5

Functional Programming

Functional programming (FP) is a big topic, not to be learned in twenty-one days[1] or in a single chapter of a book. Nevertheless, it is possible to reach a first level of effectiveness using lazy and recursive techniques in Clojure fairly quickly, and that is the goal of this chapter.

The chapter is organized as follows:

- Section 5.1, *Functional Programming Concepts*, on the next page begins with a quick overview of FP terms and concepts. This section also introduces the "Six Rules of Clojure FP" that we will refer to throughout the chapter.

- Section 5.2, *How to Be Lazy*, on page 132 demonstrates the power of lazy sequences. You will create several implementations of the Fibonacci numbers, starting with a terrible approach and improving it to an elegant, lazy solution.

- As cool as lazy sequences are, you rarely need to work with them directly. Section 5.3, *Lazier Than Lazy*, on page 140 shows how to rethink problems so that they can be solved directly using the sequence library described in Chapter 4, *Unifying Data with Sequences*, on page 91.

- Section 5.4, *Recursion Revisited*, on page 147 explores advanced issues. Some programmers will never need the techniques discussed here. If you are new to FP, it is OK to skip this section.

---

1. http://norvig.com/21-days.html

5.1 Functional Programming Concepts

Functional programming leads to code that is easier to write, read, test, and reuse. Here's how it works.

Pure Functions

Programs are built out of *pure functions*. A pure function has no *side effects*; that is, it does not depend on anything but its arguments, and its only influence on the outside world is through its return value.

Mathematical functions are pure functions. Two plus two is four, no matter where and when you ask. Also, asking doesn't *do* anything other than return the answer.

Program output is decidedly *impure*. For example, when you println, you change the outside world by pushing data onto an output stream. Also, the results of println depend on state outside the function: the standard output stream might be redirected, closed, or broken.

If you start writing pure functions, you will quickly realize that pure functions and *immutable* data go hand in hand. Consider the following mystery function:

```
(defn mystery [input]
  (if input data-1 data-2))
```

If mystery is a pure function, then regardless of what it does, data-1 and data-2 have to be immutable! Otherwise, changes to the data would cause the function to return different values for the same input.

A single piece of mutable data can ruin the game, rendering an entire call chain of functions impure. So, once you make a commitment to writing pure functions, you end up using immutable data in large sections of your application.

Persistent Data Structures

Immutable data is critical to Clojure's approach to both FP and concurrency. On the FP side, pure functions cannot have side effects, such as updating the state of a mutable object. On the concurrency side, Clojure's concurrency primitives require immutable data structures to implement their thread-safety guarantees.

The fly in the ointment is performance. When all data is immutable, "update" translates into "create a copy of the original data, plus my changes." This will use up memory quickly! Imagine that you have an address book that takes up 5MB of memory. Then, you make five small updates. With a mutable address book, you are still consuming about 5MB of memory. But if you have to copy the whole address book for each update, then an immutable version would balloon to 25MB!

Clojure's data structures do not take this naive "copy everything" approach. Instead, all Clojure data structures are *persistent*. In this context, persistent means that the data structures preserve old copies of themselves by efficiently *sharing structure* between older and newer versions.

Structural sharing is easiest to visualize with a list. Consider list a with two elements:

```
(def a '(1 2))
    #'user/a
```

Then, from a you can create a b with an additional element added:

```
(def b (cons 0 a))
    #'user/b
```

b is able to reuse all of a's structure, rather than having its own private copy:

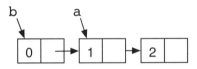

All of Clojure's data structures share structure where possible. For structures other than simple lists, the mechanics are more complex, of course. If you are interested in the details, check out the following articles:

- "Ideal Hash Trees"[2] by Phil Bagwell

- "Understanding Clojure's PersistentVector Implementation"[3] by Karl Krukow

Laziness and Recursion

Functional programs make heavy use of *recursion* and *laziness*. A recursion occurs when a function calls itself, either directly or indirectly. Laziness is when an expression's evaluation is postponed until it is

---

2. http://lamp.epfl.ch/papers/idealhashtrees.pdf
3. http://tinyurl.com/clojure-persistent-vector

actually needed. Evaluating a lazy expression is called *realizing* the expression.

In Clojure, functions and expressions are not lazy. However, sequences *are* generally lazy. Because so much Clojure programming is sequence manipulation, you get many of the benefits of a fully lazy language. In particular, you can build complex expressions using lazy sequences and then pay only for the elements you actually need.

Lazy techniques imply pure functions. You never have to worry about when to call a pure function, since it always returns the same thing. Impure functions, on the other hand, do not play well with lazy techniques. As a programmer you must explicitly control when an impure function is called, because if you call it at some other time, it may behave differently!

Referential Transparency

Laziness depends on the ability to replace a function call with its result at any time. Functions that have this ability are called *referentially transparent*, because calls to such functions can be replaced without affecting the behavior of the program. In addition to laziness, referentially transparent functions can also benefit from the following:

- *Memoization*, automatic caching of results

- Automatic *parallelization*, moving function evaluation to another processor or machine

Pure functions are referentially transparent *by definition*. Most other functions are *not* referentially transparent, and those that are must be proven safe by code review.

Benefits of FP

Well, that is a lot of terminology, and I promised it would make your code easier to write, read, test, and compose. Here's how.

Functional code is easier to *write* because the relevant information is right in front of you, in a function's argument list. You do not have to worry about global scope, session scope, application scope, or thread scope. Functional code is easier to *read* for exactly the same reason.

Code that is easier to read and write is going to be easier to test, but functional code brings an additional benefit for testing. As projects get large, it often takes a lot of effort to set up the right environment to execute a test. This is much less of a problem with functional code, because there *is no relevant environment* beyond the function's arguments.

Functional code improves *reuse*. In order to reuse code, you must be able to do the following:

- Find and understand a piece of useful code.
- Compose the reusable code with other code.

The readability of functional code helps you find and understand the functions you need, but the benefit for *composing* code is even more compelling.

Composability is a hard problem. For years programmers have used *encapsulation* to try to create composable code. Encapsulation creates a firewall, providing access to data only through a public API.

Encapsulation helps, but it is nowhere near enough. Even with encapsulated objects, there are far too many surprising interactions when you try to compose entire systems. The problem is those darn side effects. *Impure functions* violate encapsulation, because they let the outside world reach in (invisibly!) and change the behavior of your code. Pure functions, on the other hand, are truly encapsulated and composable. Put them anywhere you want in a system, and they will always behave in the same way.

The Six Rules

Although the benefits of FP are compelling, FP is a wholesale change from the imperative programming style that dominates much of the programming world today. Plus, Clojure takes a unique approach to FP that strikes a balance between academic purity and the reality of running well on the JVM. That means there is a lot to learn all at once. But fear not. If you are new to FP, the following "Six Rules of Clojure FP" will help you on your initial steps toward FP mastery, Clojure style:

1. Avoid direct recursion. The JVM cannot optimize recursive calls, and Clojure programs that recurse will blow their stack.

2. Use recur when you are producing scalar values or small, fixed sequences. Clojure *will* optimize calls that use an explicit recur.

3. When producing large or variable-sized sequences, always be lazy. (Do *not* recur.) Then, your callers can consume just the part of the sequence they actually need.

4. Be careful not to realize more of a lazy sequence than you need.

5. Know the sequence library. You can often write code without using recur or the lazy APIs at all.

6. Subdivide. Divide even simple-seeming problems into smaller pieces, and you will often find solutions in the sequence library that lead to more general, reusable code.

Rules 5 and 6 are particularly important. If you are new to FP, you can translate these two rules to this: "Ignore this chapter and just use the techniques in Chapter 4, *Unifying Data with Sequences*, on page 91 until you hit a wall."

Like most rules, the six rules are guidelines, not absolutes. As you become comfortable with FP, you will find reasons to break them.

Now, let's get started writing functional code.

5.2 How to Be Lazy

Functional programs make great use of *recursive definitions*. A recursive definition consists of two parts:

- A *basis*, which explicitly enumerates some members of the sequence
- An *induction*, which provides rules for combining members of the sequence to produce additional members

Our challenge in this section is converting a recursive definition into working code. There are many ways you might do this:

- A simple recursion, using a function that calls itself in some way to implement the induction step.
- A tail recursion, using a function only calling itself at the tail end of its execution. Tail recursion enables an important optimization.
- A lazy sequence that eliminates actual recursion and calculates a value later, when it is needed.

Choosing the right approach is important. Implementing a recursive definition poorly can lead to code that performs terribly, consumes all available stack and fails, consumes all available heap and fails, or does all of these. In Clojure, being lazy is often the right approach.

We will explore all of these approaches by applying them to the Fibonacci numbers. Named for the Italian mathematician Leonardo (Fibonacci) of Pisa (c.1170 – c.1250), the Fibonacci numbers were actually known to Indian mathematicians as far back as 200 BC. The Fibonacci numbers have many interesting properties, and they crop up again and again in algorithms, data structures, and even biology.[4] The Fibonaccis have a very simple recursive definition:

- Basis: F_0, the zeroth Fibonacci number, is zero. F_1, the first Fibonacci number, is one.
- Induction: For *n > 1*, F_n equals $F_{n-1}+F_{n-2}$.

Using this definition, the first ten Fibonacci numbers are as follows:

(0 1 1 2 3 5 8 13 21 34)

Let's begin by implementing the Fibonaccis using a simple recursion. The following Clojure function will return the *nth* Fibonacci number:

`examples/functional.clj`

```
Line 1    ; bad idea
2    (defn stack-consuming-fibo [n]
3      (cond
4        (= n 0) 0
5        (= n 1) 1
6        :else (+ (stack-consuming-fibo (- n 1))
7                 (stack-consuming-fibo (- n 2)))))
```

Lines 4 and 5 define the basis, and line 6 defines the induction. The implementation is recursive because stack-consuming-fibo calls itself on lines 6 and 7.

Test that stack-consuming-fibo works correctly for small values of n:

(stack-consuming-fibo 9)

⇒   34

Good so far, but there is a problem calculating larger Fibonacci numbers such as $F_{1000000}$:

(stack-consuming-fibo 1000000)

⇒   java.lang.StackOverflowError

Because of the recursion, each call to stack-consuming-fibo for *n > 1* begets two more calls to stack-consuming-fibo. At the JVM level, these calls are translated into method calls, each of which allocates a data structure called a *stack frame*.[5]

---

4. http://en.wikipedia.org/wiki/Fibonacci_number
5. For more on how the JVM manages its stack, see "Runtime Data Areas" at http://tinyurl.com/jvm-spec-toc.

The stack-consuming-fibo creates a depth of stack frames proportional to n, which quickly exhausts the JVM stack and causes the StackOverflow-Error shown earlier. (It also creates a total number of stack frames that is exponential in n, so its performance is terrible even when the stack does not overflow.)

Clojure function calls are designated as *stack-consuming* because they allocate stack frames that use up stack space. In Clojure, you should almost always avoid stack-consuming recursion as shown in stack-consuming-fibo.

Tail Recursion

Functional programs can solve the stack-usage problem with *tail recursion*. A tail-recursive function is still defined recursively, but the recursion must come at the tail, that is, at an expression that is a return value of the function. Languages can then perform *tail-call optimization* (TCO), converting tail recursions into iterations that do not consume the stack.

The stack-consuming-fibo definition of Fibonacci is not tail-recursive, because it calls add (+) *after* both calls to stack-consuming-fibo. To make fibo tail-recursive, you must create a function whose arguments carry enough information to move the induction forward, without any extra "after" work (like an addition) that would push the recursion out of the tail position. For fibo, such a function needs to know two Fibonacci numbers, plus an ordinal n that can count down to zero as new Fibonaccis are calculated. You can write tail-fibo thusly:

`examples/functional.clj`

```
Line 1  (defn tail-fibo [n]
     2    (letfn [(fib
     3            [current next n]
     4            (if (zero? n)
     5                current
     6                (fib next (+ current next) (dec n))))]
     7      (fib 0 1 n)))
```

Line 2 introduces the letfn macro:

```
(letfn fnspecs & body)
; fnspecs ==> [(fname [params*] exprs)+]
```

letfn is like let but is dedicated to letting local functions. Each function declared in a letfn can call itself, or any other function in the same letfn block. Line 3 declares that fib has three arguments: the current Fibonacci, the next Fibonacci, and the number n of steps remaining.

Line 5 returns current when there are no steps remaining, and line 6 continues the calculation, decrementing the remaining steps by one. Finally, line 7 kicks off the recursion with the basis values 0 and 1, plus the ordinal n of the Fibonacci we are looking for.

tail-fibo works for small values of n:

```
(tail-fibo 9)
⇒    34
```

But even though it is tail-recursive, it still fails for large n:

```
(tail-fibo 1000000)
⇒    java.lang.StackOverflowErrow
```

The problem here is the JVM. While functional languages such as Haskell can perform TCO, the JVM was not designed for functional languages. No language that runs directly on the JVM can perform automatic TCO.[6]

The absence of TCO is unfortunate but not a showstopper for functional programs. Clojure provides several pragmatic workarounds: explicit self-recursion with recur, lazy sequences, and explicit mutual recursion with trampoline.

Self-recursion with recur

One special case of recursion that *can* be optimized away on the JVM is a self-recursion. Fortunately, the tail-fibo is an example: it calls itself directly, not through some series of intermediate functions.

In Clojure, you can convert a function that tail calls itself into an explicit self-recursion with recur. Using this approach, convert tail-fibo into recur-fibo:

examples/functional.clj

```
Line 1   ; better but not great
     2   (defn recur-fibo [n]
     3     (letfn [(fib
     4               [current next n]
     5               (if (zero? n)
     6                 current
     7                 (recur next (+ current next) (dec n))))]
     8       (fib 0 1 n)))
```

---

6. On today's JVMs, languages can provide automatic TCO for *some* kinds of recursion but not for *all*. Since there is no general solution, Clojure forces you to be explicit. When and if general TCO becomes widely supported on the JVM, Clojure will support it as well.

The critical difference between tail-fibo and recur-fibo is on line 7, where recur replaces the call to fib.

The recur-fibo will not consume stack as it calculates Fibonacci numbers and can calculate F_n for large n if you have the patience:

```
(recur-fibo 9)
```
⇒   34

```
(recur-fibo 1000000)
```
⇒   195 ... 208,982 other digits ... 875

The complete value of $F_{1000000}$ is included in the sample code at output/f-1000000.

The recur-fibo calculates one Fibonacci number. But what if you want several? Calling recur-fibo multiple times would be wasteful, since none of the work from any call to recur-fibo is ever cached for the next call. But how many values should be cached? Which ones? These choices should be made by the *caller* of the function, not the implementer.

Ideally you would define sequences with an API that makes *no reference* to the specific range that a particular client cares about and then let clients pull the range they want with take and drop. This is exactly what lazy sequences provide.

Lazy Sequences

Lazy sequences are constructed using the macro lazy-seq:

```
(lazy-seq & body)
```

A lazy-seq will invoke its body only when needed, that is, when seq is called directly or indirectly. lazy-seq will then cache the result for subsequent calls. You can use lazy-seq to define a lazy Fibonacci series as follows:

examples/functional.clj

```
Line 1  (defn lazy-seq-fibo
     2    ([]
     3      (concat [0 1] (lazy-seq-fibo 0 1)))
     4    ([a b]
     5      (let [n (+ a b)]
     6        (lazy-seq
     7          (cons n (lazy-seq-fibo b n))))))
```

On line 3, the zero-argument body returns the concatenation of the basis values [0 1] and then calls the two-argument body to calculate the rest of the values. On line 5, the two-argument body calculates the next value n in the series, and on line 7 it conses n onto the rest of the values.

The key is line 6, which makes its body lazy. Without this, the recursive call to lazy-seq-fibo on line 7 would happen immediately, and lazy-seq-fibo would recurse until it blew the stack. This illustrates the general pattern: wrap the recursive part of a function body with lazy-seq to replace recursion with laziness.

lazy-seq-fibo works for small values:

```
(take 10 (lazy-seq-fibo))
    (0 1 1 2 3 5 8 13 21 34)
```

lazy-seq-fibo also works for large values. Use (rem ... 1000) to print only the last three digits of the one millionth Fibonacci number:

```
(rem (nth (lazy-seq-fibo) 1000000) 1000)
    875
```

The lazy-seq-fibo approach follows rule 3, using laziness to implement an infinite sequence. But as is often the case, you do not need to explicitly call lazy-seq yourself. By rule 5, you can reuse existing sequence library functions that return lazy sequences. Consider this use of iterate:

```
(take 5 (iterate (fn [[a b]] [b (+ a b)]) [0 1]))
    ([0 1] [1 1] [1 2] [2 3] [3 5])
```

The iterate begins with the first pair of Fibonacci numbers [0 1]. By working pairwise, it then calculates the Fibonaccis by carrying along just enough information (two values) to calculate the next value.

The Fibonaccis are simply the first value of each pair. They can be extracted by calling map first over the entire sequence, leading to the following definition of fibo suggested by Christophe Grand:

examples/functional.clj

```
(defn fibo []
 (map first (iterate (fn [[a b]] [b (+ a b)]) [0 1])))
```

fibo returns a lazy sequence because it builds on map and iterate, which themselves return lazy sequences. fibo is also *simple*. fibo is the shortest implementation we have seen so far. But if you are accustomed to writing imperative, looping code, correctly *choosing* fibo over other approaches may not seem simple at all! Learning to think recursively, lazily, and within the JVM's limitations on recursion—all at the same time—can be intimidating. Let the rules help you. The Fibonacci numbers are infinite: rule 3 correctly predicts that the right approach in

Clojure will be a lazy sequence, and rule 5 lets the existing sequence functions do most of the work.

Lazy definitions consume *some* stack and heap. But they do not consume resources proportional to the size of an entire (possibly infinite!) sequence. Instead, *you choose* how many resources to consume when you traverse the sequence. If you want the one millionth Fibonacci number, you can get it from fibo, without having to consume stack or heap space for all the previous values.

There is no such thing as a free lunch. But with lazy sequences, you can have an infinite menu and pay only for the menu items you are eating at a given moment. When writing Clojure programs, you should prefer lazy sequences over loop/recur for any sequence that varies in size and for any large sequence.

Coming to Realization

Lazy sequences consume significant resources only as they are *realized*, that is, as a portion of the sequence is actually instantiated in memory. Clojure works hard to be lazy and avoid realizing sequences until it is absolutely necessary. For example, take returns a lazy sequence and does no realization at all. You can see this by creating a var to hold, say, the first billion Fibonacci numbers:

```
(def lots-o-fibs (take 1000000000 (fibo)))
```
⇒   #'user/lots-o-fibs

The creation of lots-o-fibs returns almost immediately, because it does *almost nothing*. If you ever call a function that needs to *actually use* some values in lots-o-fibs, Clojure will calculate them. Even then, it will do only what is necessary. For example, the following will return the 100th Fibonacci number from lots-o-fibs, without calculating the millions of other numbers that lots-o-fibs promises to provide:

```
(nth lots-o-fibs 100)
```
⇒   354224848179261915075

Most sequence functions return lazy sequences. If you are not sure whether a function returns a lazy sequence, the function's documentation string typically will tell you the answer:

```
(doc take)
-------------------------
clojure.core/take
([n coll])
  Returns a lazy seq of the first n items in coll, or all items if
  there are fewer than n.
```

The REPL, however, is *not lazy*. The printer used by the REPL will, by default, print the entirety of a collection. That is why we stuffed the first billion Fibonaccis into lots-o-fibs, instead of evaluating them at the REPL. Don't enter the following at the REPL:

```
; don't do this
(take 1000000000 (fibo))
```

If you enter the previous expression, the printer will attempt to print a billion Fibonacci numbers, realizing the entire collection as it goes. You will probably get bored and exit the REPL before Clojure runs out of memory.

As a convenience for working with lazy sequences, you can configure how many items the printer will print by setting the value of *print-length*:

```
(set! *print-length* 10)
```
⇒   10

For collections with more than ten items, the printer will now print only the first ten followed by an ellipsis. So, you can safely print a billion fibos:

```
(take 1000000000 (fibo))
```
⇒   (0 1 1 2 3 5 8 13 21 34 ...)

Or even all the fibos:

```
(fibo)
```
⇒   (0 1 1 2 3 5 8 13 21 34 ...)

Lazy sequences are wonderful. They do only what is needed, and for the most part you don't have to worry about them. If you ever want to force a sequence to be fully realized, you can use either doall or dorun, discussed in Section 4.3, *Forcing Sequences*, on page 106.

Losing Your Head

There is one last thing to consider when working with lazy sequences. Lazy sequences let you define a large (possibly infinite) sequence and then work with a small part of that sequence in memory at a given moment. This clever ploy will fail if you (or some API) unintentionally hold a reference to the part of the sequence you no longer care about.

The most common way this can happen is if you accidentally hold the head (first item) of a sequence. In the examples in the previous sections, each variant of the Fibonacci numbers was defined as a function returning a sequence, not the sequence itself.

You could define the sequence directly as a top-level var:

examples/functional.clj

```
; holds the head (avoid!)
(def head-fibo (lazy-cat [0 1] (map + head-fibo (rest head-fibo))))
```

This definition uses lazy-cat, which is like concat except that the arguments are evaluated only when needed. This is a very pretty definition in that it defines the recursion by mapping a sum over (each element of the Fibonaccis) and (each element of the *rest* of the Fibonaccis).

head-fibo works great for small Fibonacci numbers:

```
(take 10 head-fibo)
```
⇒   (0 1 1 2 3 5 8 13 21 34)

but not so well for huge ones:

```
(nth head-fibo 1000000)
```
⇒   java.lang.OutOfMemoryError: Java heap space

The problem is that the top-level var head-fibo *holds the head* of the collection. This prevents the garbage collector from reclaiming elements of the sequence after you have moved past those elements. So, any part of the Fibonacci sequence that you actually use gets cached for the life of the value referenced by head-fibo, which is likely to be the life of the program.

Unless you want to cache a sequence as you traverse it, you must be careful not to keep a reference to the head of the sequence. As the head-fibo example demonstrates, you should normally expose lazy sequences as a function that *returns* the sequence, not as a var that *contains* the sequence. If a caller of your function wants an explicit cache, the caller can always create its own var.

With lazy sequences, losing your head is often a good idea.

5.3 Lazier Than Lazy

Clojure's lazy sequences are a great form of laziness at the language level. As a programmer, you can be *even lazier* by finding solutions that do not require explicit sequence manipulation at all. You can often combine existing sequence functions to solve a problem, without having to get your hands dirty at the level of recur or lazy sequences at all.

As an example of this, you will implement several solutions to the following problem.[7] You are given a sequence of coin toss results, where heads is :h and tails is :t:

```
[:h :t :t :h :h :h]
```

How many times in the sequence does heads come up twice in a row? In the previous example, the answer is two. Toss 3 and 4 are both heads, and toss 4 and 5 are both heads.

The sequence of coin tosses might be very large, but it will be finite. Since you are looking for a scalar answer (a count), by rule 2 it is acceptable to use recur:

examples/functional.clj

```
Line 1  (defn count-heads-pairs [coll]
     2    (loop [cnt 0 coll coll]
     3      (if (empty? coll)
     4        cnt
     5        (recur (if (= :h (first coll) (second coll))
     6                 (inc cnt)
     7                 cnt)
     8               (rest coll)))))
```

Since the purpose of the function is to count something, the loop introduces a cnt binding, initially zero on line 2. The loop also introduces its own binding for the coll so that we can shrink the coll each time through the recur.

Line 3 provides the basis for the recurrence. If a sequence of coins tosses is empty, it certainly has zero runs of two heads in a row.

Line 5 is the meat of the function, incrementing the cnt by one if the first and second items of coll are both heads (:h).

Try a few inputs to see that count-heads-pairs works as advertised:

```
(count-heads-pairs [:h :h :h :t :h])
```
⇒   2

```
(count-heads-pairs [:h :t :h :t :h])
```
⇒   0

Although count-heads-pairs works, it fails as code prose. The key notion of "two in a rowness" is completely obscured by the boilerplate for

---

7. Hat tip to Jeff Brown, who posed this problem over breakfast at a No Fluff, Just Stuff symposium.

loop/recur. To fix this, you will need to use rules 5 and 6, subdividing the problem to take advantage of Clojure's sequence library.

The first problem you will encounter is that almost all the sequence functions do something to each element in a sequence in turn. This doesn't help us at all, since we want to look at each element in the context of its immediate neighbors. So, let's transform the sequence. When you see this:

```
[:h :t :t :h :h :h]
```

you should mentally translate that into a sequence of every adjacent pair:

```
[[:h :t] [:t :t] [:t :h] [:h :h] [:h :h]]
```

Write a function named by-pairs that performs this transformation. Because the output of by-pairs varies based on the size of its input, by rule 3 you should build this sequence lazily:

`examples/functional.clj`

```
Line 1  ; overly complex, better approaches follow...
     2  (defn by-pairs [coll]
     3    (let [take-pair (fn [c]
     4                        (when (next c) (take 2 c)))]
     5      (lazy-seq
     6        (when-let [pair (seq (take-pair coll))]
     7          (cons pair (by-pairs (rest coll)))))))
```

Line 3 defines a function that takes the first pair of elements from the collection. Line 5 ensures that the recursion is evaluated lazily. Line 6 is a conditional: if the next pair does not actually contain two elements, we must be (almost) at the end of the list, and we implicitly terminate. If we did get two elements, then on line 7 we continue building the sequence by consing our pair onto the pairs to be had from the rest of the collection.

Check that by-pairs works:

```
(by-pairs [:h :t  :t :h :h :h])
⇒   ((:h :t) (:t :t) (:t :h) (:h :h) (:h :h))
```

Now that you can think of the coin tosses as a sequence *of pairs* of results, it is easy to describe count-heads-pairs in English:

"Count the pairs of results that are all heads."

This English description translates directly into existing sequence library functions: "Count" is count, of course, and "that are all heads" suggests a filter:

examples/functional.clj

```
(defn count-heads-pairs [coll]
  (count (filter (fn [pair] (every? #(= :h %) pair))
                 (by-pairs coll))))
```

This is much more expressive than the recur-based implementation, and it makes clear that we are counting all the adjacent pairs of heads. But we can make things even simpler. Clojure already has a more general version of by-pairs named partition:

```
(partition size step? coll)
```

partition breaks a collection into chunks of size size. So, you could break a heads/tails vector into a sequence of pairs:

```
(partition 2 [:h :t  :t :h :h :h])
```
⇒   `((:h :t) (:t :h) (:h :h))`

That isn't quite the same as by-pairs, which yields overlapping pairs. But partition can do overlaps too. The optional step argument determines how far partition moves down the collection before starting its next chunk. If not specified, step is the same as size. To make partition work like by-pairs, set size to 2 and step to 1:

```
(partition 2 1 [:h :t  :t :h :h :h])
```
⇒   `((:h :t) (:t :t) (:t :h) (:h :h) (:h :h))`

```
(by-pairs [:h :t  :t :h :h :h])
```
⇒   `((:h :t) (:t :t) (:t :h) (:h :h) (:h :h))`

Another possible area of improvement is the count/filter idiom used to count the pairs that are both heads. This combination comes up often enough that it is worth encapsulating in a count-if function:

examples/functional.clj

```
(use '[clojure.contrib.def :only (defvar)])
(defvar count-if (comp count filter)  "Count items matching a filter")
```

The definition of count-if introduces two new forms. defvar is a convenience wrapper around def and is described in the sidebar on the following page. comp is used to *compose* two or more functions:

```
(comp f & fs)
```

The composed function is a new function that applies the rightmost function to its arguments, the next-rightmost function to that result,

> ### Faces of def
>
> Throughout the book you will use various def forms to create vars, such as defn, defmacro, and defmulti. These forms are all eventually wrappers around the def special form.
>
> A number of other def variants are less often used but still worth knowing. defvar provides a convenient way to add a documentation string to a var:
>
> ```
> (clojure.contrib.def/defvar a-symbol initial-value? docstring?)
> ```
>
> defonce ensures that a var exists and sets the root binding for the var *only if it is not already set*:
>
> ```
> (defonce a-symbol initial-value?)
> ```
>
> defhinted will create a var and set its type information based on the initial value of the var:
>
> ```
> (clojure.contrib.def/defhinted a-symbol initial-value?)
> ```
>
> defn- works just like defn but yields a *private* function that is accessible only in the namespace where it was defined.
>
> ```
> (defn- name & args-as-for-defn)
> ```
>
> Many other def forms also have dash-suffixed variants that are private.
>
> For more def variants, see the source code for clojure.contrib.def.

and so on. So, count-if will first filter and then count the results of the filter:

```
(count-if odd? [1 2 3 4 5])
```
⇒   3

Finally, you can use count-if and partition to create a count-runs function that is more general than count-heads-pairs:

examples/functional.clj
```
(defn
 count-runs
 "Count runs of length n where pred is true in coll."
 [n pred coll]
 (count-if #(every? pred %) (partition n 1 coll)))
```

count-runs is a winning combination: both simpler and more general than the previous versions of count-heads-pairs. You can use it to count pairs of heads:

```
(count-runs 2 #(= % :h) [:h :t :t :h :h :h])
```
⇒   2

But you can just as easily use it to count pairs of tails:

```
(count-runs 2 #(= % :t) [:h :t :t :h :h :h])
```
⇒   1

Or, instead of pairs, how about runs of three heads in a row?

```
(count-runs 3 #(= % :h) [:h :t :t :h :h :h])
```
⇒   1

If you still want to have a function named count-heads-pairs, you can implement it in terms of count-runs:

examples/functional.clj

```
(defvar count-heads-pairs (partial count-runs 2 #(= % :h))
  "Count runs of length two that are both heads")
```

This version of count-heads-pairs builds a new function using partial:

```
(partial f & partial-args)
```

partial performs a *partial application* of a function. You specify a function f and part of the argument list when you perform the partial. You specify the remainder of the argument list later, when you call the function created by partial. So, the following:

```
(partial count-runs 1 #(= % :h))
```

is a more expressive way of saying this:

```
(fn [coll] (count-runs 1 #(= % :h) coll))
```

Partial application is similar but not identical to *currying*.

Currying and Partial Application

When you *curry* a function, you get a new function that takes one argument and returns the original function with that one argument fixed. (Curry is named for Haskell Curry, an American logician best known for his work in combinatory logic.) If Clojure had a curry, it might be implemented like this:

```
; almost a curry
(defn faux-curry [& args] (apply partial partial args))
```

One use of curry is partial application. Here is partial application in Clojure:

```
(def add-3 (partial + 3))
(add-3 7)
```
⇒   10

And here is partial application using our faux-curry:

```
(def add-3 ((faux-curry +) 3))
(add-3 7)
```
⇒   10

If all you want is partial application, currying is just an intermediate step. Our faux-curry is not a real curry. A real curry would return a result, not a function of no arguments, once all the arguments were fixed. You can see the difference here, using the function true?, which takes only one argument:

```
; faux curry
((faux-curry true?) (= 1 1))
```
⇒   #<... mangled function name ...>

```
; if the curry were real
((curry true?) (= 1 1))
```
⇒   true

Since Clojure functions can have variable-length argument lists, Clojure cannot know when all the arguments are fixed. But you, the programmer, do know when you are done adding arguments. Once you have curried as many arguments as you want, just invoke the function. That amounts to adding an extra set of parentheses around the earlier expression:

```
(((faux-curry true?) (= 1 1)))
```
⇒   true

The absence of curry from Clojure is not a major problem, since partial is available, and that is what people generally want out of curry anyway. In fact, many programmers use the terms *currying* and *partial application* interchangeably.

You have seen a lot of new forms in this section. Do not let all the details obscure the key idea: by combining existing functions from the sequence library, you were able to create a solution that was both simpler and more general than the direct approach. And, you did not have to worry about laziness or recursion at all. Instead, you worked at a higher level of abstraction and let Clojure deal with laziness and recursion for you.

5.4 Recursion Revisited

Clojure works very hard to balance the power of functional programming with the reality of the Java Virtual Machine. One example of this is the well-motivated choice of explicit TCO through loop/recur.

But blending the best of two worlds always runs the risk of unpleasant compromises, and it certainly makes sense to ask the question "Does Clojure contain hidden design compromises that, while not obvious on day one, will bite me later?"

This question is *never* fully answerable for any language, but let's consider by exploring some more complex recursions. First, we will look at *mutual recursion*.

A mutual recursion occurs when the recursion bounces between two or more functions. Instead of A calls A calls A, you have A calls B calls C calls A again. As a simple example, you could define my-odd? and my-even? using mutual recursion:

```
examples/functional.clj
(declare my-odd? my-even?)

(defn my-odd? [n]
  (if (= n 0)
    false
    (my-even? (dec n))))

(defn my-even? [n]
  (if (= n 0)
    true
    (my-odd? (dec n))))
```

Because my-odd? and my-even? each call the other, you need to create both vars before actually defining the functions. You could do this with def, but the declare macro lets you create both vars (with no initial binding) in a single line of code.

Verify that my-odd? and my-even? work for small values:

```
(map my-even? (range 10))
```
⇒
```
    (true false true false true false true false true false)
```

```
(map my-odd? (range 10))
```
⇒
```
    (false true false true false true false true false true)
```

my-odd? and my-even? consume stack frames proportional to the size of their argument, so they will fail with large numbers.

```
(my-even? (* 1000 1000 1000))
```
⇒ `java.lang.StackOverflowError`

This is very similar to the problem that motivated the introduction of recur. But you cannot use recur to fix it, because recur works with self-recursion, not mutual recursion.

Of course, odd/even can be implemented more efficiently *without* recursion anyway. Clojure's implementation uses bit-and (bitwise and) to implement odd? and even?:

```
; from core.clj
(defn even? [n] (zero? (bit-and n 1)))
(defn odd? [n] (not (even? n)))
```

I picked odd/even for its simplicity. Other recursive problems are not so simple and do not have an elegant nonrecursive solution. We will examine four approaches that you can use to solve such problems:

- Converting to self-recursion
- Trampolining a mutual recursion
- Replacing recursion with laziness
- Shortcutting recursion with memoization

Converting to Self-recursion

Mutual recursion is often a nice way to model separate but related concepts. For example, oddness and evenness are separate concepts but clearly related to one another.

You can convert a mutual recursion to a self-recursion by coming up with a single abstraction that deals with multiple concepts simultaneously. For example, you can think of oddness and evenness in terms of a single concept: *parity*. Define a parity function that uses recur and returns 0 for even numbers and 1 for odd numbers:

examples/functional.clj

```
(defn parity [n]
  (loop [n n par 0]
    (if (= n 0)
      par
      (recur (dec n) (- 1 par)))))
```

Test that parity works for small values:

```
(map parity (range 10))
```
⇒ `(0 1 0 1 0 1 0 1 0 1)`

At this point, you can trivially implement my-odd? and my-even? in terms of parity:

examples/functional.clj

```
(defn my-even? [n] (= 0 (parity n)))
(defn my-odd? [n] (= 1 (parity n)))
```

Parity is a straightforward concept. Unfortunately, many mutual recursions will not simplify down into an elegant self-recursion. If you try to convert a mutual recursion into a self-recursion and you find the resulting code to be full of conditional expressions that obfuscate the definition, then do not use this approach.

Trampolining Mutual Recursion

A *trampoline* is a technique for optimizing mutual recursion. A trampoline is like an after-the-fact recur, imposed by the *caller* of a function instead of the *implementer*. Since the caller can call more than one function inside a trampoline, trampolines can optimize mutual recursion.

Clojure's trampoline function invokes one of your mutually recursive functions:

```
(trampoline f & partial-args)
```

If the return value is not a function, then a trampoline works just like calling the function directly. Try trampolining a few simple Clojure functions:

```
(trampoline list)
```
⇒   ()
```
(trampoline + 1 2)
```
⇒   3

If the return value *is* a function, then trampoline assumes you want to call it recursively and calls it for you. trampoline manages its own recur, so it will keep calling your function until it stops returning functions.

Back in Section 5.2, *Tail Recursion*, on page 134, you implemented a tail-fibo function. You saw how the function consumed stack space and replaced the tail recursion with a recur. Now you have another option. You can take the code of tail-fibo and prepare it for trampolining by wrapping the recursive return case inside a function.

This requires adding only a single character, the #, to introduce an anonymous function:

examples/trampoline.clj

```
Line 1   ; Example only. Don't write code like this.
    -    (defn trampoline-fibo [n]
    -      (let [fib (fn fib [f-2 f-1 current]
    -                  (let [f (+ f-2 f-1)]
    5                    (if (= n current)
    -                      f
    -                      #(fib f-1 f (inc current)))))]
    -        (cond
    -          (= n 0) 0
    10         (= n 1) 1
    -          :else (fib 0 1 2)))))
```

The only difference between this and the original version of tail-fibo is the initial # on line 7. Try bouncing trampoline-fibo on a trampoline:

```
(trampoline trampoline-fibo 9)
```
⇒   34

Since trampoline does a recur for you, it can handle large inputs just fine, without throwing a StackOverflowError:

```
(rem (trampoline trampoline-fibo 1000000) 1000)
```
⇒   875

We have ported tail-fibo to use trampoline in order to compare and contrast trampoline and recur. For self-recursions like trampoline-fibo, trampoline offers no advantage, and you should prefer recur. But with mutual recursion, trampoline comes into its own.

Consider the mutually recursive definition of my-odd? and my-even? which was presented at the beginning of Section 5.4, *Recursion Revisited*, on page 147. You can convert these broken, stack-consuming implementations to use trampoline using the same approach you used to convert tail-fibo: simply prepend a # to any recursive tail calls:

examples/trampoline.clj

```
Line 1   (declare my-odd? my-even?)
    -
    -    (defn my-odd? [n]
    -      (if (= n 0)
    5        false
    -        #(my-even? (dec n))))
    -
    -    (defn my-even? [n]
    -      (if (= n 0)
    10       true
    -        #(my-odd? (dec n))))
```

The only difference from the original implementation is the # wrappers on lines 6 and 11. With this change in place, you can trampoline large values of n without blowing the stack:

```
(trampoline my-even? 1000000)
```
⇒   true

A trampoline is a special-purpose solution to a specific problem. It requires doctoring your original functions to return a different type to indicate recursion. If one of the other techniques presented here provides a more elegant implementation for a particular recursion, that is great. If not, you will be happy to have trampoline in your box of tools.

Replacing Recursion with Laziness

Of all the techniques for eliminating or optimizing recursion discussed in this chapter, laziness is the one you will probably use most often.

For our example, we will implement the replace function developed by Eugene Wallingford to demonstrate mutual recursion. (See http://www. cs.uni.edu/~wallingf/patterns/recursion.html.)

replace works with an s-list data structure, which is a list that can contain both symbols and lists of symbols. replace takes an s-list, an oldsym, and a newsym and replaces all occurrences of oldsym with newsym. For example, this call to replace replaces all occurrences of b with a:

```
(replace '((a b) (((b g r) (f r)) c (d e)) b) 'b 'a)
```
⇒   ((a a) (((a g r) (f r)) c (d e)) a)

The following is a fairly literal translation of the Scheme implementation from Wallingford's paper. I have converted from Scheme functions to Clojure functions, changed the name to replace-symbol to avoid collision with Clojure's replace, and shortened names to better fit the printed page, but I otherwise have preserved the structure of the original:

examples/wallingford.clj
```
; overly-literal port, do not use
(declare replace-symbol replace-symbol-expression)

(defn replace-symbol [coll oldsym newsym]
  (if (empty? coll)
    ()
    (cons (replace-symbol-expression
            (first coll) oldsym newsym)
          (replace-symbol
            (rest coll) oldsym newsym))))
```

```clojure
(defn replace-symbol-expression [symbol-expr oldsym newsym]
  (if (symbol? symbol-expr)
    (if (= symbol-expr oldsym)
      newsym
      symbol-expr)
    (replace-symbol symbol-expr oldsym newsym)))
```

The two functions replace-symbol and replace-symbol-expression are mutually recursive, so a deeply nested structure could blow the stack. To demonstrate the problem, create a deeply-nested function that builds deeply nested lists containing a single bottom element:

examples/replace_symbol.clj

```clojure
(defn deeply-nested [n]
  (loop [n n
         result '(bottom)]
    (if (= n 0)
      result
      (recur (dec n) (list result)))))
```

Try deeply-nested for a few small values of n:

```clojure
(deeply-nested 5)
```
⇒   ((((((bottom))))))

```clojure
(deeply-nested 25)
```
⇒   ((((((((((((((((((((((((((bottom))))))))))))))))))))))))))

Clojure provides a *print-level* that controls how deeply the Clojure printer will go into a nested data structure. Set the *print-level* to a modest value so that the printer doesn't go crazy trying to print a deeply nested structure. You will see when nesting deeper, the printer simply prints a # and stops:

```clojure
(set! *print-level* 25)
```
⇒   25

```clojure
(deeply-nested 5)
```
⇒   ((((((bottom))))))

```clojure
(deeply-nested 25)
```
⇒   (((((((((((((((((((((((((#))))))))))))))))))))))))))

Now, try to use replace-symbol to change bottom to deepest for different levels of nesting. You will see that large levels blow the stack. Depending on your particular JVM implementation, you may need a larger value than the 10000 shown here:

```clojure
(replace-symbol (deeply-nested 5) 'bottom 'deepest)
```
⇒   ((((((deepest))))))

```
(replace-symbol (deeply-nested 10000) 'bottom 'deepest)
```
⇒   java.lang.StackOverflowError

All of the recursive calls to replace-symbol are inside a cons. To break
the recursion, all you have to do is wrap the recursion with lazy-seq.

It's really that simple. You can break a sequence-generating recursion
by wrapping it with a lazy-seq. Here's the improved version. Since the
transition to laziness was so simple, I could not resist the temptation
to make the function more Clojurish in another way as well:

examples/replace_symbol.clj

```
Line 1  (defn- coll-or-scalar [x & _] (if (coll? x) :collection :scalar))
   -    (defmulti replace-symbol coll-or-scalar)
   -
   -    (defmethod replace-symbol :collection [coll oldsym newsym]
   5      (lazy-seq
   -        (when (seq coll)
   -          (cons (replace-symbol (first coll) oldsym newsym)
   -                (replace-symbol (rest coll) oldsym newsym)))))
   -
  10    (defmethod replace-symbol :scalar [obj oldsym newsym]
   -      (if (= obj oldsym) newsym obj))
```

On line 5, the lazy-seq breaks the recursion, preventing stack overflow
on deeply nested structures. The other improvement is on line 2. Rather
than have two different functions to deal with symbols and lists, there
is a single multimethod replace-symbol with one method for lists and
another for symbols. (Multimethods are covered in detail in Chapter 8,
Multimethods, on page 225.) This gets rid of an if form and improves
readability.

Make sure the improved replace-symbol can handle deep nesting:

```
(replace-symbol (deeply-nested 10000) 'bottom 'deepest)
```
⇒   (((((((((((((((((((((((((((#))))))))))))))))))))))))))))

Laziness is a powerful ally. You can often write recursive and even
mutually recursive functions and then break the recursion with laziness.

Shortcutting Recursion with Memoization

To demonstrate a more complex mutual recursion, we will look at the
Hofstadter Female and Male sequences. The first Hofstadter sequences

were described in *Gödel, Escher, Bach: An Eternal Golden Braid* [Hof99]. The Female and Male sequences are defined as follows:[8]

$F(0) = 1; M(0) = 0$

$F(n) = n - M(F(n-1)), n > 0$

$M(n) = n - F(M(n-1)), n > 0$

This suggests a straightforward definition in Clojure:

examples/male_female.clj

```
; do not use these directly
(declare m f)
(defn m [n]
  (if (zero? n)
    0
    (- n (f (m (dec n)))))))

(defn f [n]
  (if (zero? n)
    1
    (- n (m (f (dec n)))))))
```

The Clojure definition is easy to read and closely parallels the mathematical definition. However, it performs *terribly* for large values of n. Each value in the sequence requires calculating two other values from scratch, which in turn requires calculating two other values from scratch. On my MacBook Pro[9] it takes more than a minute to calculate (m 250):

```
(time (m 250))
"Elapsed time: 78482.038 msecs"
⇒    155
```

Is it possible to preserve the clean, mutually recursive definition *and* have decent performance? Yes, with a little help from *memoization*. Memoization trades space for time by caching the results of past calculations. When you call a memoized function, it first checks your input against a map of previous inputs and their outputs. If it finds the input in the map, it can return the output immediately, without having to perform the calculation again.

---

8. http://en.wikipedia.org/wiki/Hofstadter_sequence
9. 2.4 GHz Intel Core 2 Duo, 4 GB 667 MHz DDR2 SDRAM, OS X 10.5.5

Rebind m and f to memoized versions of themselves, using Clojure's memoize function:

```
examples/memoized_male_female.clj
```
```
(def m (memoize m))
(def f (memoize f))
```

Now Clojure needs to calculate F and M only once for each n. The speedup is enormous. Calculating (m 250) is thousands of times faster:

```
(time (m 250))
"Elapsed time: 18.197 msecs"
```
⇒   155

And, of course, once the memoization cache is built, "calculation" of a cached value is almost instantaneous:

```
(time (m 250))
"Elapsed time: 0.084 msecs"
```
⇒   155

Memoization alone is not enough, however. Memoization shortcuts the recursion only if the memoization cache is already populated. If you start with an empty cache and ask for m or f of a large number, you will blow the stack before the cache can be built:

```
(m 10000)
```
⇒   java.lang.StackOverflowError

The final trick is to guarantee that the cache is built from the ground up by exposing *sequences*, instead of *functions*. Create m-seq and f-seq by mapping m and f over the whole numbers:

```
examples/male_female_seq.clj
```
```
(def m-seq (map m (iterate inc 0)))
(def f-seq (map f (iterate inc 0)))
```

Now callers can get *M(n)* or *F(n)* by taking the nth value from a sequence:

```
(nth m-seq 250)
```
⇒   155

The approach is quite fast, even for larger values of n:

```
(time (nth m-seq 10000))
"Elapsed time: 483.069 msecs"
```
⇒   6180

The approach we have used here is as follows:

- Define a mutually recursive function in a natural way.

- Use memoization in order to shortcut recursion for values that have already been calculated.

- Expose a sequence so that dependent values are cached before they are needed.

This approach *is* heap-consuming, in that it does cache all previously seen values. If this is a problem, you can in some situations eliminate it by selecting a more complex caching policy.

5.5 Wrapping Up

Clojure's support for FP strikes a well-motivated balance between academic purity and effectiveness on the Java Virtual Machine. Clojure gives you access to a wide variety of techniques including self-recursion with recur, mutual recursion with trampoline, lazy sequences, and memoization.

Better still, for a wide variety of everyday programming tasks, you can use the sequence library, without ever having to define your own explicit recursions of lazy sequences. Functions like partition create clean, expressive solutions that are much easier to write.

If Clojure were an exclusively FP language, we would turn our attention next to the challenges of living in a world without mutable state and perhaps begin discussing the state monad. But Clojure leads us in a different direction with its most innovative feature: explicit APIs for managing mutable state. The Clojure concurrency API provides four different ways to model mutable state and is the subject of the next chapter.

Chapter 6

Concurrency

Concurrency is a fact of life and, increasingly, a fact of software. There are several reasons that programs need to do more than one thing at a time:

- Expensive computations may need to execute in parallel on multiple cores (or multiple boxes) in order to complete in a timely manner.
- Tasks that are blocked waiting for a resource should stand down and let other tasks use available processors.
- User interfaces need to remain responsive while performing long-running tasks.
- Operations that are logically independent are easier to implement if the platform can recognize and take advantage of their independence.

The challenge of concurrency is not making multiple things happen at once. It is easy enough to launch a bunch of threads or a bunch of processes. Rather, the challenge is *coordinating* multiple activities happening at the same time.

Clojure provides a powerful concurrency library, consisting of four APIs that enforce different concurrency models: refs, atoms, agents, and vars.

- Refs manage *coordinated, synchronous* changes to shared state.
- Atoms manage *uncoordinated, synchronous* changes to shared state.
- Agents manage *asynchronous* changes to shared state.
- Vars manage *thread-local* state.

Refs are updated within transactions managed by Clojure's Software Transactional Memory (STM) system. Agents also have the option of interacting with STM.

Each of these APIs is discussed in this chapter. At the end of the chapter, we will develop two sample applications:

- The Snake game demonstrates how to divide an application model into immutable and mutable components.

- Continuing the Lancet example, we will add a thread-safe runonce capability to make sure each Lancet target runs only once per build.

Before we dive in, let's review the problem these APIs were designed to solve: the difficulty of using locks.

6.1 The Problem with Locks

A big challenge for concurrent programs is managing mutable state. If mutable state can be accessed concurrently, then as a programmer you must be careful to protect that access. In most programming languages today, development proceeds as follows:

- Mutable state is the default, so mutable state is commingled through all layers of the codebase.

- Concurrency is implemented using independent flows of execution called *threads*.

- If mutable state can be reached by multiple threads, you must protect that state with *locks* that allow only one thread to pass at a time.

Choosing what and where to lock is a difficult task. If you get it wrong, all sorts of bad things can happen. *Race conditions* between threads can corrupt data. *Deadlocks* can stop an entire program from functioning at all. *Java Concurrency in Practice* [Goe06] covers these and other problems, plus their solutions, in detail. It is a terrific book, but it is difficult to read it and not be asking yourself "Is there another way?"

Yes, there is. In Clojure, *immutable state* is the default. Most data is immutable. The small parts of the codebase that truly benefit from mutability are distinct and must explicitly select one or more concurrency APIs. Using these APIs, you can split your models into two layers:

- A *functional model* that has no mutable state. Most of your code will normally be in this layer, which is easier to read, easier to test, and easier to run concurrently.

- A *mutable model* for the parts of the application that you find more convenient to deal with using mutable state (despite its disadvantages).

To manage the mutable model, you can use Clojure's concurrency library. In addition, you can still use locks and all the low-level APIs for Java concurrency. If after reviewing Clojure's options you decide that Java's concurrency APIs are a better fit, use Clojure's Java interop to call them from your Clojure program. Consult *Java Concurrency in Practice* [Goe06] for API details.

Now, let's get started working with mutable state in Clojure, using what is probably the most important part of the Clojure concurrency library: refs.

6.2 Refs and Software Transactional Memory

Most objects in Clojure are immutable. When you really want mutable data, you must be explicit about it, such as by creating a mutable *reference* (ref) to an immutable object. You create a ref with this:

```
(ref initial-state)
```

For example, you could create a reference to the current song in your music playlist:

```
(def current-track (ref "Mars, the Bringer of War"))
```
⇒ `#'user/current-track`

The ref wraps and protects access to its internal state. To read the contents of the reference, you can call deref:

```
(deref reference)
```

The deref function can be shortened to the @ reader macro. Try using both deref and @ to dereference current-track:

```
(deref current-track)
```
⇒ `"Mars, the Bringer of War"`

```
@current-track
```
⇒ `"Mars, the Bringer of War"`

Notice how in this example the Clojure model fits the real world. A track is an immutable entity. It doesn't change into another track when you are finished listening to it. But the *current* track is a reference to an entity, and it does change.

ref-set

You can change where a reference points with ref-set:

```
(ref-set reference new-value)
```

Call ref-set to listen to a different track:

```
(ref-set current-track "Venus, the Bringer of Peace")
```
⇒   java.lang.IllegalStateException: No transaction running

Oops. Because refs are mutable, you must protect their updates. In many languages, you would use a *lock* for this purpose. In Clojure, you can use a *transaction*. Transactions are wrapped in a dosync:

```
(dosync & exprs)
```

Wrap your ref-set with a dosync, and all is well:

```
(dosync (ref-set current-track "Venus, the Bringer of Peace"))
```
⇒   "Venus, the Bringer of Peace"

The current-track reference now refers to a different track.

Transactional Properties

Like database transactions, STM transactions guarantee some important properties:

- Updates are *atomic*. If you update more than one ref in a transaction, the cumulative effect of all the updates will appear as a single instantaneous event to anyone not inside your transaction.

- Updates are *consistent*. Refs can specify validation functions. If any of these functions fail, the entire transaction will fail.

- Updates are *isolated*. Running transactions cannot see partially completed results from other transactions.

Databases provide the additional guarantee that updates are *durable*. Because Clojure's transactions are in-memory transactions, Clojure does not guarantee that updates are durable. If you want a durable transaction in Clojure, you should use a database.

Together, the four transactional properties are called ACID. Databases provide ACID; Clojure's STM provides ACI.

If you change more than one ref in a single transaction, those changes are all coordinated to "happen at the same time" from the perspective of any code outside the transaction. So, you can make sure that updates to current-track and current-composer are *coordinated*:

```
(def current-track (ref "Venus, the Bringer of Peace"))
```
⇒   `#'user/current-track`
```
(def current-composer (ref "Holst"))
```
⇒   `#'user/current-composer`

```
(dosync
  (ref-set current-track "Credo")
  (ref-set current-composer "Byrd"))
```
⇒   `"Byrd"`

Because the updates are in a transaction, no other thread will ever see an updated track with an out-of-date composer, or vice versa.

alter

The current-track example is deceptively easy, because updates to the ref are totally independent of any previous state. Let's build a more complex example, where transactions need to update existing information. A simple chat application fits the bill. First, create a message struct that has a sender and some text:

`examples/chat.clj`

```
(defstruct message :sender :text)
```

Now, you can create messages by calling struct:

```
(struct message "stu" "test message")
```
⇒   `{:sender "stu", :text "test message"}`

Users of the chat application want to see the most recent message first, so a list is a good data structure. Create a messages reference that points to an initially empty list:

```
(def messages (ref ()))
```

Now you need a function to add a new message to the front of messages. You could simply deref to get the list of messages, cons the new message, and then ref-set the updated list back into messages:

```
; bad idea
(defn naive-add-message [msg]
  (dosync (ref-set messages (cons msg @messages))))
```

But there is a better option. Why not perform the read and update in a single step? Clojure's alter will apply an update function to a referenced object within a transaction:

```
(alter ref update-fn & args...)
```

alter returns the new value of the ref within the transaction. When a transaction successfully completes, the ref will take on its last in-transaction value. Using alter instead of ref-set makes the code more readable:

```
(defn add-message [msg]
  (dosync (alter messages conj msg)))
```

Notice that the update function is conj (short for "conjoin"), not cons. This is because conj takes arguments in an order suitable for use with alter:

```
(cons item sequence)
(conj sequence item)
```

The alter function calls its update-fn with the current reference value as its first argument, as conj expects. If you plan to write your own update functions, they should follow the same structure as conj:

```
(your-func thing-that-gets-updated & optional-other-args)
```

Try adding a few messages to see that the code works as expected:

```
(add-message (struct message "user 1" "hello"))
    ({:sender "user 1", :text "hello"})

(add-message (struct message "user 2" "howdy"))
    ({:sender "user 2", :text "howdy"}
     {:sender "user 1", :text "hello"})
```

alter is the workhorse of Clojure's STM and is the primary means of updating refs. But if you know a little about how the STM works, you may be able to optimize your transactions in certain scenarios.

How STM Works: MVCC

Clojure's STM uses a technique called Multiversion Concurrency Control (MVCC), which is also used in several major databases. Here's how MVCC works in Clojure:

Transaction A begins by taking a *point*, which is simply a number that acts as a unique timestamp in the STM world. Transaction A has access to its own *effectively private* copy of any reference it needs, associated with the point. Clojure's persistent data structures (Section 5.1, *Persistent Data Structures*, on page 128) make it cheap to provide these effectively private copies.

During Transaction A, operations on a ref work against (and return) the transaction's private copy of the ref's data, called the *in-transaction-value*.

If at any point the STM detects that another transaction has already set/altered a ref that Transaction A wants to set/alter, Transaction A will be forced to retry. If you throw an exception out of the dosync block, then Transaction A will abort *without* a retry.

If and when Transaction A commits, its heretofore private writes will become visible to the world, associated with a single point in the transaction timeline.

Sometimes the approach implied by alter is too cautious. What if you *don't care* that another transaction altered a reference out from under you in the middle of your transaction? If in such a situation you would be willing to commit your changes anyway, you can beat alter's performance with commute.

commute

commute is a specialized variant of alter allowing for more concurrency:

```
(commute ref update-fn & args...)
```

Of course, there is a trade-off. Commutes are so named because they must be *commutative*. That is, updates must be able to occur in any order. This gives the STM system freedom to reorder commutes.

To use commute, simply replace alter with commute in your implementation of add-message:

```
(defn add-message-commute [msg]
  (dosync (commute messages conj msg)))
```

commute returns the new value of the ref. However, the last in-transaction-value you see from a commute will *not* always match the end-of-transaction value of a ref, because of reordering. If another transaction sneaks in and alters a ref that you are trying to commute, the STM will not restart your transaction. Instead, it will simply run your commute function again, out of order. Your transaction will *never even see* the ref value that your commute function finally ran against.

Since Clojure's STM can reorder commutes behind your back, you can use them only when you do not care about ordering. Literally speaking, this is not true for a chat application. The list of messages most certainly has an order, so if two message adds get reversed, the resulting list will not correctly show the order in which the messages arrived.

Practically speaking, chat message updates are *commutative enough*. STM-based reordering of messages will likely happen on time scales of microseconds or less. For users of a chat application, there are already reorderings on much larger time scales due to network and human latency. (Think about times that you have "spoken out of turn" in an online chat room because another speaker's message had not reached you yet.) Since these larger reorderings are unfixable, it is reasonable for a chat application to ignore the smaller reorderings that might bubble up from Clojure's STM.

Prefer alter

Many updates are not commutative. For example, consider a counter that returns an increasing sequence of numbers. You might use such a counter to build unique IDs in a system. The counter can be a simple reference to a number:

examples/concurrency.clj

```
(def counter (ref 0))
```

You should not use commute to update the counter. commute returns the in-transaction value of the counter at the time of the commute, but reorderings could cause the actual end-of-transaction value to be different. This could lead to more than one caller getting the same counter value. Instead, use alter:

```
(defn next-counter [] (dosync (alter counter inc)))
```

Try calling next-counter a few times to verify that the counter works as expected:

```
(next-counter)
```
⇒ 1

```
(next-counter)
```
⇒ 2

In general, you should prefer alter over commute. Its semantics are easy to understand and error-proof. commute, on the other hand, requires that you think carefully about transactional semantics. If you use alter when commute would suffice, the worst thing that might happen is performance degradation. But if you use commute when alter is required, you will introduce a subtle bug that is difficult to detect with automated tests.

Adding Validation to Refs

Database transactions maintain consistency through various integrity checks. You can do something similar with Clojure's transactional memory, by specifying a validation function when you create a ref:

```
(ref initial-state options*)
; options include:
;   :validator validate-fn
;   :meta metadata-map
```

The options to ref include an optional validation function that can throw an exception to prevent a transaction from completing. Note that options is *not* a map; it is simply a sequence of key/value pairs spliced into the function call.

Continuing the chat example, add a validation function to the messages reference that guarantees that all messages have non-nil values for :sender and :text:

examples/chat.clj

```
(def validate-message-list
  (partial every? #(and (:sender %) (:text %))))

(def messages (ref () :validator validate-message-list))
```

This validation acts like a key constraint on a table in a database transaction. If the constraint fails, the entire transaction rolls back. Try adding an ill-formed message such as a simple string:

```
(add-message "not a valid message")
```
⇒   java.lang.IllegalStateException: Invalid reference state

```
@messages
```
⇒   ()

Messages that match the constraint are no problem:

```
(add-message (struct message "stu" "legit message"))
```
⇒   ({:sender "stu", :text "legit message"})

Refs are great for coordinated access to shared state, but not all tasks require such coordination. For updating a single piece of isolated data, prefer an atom.

6.3 Use Atoms for Uncoordinated, Synchronous Updates

Atoms are a lighter-weight mechanism than refs. Where multiple ref updates can be coordinated in a transaction, atoms allow updates of a single value, uncoordinated with anything else.

You create atoms with atom, which has a signature very similar to ref:

```
(atom initial-state options?)
; options include:
;    :validator validate-fn
;    :meta metadata-map
```

Returning to our music player example, you could store the current-track in an atom instead of a ref:

```
(def current-track (atom "Venus, the Bringer of Peace"))
⇒    #'user/current-track
```

You can dereference an atom to get its value, just as you would a ref:

```
(deref current-track)
⇒    "Venus, the Bringer of Peace"
```

```
@current-track
⇒    "Venus, the Bringer of Peace"
```

Atoms do not participate in transactions and thus do not require a dosync. To set the value of an atom, simply call reset!

```
(reset! an-atom newval)
```

For example, you can set current-track to "Credo":

```
(reset! current-track "Credo")
⇒    "Credo"
```

What if you want to coordinate an update of both current-track and current-composer with an atom? The short answer is "You can't." That is the difference between refs and atoms. If you need coordinated access, use a ref.

The longer answer is "You can...if you are willing to change the way you model the problem." What if you store the track title and composer in a map and then store the whole map in a single atom?

```
(def current-track (atom {:title "Credo" :composer "Byrd"}))
⇒    #'user/current-track
```

Now you can update both values in a single reset!

```
(reset! current-track {:title "Spem in Alium" :composer "Tallis"})
⇒    {:title "Spem in Alium", :composer "Tallis"}
```

Maybe you like to listen to several tracks in a row by the same composer. If so, you want to change the track title but keep the same composer. swap! will do the trick:

```
(swap! an-atom f & args)
```

swap! updates an-atom by calling function f on the current value of an-atom, plus any additional args.

To change just the track title, use swap! with assoc to update only the :title:

```
(swap! current-track assoc :title "Sancte Deus")
```
⇒   {:title "Sancte Deus", :composer "Tallis"}

swap! returns the new value. Calls to swap! might be retried, if other threads are attempting to modify the same atom. So, the function you pass to swap! should have no side effects.

Both refs and atoms perform synchronous updates. When the update function returns, the value is already changed. If you do not need this level of control and can tolerate updates happening asynchronously at some later time, prefer an agent.

6.4 Use Agents for Asynchronous Updates

Some applications have tasks that can proceed independently with minimal coordination between tasks. Clojure *agents* support this style of task.

Agents have much in common with refs. Like refs, you create an agent by wrapping some piece of initial state:

```
(agent initial-state)
```

Create a counter agent that wraps an initial count of zero:

```
(def counter (agent 0))
```
⇒   #'user/counter

Once you have an agent, you can send the agent a function to update its state. send queues an update-fn to run later, on a thread in a thread pool:

```
(send agent update-fn & args)
```

Sending to an agent is very much like commuting a ref. Tell the counter to inc:

```
(send counter inc)
    #<clojure.lang.Agent@23451c74: 0>
```

Notice that the call to send does not return the new value of the agent, returning instead the agent itself. That is because send *does not know* the new value. After send queues the inc to run later, it returns immediately.

Although send does not know the new value of an agent, the REPL *might* know. Depending on whether the agent thread or the REPL thread runs first, you might see a 1 or a 0 after the colon in the previous output.

You can check the current value of an agent with deref/@, just as you would a ref. By the time you get around to checking the counter, the inc will almost certainly have completed on the thread pool, raising the value to one:

```
@counter
    1
```

If the race condition between the REPL and the agent thread bothers you, there is a solution. If you want to be sure that the agent has completed the actions *you sent* to it, you can call await or await-for:

```
(await & agents)
```

```
(await-for timeout-millis & agents)
```

These functions will cause the current thread to block until all actions sent from the current thread or agent have completed. await-for will return nil if the timeout expires and will return a non-nil value otherwise. await has no timeout, so be careful: await is willing to wait forever.

Validating Agents and Handling Errors

Agents have other points in common with refs. They also can take a validation function:

```
(agent initial-state options*)
; options include:
;    :validator validate-fn
;    :meta metadata-map
```

Re-create the counter with a validator that ensures it is a number:

```
(def counter (agent 0 :validator number?))
    #'user/counter
```

Try to set the agent to a value that is not a number by passing an update function that ignores the current value and simply returns a string:

```
(send counter (fn [_] "boo"))
```
⇒   `#<clojure.lang.Agent@4de8ce62: 0>`

Everything looks fine (so far) because send still returns immediately. After the agent tries to update itself on a pooled thread, it will enter an exceptional state. You will discover the error when you try to dereference the agent:

```
@counter
```
⇒   `java.lang.Exception: Agent has errors`

To discover the specific error (or errors), call agent-errors, which will return a sequence of errors thrown during agent actions:

```
(agent-errors counter)
    (#<IllegalStateException ...>)
```
⇒

Once an agent has errors, all subsequent attempts to query the agent will return an error. You make the agent usable again by calling clear-agent-errors:

```
(clear-agent-errors agent)
```

which returns the agent to its pre-error state. Clear the counter's errors, and verify that its state is the same as before the error occurred:

```
(clear-agent-errors counter)
```
⇒   `nil`

```
@counter
```
⇒   `0`

Now that you know the basics of agents, let's use them in conjunction with refs and transactions.

Including Agents in Transactions

Transactions should not have side effects, because Clojure may retry a transaction an arbitrary number of times. However, sometimes you *want* a side effect when a transaction succeeds. Agents provide a solution. If you send an action to an agent from within a transaction, that action will be sent exactly once, if and only if the transaction succeeds.

As an example of where this would be useful, consider an agent that writes to a file when a transaction succeeds. You could combine such an agent with the chat example from Section 6.2, *commute*, on page 163 to automatically back up chat messages. First, create a backup-agent that stores the filename to write to:

examples/concurrency.clj

```
(def backup-agent (agent "output/messages-backup.clj"))
```

Then, create a modified version of add-message. The new function add-message-with-backup should do two additional things:

- Grab the return value of commute, which is the current database of messages, in a let binding.

- While still inside a transaction, send an action to the backup agent that writes the message database to filename. For simplicity, have the action function return filename so that the agent will use the same filename for the next backup.

```
(use '[clojure.contrib.duck-streams :only (spit)])
(defn add-message-with-backup [msg]
  (dosync
    (let [snapshot (commute messages conj msg)]
      (send-off backup-agent (fn [filename]
                               (spit filename snapshot)
                               filename))
      snapshot)))
```

The new function has one other critical difference: it calls send-off instead of send to communicate with the agent. send-off is a variant of send for actions that expect to block, as a file write might do. send-off actions get their own expandable thread pool. Never send a blocking function, or you may unnecessarily prevent other agents from making progress.

Try adding some messages using add-message-with-backup:

```
(add-message-with-backup (struct message "john" "message one"))
```
⇒ `({:sender "john", :text "message one"})`

```
(add-message-with-backup (struct message "jane" "message two"))
```
⇒ `({:sender "jane", :text "message two"}`
   `{:sender "john", :text "message one"})`

You can check both the in-memory messages as well as the backup file messages-backup to verify that they contain the same structure.

You could enhance the backup strategy in this example in various ways. You could provide the option to back up less often than on every update or back up only information that has changed since the last backup.

Since Clojure's STM provides the ACI properties of ACID and writing to file provides the D (Durability), it is tempting to think that STM plus a

Update Mechanism	Ref Function	Atom Function	Agent Function
Function application	alter	swap!	send-off
Function (commutative)	commute	N/A	N/A
Function (nonblocking)	N/A	N/A	send
Simple setter	ref-set	reset!	N/A

Figure 6.1: UPDATING STATE IN REFS, ATOMS, AND AGENTS

backup agent equals a database. This is *not* the case. A Clojure transaction only promises to send(-off) an action to the agent; it does not actually *perform* the action under the ACI umbrella. So, for example, a transaction could complete, and then someone could unplug the power cord before the agent writes to the database. The moral is simple. If your problem calls for a real database, use a real database. Section 9.2, *Data Access*, on page 252 demonstrates using Clojure to read and write a database.

The Unified Update Model

As you have seen, refs, atoms, and agents all provide functions for updating their state by applying a function to their previous state. This unified model for handling shared state is one of the central concepts of Clojure. The unified model and various ancillary functions are summarized in Figure 6.1.

The unified update model is by far the most important way to update refs, atoms, and agents. The ancillary functions, on the other hand, are optimizations and options that stem from the semantics peculiar to each API:

- The opportunity for the commute optimization arises when coordinating updates. Since only refs provide coordinated updates, commute makes sense only for refs.

- Updates to refs and atoms take place on the thread they are called on, so they provide no scheduling options. Agents update later, on a thread pool, making blocking/nonblocking a relevant scheduling option.

Clojure's final concurrency API, vars, are a different beast entirely. They do not participate in the unified update model and are instead used to manage thread-local, private state.

6.5 Managing Per-Thread State with Vars

When you call def or defn, you create a *dynamic var*, often called just a var. In all the examples so far in the book, you pass an initial value to def, which becomes the *root binding* for the var. For example, the following code creates a root binding for foo of 10:

```
(def foo 10)
```
⇒   #'user/foo

The binding of foo is shared by all threads. You can check the value of foo on your own thread:

```
foo
```
⇒   10

You can also verify the value of foo from another thread. Create a new thread, passing it a function that prints foo. Don't forget to start the thread:

```
user=> (.start (Thread. (fn [] (println foo))))
```
⇒   nil
| 10

In the previous example, the call to start() returns nil, and then the value of foo is printed from a new thread.

Most vars are content to keep their root bindings forever. However, you can create a *thread-local* binding for a var with the binding macro:

```
(binding [bindings] & body)
```

Bindings have *dynamic scope*. In other words, a binding is visible anywhere a thread's execution takes it, until the thread exits the scope where the binding began. A binding is not visible to any other threads.

Structurally, a binding looks a lot like a let. Create a thread-local binding for foo and check its value:

```
(binding [foo 42] foo)
```
⇒   42

To see the difference between binding and let, create a simple function that prints the value of foo:

```
(defn print-foo [] (println foo))
```
⇒   #'user/print-foo

Now, try calling print-foo from both a let and a binding:

```
(let [foo "let foo"] (print-foo))
```
| 10

```
(binding [foo "bound foo"] (print-foo))
| bound foo
```

As you can see, the let has no effect outside its own form, so the first print-foo prints the root binding 10. The binding, on the other hand, stays in effect down any chain of calls that begins in the binding form, so the second print-foo prints bound foo.

Acting at a Distance

Vars intended for dynamic binding are sometimes called *special* variables. It is good style to name them with leading and trailing asterisks. For example, Clojure uses dynamic binding for thread-wide options such as the standard I/O streams *in*, *out*, and *err*. Dynamic bindings enable *action at a distance*. When you change a dynamic binding, you can change the behavior of distant functions without changing any function arguments.

One kind of action at a distance is temporarily augmenting the behavior of a function. In some languages this would be classified as aspect-oriented programming; in Clojure it is simply a side effect of dynamic binding.

As an example, imagine that you have a function that performs an expensive calculation. To simulate this, write a function named slow-double that sleeps for a tenth of a second and then doubles its input.

```
(defn slow-double [n]
  (Thread/sleep 100)
  (* n 2))
```

Next, write a function named calls-slow-double that calls slow-double for each item in [1 2 1 2 1 2]:

```
(defn calls-slow-double []
  (map slow-double [1 2 1 2 1 2]))
```

Time a call to calls-slow-double. With six internal calls to slow-double, it should take a little over six tenths of a second. Note that you will have to run through the result with dorun; otherwise, Clojure's map will outsmart you by immediately returning a lazy sequence.

```
(time (dorun (calls-slow-double)))
| "Elapsed time: 601.418 msecs"
⇒    nil
```

Reading the code, you can tell that calls-slow-double is slow because it does the same work over and over again. One times two is two, no matter how many times you ask.

Calculations such as slow-double are good candidates for *memoization*. When you memoize a function, it keeps a cache mapping past inputs to past outputs. If subsequent calls hit the cache, they will return almost immediately. Thus, you are trading space (the cache) for time (calculating the function again for the same inputs).

Clojure provides memoize, which takes a function and returns a memoization of that function:

```
(memoize function)
```

slow-double is a great candidate for memoization, but it isn't memoized yet, and clients like calls-slow-double already use the slow, unmemoized version. With dynamic binding, this is no problem. Simply create a binding to a memoized version of slow-double, and call calls-slow-double from within the binding.

```
(defn demo-memoize []
  (time
   (dorun
    (binding [slow-double (memoize slow-double)]
      (calls-slow-double)))))
```

With the memoized version of slow-double, calls-slow-double runs three times faster, completing in about two tenths of a second:

```
(demo-memoize)
"Elapsed time: 203.115 msecs"
```

This example demonstrates the power and the danger of action at a distance. By dynamically rebinding a function such as slow-double, you change the behavior of *other* functions such as calls-slow-double without their knowledge or consent. With lexical binding forms such as let, it is easy to see the entire range of your changes. Dynamic binding is not so simple. It can change the behavior of other forms in other files, far from the point in your source where the binding occurs.

Used occasionally, dynamic binding has great power. But it should not become your primary mechanism for extension or reuse. Functions that use dynamic bindings are not pure functions and can quickly lose the benefits of Clojure's functional style.

Working with Java Callback APIs

Several Java APIs depend on callback event handlers. GUI frameworks such as Swing use event handlers to respond to user input. XML parsers such as SAX depend on the user implementing a callback handler interface.

These callback handlers are written with mutable objects in mind. Also, they tend to be single-threaded. In Clojure, the best way to meet such APIs halfway is to use dynamic bindings. This will involve mutable references that feel almost like variables, but because they are used in a single-threaded setting, they will not present any concurrency problems.

Clojure provides the set! special form for setting a thread-local dynamic binding:

```
(set! var-symbol new-value)
```

set! should be used rarely. In fact, the only place in the entire Clojure core that uses set! is the Clojure implementation of a SAX ContentHandler.

A ContentHandler receives callbacks as a parser encounters various bits of an XML stream. In nontrivial scenarios, the ContentHandler needs to keep track of *where it is* in the XML stream: the current stack of open elements, current character data, and so on.

In Clojure-speak, you can think of a ContentHandler's current position as a mutable pointer to a specific spot in an immutable XML stream. It is unnecessary to use references in a ContentHandler, since everything will happen on a single thread. Instead, Clojure's ContentHandler uses dynamic variables and set!. Here is the relevant detail:

```
; redacted from Clojure's xml.clj to focus on dynamic variable usage
(startElement
 [uri local-name q-name #^Attributes atts]
 ; details omitted
 (set! *stack* (conj *stack* *current*))
 (set! *current* e)
 (set! *state* :element))
nil)
(endElement
 [uri local-name q-name]
 ; details omitted
 (set! *current* (push-content (peek *stack*) *current*))
 (set! *stack* (pop *stack*))
 (set! *state* :between)
nil)
```

Model	Usage	Functions
Refs and STM	Coordinated, synchronous updates	Pure
Atoms	Uncoordinated, synchronous updates	Pure
Agents	Uncoordinated, asynchronous updates	Any
Vars	Thread-local dynamic scopes	Any
Java locks	Coordinated, synchronous updates	Any

Figure 6.2: CONCURRENCY MODELS

A SAX parser calls startElement when it encounters an XML start tag. The callback handler updates three thread-local variables. The *stack* is a stack of all the elements the current element is nested inside. The *current* is the current element, and the *state* keeps track of what kind of content is inside. (This is important primarily when inside character data, which is not shown here.)

endElement reverses the work of startElement by popping the *stack* and placing the top of the *stack* in *current*.

It is worth noting that this style of coding is the industry norm: objects are mutable, and programs are single-threadedly oblivious to the possibility of concurrency. Clojure permits this style as an explicit special case, and you should use it for interop purposes only.

The ContentHandler's use of set! does not leak mutable data out into the rest of Clojure. Clojure uses the ContentHandler implementation to build an immutable Clojure structure, which then gets all the benefits of the Clojure concurrency model.

You have now seen four different models for dealing with concurrency. And since Clojure is built atop Java, you can also use Java's lock-based model. The models, and their use, are summarized in Figure 6.2.

Now let's put these models to work in designing a small but complete application.

6.6 A Clojure Snake

The Snake game features a player-controlled snake that moves around a game grid hunting for an apple. When your snake eats an apple, it grows longer by a segment, and a new apple appears. If your snake reaches a certain length, you win. But if your snake crosses over its own body, you lose.

Before you start building your own snake, take a minute to try the completed version. From the book's REPL, enter the following:

```
(use 'examples.snake)
```

```
(game)
    [#<Ref clojure.lang.Ref@65694ee6>
     #<Ref clojure.lang.Ref@261ae209>
     #<Timer javax.swing.Timer@7f0df737>]
```

Select the Snake window, and use the arrow keys to control your snake.

Our design for the snake is going to take advantage of Clojure's functional nature and its support for explicit mutable state by dividing the game into three layers:

- The *functional model* will use pure functions to model as much of the game as possible.

- The *mutable model* will handle the mutable state of the game. The mutable model will use one or more of the concurrency models discussed in this chapter. Mutable state is much harder to test, so we will keep this part small.

- The *GUI* will use Swing to draw the game and to accept input from the user.

These layers will make the Snake easy to build, test, and maintain.

As you work through this example, add your code to the file reader/snake.clj in the sample code. When you open the file, you will see that it already imports/uses the Swing classes and Clojure libraries you will need:

```
reader/snake.clj
```

```
(ns reader.snake
  (:import (java.awt Color Dimension)
           (javax.swing JPanel JFrame Timer JOptionPane)
           (java.awt.event ActionListener KeyListener))
  (:use clojure.contrib.import-static
        [clojure.contrib.seq-utils :only (includes?)]))
(import-static java.awt.event.KeyEvent VK_LEFT VK_RIGHT VK_UP VK_DOWN)
```

Now you are ready to build the functional model.

Other Snake Implementations

There's more than one way to skin a snake. You may enjoy comparing the snake presented here with these other snakes:

- David Van Horn's Snake,[*] written in Typed Scheme, has no mutable state.

- Jeremy Read wrote a Java Snake[†] designed to be "just about as small as you can make it in Java and still be readable."

- Abhishek Reddy wrote a tiny (35-line) Snake[‡] in Clojure. The design goal was to be abnormally terse.

- Dale Vaillancourt's Worm Game.[§]

- Mark Volkmann wrote a Clojure Snake[¶] designed for readability.

Each of the snake implementations has its own distinctive style. What would *your* style look like?

[*]. http://planet.plt-scheme.org/package-source/dvanhorn/snake.plt/1/0/main.ss
[†]. http://www.plt1.com/1069/smaller-snake/
[‡]. http://www.plt1.com/1070/even-smaller-snake/
[§]. http://www.ccs.neu.edu/home/cce/acl2/worm.html includes some verifications using the theorem prover ACL2.
[¶]. http://www.ociweb.com/mark/programming/ClojureSnake.html

The Functional Model

First, create a set of constants to describe time, space, and motion:

```
(def width 75)
(def height 50)
(def point-size 10)
(def turn-millis 75)
(def win-length 5)
(def dirs { VK_LEFT  [-1  0]
            VK_RIGHT [ 1  0]
            VK_UP    [ 0 -1]
            VK_DOWN  [ 0  1]})
```

width and height set the size of the game board, and point-size is used to convert a game point into screen pixels. turn-millis is the heartbeat of the game, controlling how many milliseconds pass before each update of the game board. win-length is how many segments your snake needs before you win the game. (Five is a boringly small number suitable for testing.) The dirs maps symbolic constants for the four directions to their vector equivalents. Since Swing already defines the VK_ constants for different directions, we will reuse them here rather than defining our own.

Next, create some basic math functions for the game:

```
(defn add-points [& pts]
  (vec (apply map + pts)))

(defn point-to-screen-rect [pt]
  (map #(* point-size %)
       [(pt 0) (pt 1) 1 1]))
```

The add-points function adds points together. You can use add-points to calculate the new position of a moving game object. For example, you can move an object at [10, 10] left by one:

```
(add-points [10 10] [-1 0])
```
⇒
```
    [9 10]
```

point-to-screen-rect simply converts a point in game space to a rectangle on the screen:

```
(point-to-screen-rect [5 10])
```
⇒
```
    (50 100 10 10)
```

Next, let's write a function to create a new apple:

```
(defn create-apple []
  {:location [(rand-int width) (rand-int height)]
   :color (Color. 210 50 90)
   :type :apple})
```

Apples occupy a single point, the :location, which is guaranteed to be on the game board. Snakes are a little bit more complicated:

```
(defn create-snake []
  {:body (list [1 1])
   :dir [1 0]
   :type :snake
   :color (Color. 15 160 70)})
```

Because a snake can occupy multiple points on the board, it has a :body, which is a list of points. Also, snakes are always in motion in some direction expressed by :dir.

Next, create a function to move a snake. This should be a pure function, returning a new snake. Also, it should take a grow option, allowing the snake to grow after eating an apple.

```
(defn move [{:keys [body dir] :as snake} & grow]
  (assoc snake :body (cons (add-points (first body) dir)
                           (if grow body (butlast body)))))
```

move uses a fairly complex binding expression. The {:keys [body dir]} part makes the snake's body and dir available as their own bindings, and the :as snake part binds snake to the entire snake. The function then proceeds as follows:

1. add-points creates a new point, which is the head of the original snake offset by the snake's direction of motion.

2. cons adds the new point to the front of the snake. If the snake is growing, the entire original snake is kept. Otherwise, it keeps all the original snake except the last segment (butlast).

3. assoc returns a new snake, which is a copy of the old snake but with an updated :body.

Test move by moving and growing a snake:

```
(move (create-snake))
```
⇒
```
    {:body ([2 1]), ; etc.
```

```
(move (create-snake) :grow)
```
⇒
```
    {:body ([2 1] [1 1]), ; etc.
```

Write a win? function to test whether a snake has won the game:

```
(defn win? [{body :body}]
  (>= (count body) win-length))
```

Test win? against different body sizes. Note that win? binds only the :body, so you don't need a "real" snake, just anything with a body:

```
(win? {:body [[1 1]]})
```
⇒
```
    false
```

```
(win? {:body [[1 1] [1 2] [1 3] [1 4] [1 5]]})
```
⇒
```
    true
```

A snake loses if its head ever comes back into contact with the rest of its body. Write a head-overlaps-body? function to test for this, and use it to define lose?:

```
(defn head-overlaps-body? [{[head & body] :body}]
  (includes? body head))
```

```
(def lose? head-overlaps-body?)
```

Test lose? against overlapping and nonoverlapping snake bodies:

```
(lose? {:body [[1 1] [1 2] [1 3]]})
```
⇒   false

```
(lose? {:body [[1 1] [1 2] [1 1]]})
```
⇒   true

A snake eats an apple if its head occupies the apple's location. Define an eats? function to test this:

```
(defn eats? [{[snake-head] :body} {apple :location}]
  (= snake-head apple))
```

Notice how clean the body of the eats? function is. All the work is done in the bindings: {[snake-head] :body} binds snake-head to the first element of the snake's :body, and {apple :location} binds apple to the apple's :location. Test eats? from the REPL:

```
(eats? {:body [[1 1] [1 2]]} {:location [2 2]})
```
⇒   false

```
(eats? {:body [[2 2] [1 2]]} {:location [2 2]})
```
⇒   true

Finally, you need some way to turn the snake, updating its :dir:

```
(defn turn [snake newdir]
  (assoc snake :dir newdir))
```

turn returns a new snake, with an updated direction:

```
(turn (create-snake) [0 -1])
```
⇒   {:body ([1 1]), :dir [0 -1], ; etc.

All of the code you have written so far is part of the functional model of the Snake game. It is easy to understand in part because it has no local variables and no mutable state. As you will see in the next section, the amount of *mutable* state in the game is quite small.[1]

Building a Mutable Model with STM

The mutable state of the Snake game can change in only three ways:

- A game can be reset to its initial state.
- Every turn, the snake updates its position. If it eats an apple, a new apple is placed.
- A snake can turn.

---

1. It is even possible to implement the Snake with *no* mutable state, but that is not the purpose of this demo.

We will implement each of these changes as functions that modify Clojure refs inside a transaction. That way, changes to the position of the snake and the apple will be synchronous and coordinated.

reset-game is trivial:

```
(defn reset-game [snake apple]
  (dosync (ref-set apple (create-apple))
          (ref-set snake (create-snake)))
  nil)
```

You can test reset-game by passing in some refs and then checking that they dereference to a snake and an apple:

```
(def test-snake (ref nil))
(def test-apple (ref nil))

(reset-game test-snake test-apple)
```
⇒   nil

```
@test-snake
```
⇒   {:body ([1 1]), :dir [1 0], ; etc.

```
@test-apple
```
⇒   {:location [52 8], ; etc.

update-direction is even simpler; it's just a trivial wrapper around the functional turn:

```
(defn update-direction [snake newdir]
  (when newdir (dosync (alter snake turn newdir))))
```

Try turning your test-snake to move in the "up" direction:

```
(update-direction test-snake [0 -1])
```
⇒   {:body ([1 1]), :dir [0 -1], ; etc.

The most complicated mutating function is update-positions. If the snake eats the apple, a new apple is created, and the snake grows. Otherwise, the snake simply moves:

```
(defn update-positions [snake apple]
  (dosync
    (if (eats? @snake @apple)
      (do (ref-set apple (create-apple))
          (alter snake move :grow))
      (alter snake move)))
  nil)
```

To test update-positions, reset the game:

```
(reset-game test-snake test-apple)
```
⇒   nil

Then, move the apple into harm's way, under the snake:

```
(dosync (alter test-apple assoc :location [1 1]))
```
⇒   `{:location [1 1], ; etc.`

Now, after you update-positions, you should have a bigger, two-segment snake:

```
(update-positions test-snake test-apple)
```
⇒   `nil`
```
(:body @test-snake)
```
⇒   `([2 1] [1 1])`

And that is all the mutable state of the Snake world: three functions, about a dozen lines of code.

The Snake GUI

The Snake GUI consists of functions that paint screen objects, respond to user input, and set up the various Swing components. Since snakes and apples are drawn from simple points, the painting functions are simple. The fill-point function fills in a single point:

```
(defn fill-point [g pt color]
  (let [[x y width height] (point-to-screen-rect pt)]
    (.setColor g color)
    (.fillRect g x y width height)))
```

The paint multimethod knows how to paint snakes and apples:

```
Line 1  (defmulti paint (fn [g object & _] (:type object)))
     2
     3  (defmethod paint :apple [g {:keys [location color]}]
     4    (fill-point g location color))
     5
     6  (defmethod paint :snake [g {:keys [body color]}]
     7    (doseq [point body]
     8      (fill-point g point color)))
```

paint takes two required arguments: g is a java.awt.Graphics instance, and object is the object to be painted. The defmulti includes an optional rest argument so that future implementations of paint have the option of taking more arguments. (See Section 8.2, *Defining Multimethods*, on page 228 for an in-depth description of defmulti.)

On line 3, the :apple method of paint binds the location and color, of the apple and uses them to paint a single point on the screen. On line 6, the :snake method binds the snake's body and color and then uses doseq to paint each point in the body.

The meat of the UI is the game-panel function, which creates a Swing JPanel with handlers for painting the game, updating on each timer tick, and responding to user input:

```
Line 1    (defn game-panel [frame snake apple]
  -         (proxy [JPanel ActionListener KeyListener] []
  -           (paintComponent [g]
  -             (proxy-super paintComponent g)
  5             (paint g @snake)
  -             (paint g @apple))
  -           (actionPerformed [e]
  -             (update-positions snake apple)
  -             (when (lose? @snake)
  10               (reset-game snake apple)
  -               (JOptionPane/showMessageDialog frame "You lose!"))
  -             (when (win? @snake)
  -               (reset-game snake apple)
  -               (JOptionPane/showMessageDialog frame "You win!"))
  15             (.repaint this))
  -           (keyPressed [e]
  -             (update-direction snake (dirs (.getKeyCode e))))
  -           (getPreferredSize []
  -             (Dimension. (* (inc width) point-size)
  20                         (* (inc height) point-size)))
  -           (keyReleased [e])
  -           (keyTyped [e])))
```

game-panel is long but simple. It uses proxy to create a panel with a set of Swing callback methods.

- Swing calls paintComponent (line 3) to draw the panel. paintComponent calls proxy-super to invoke the normal JPanel behavior, and then it paints the snake and the apple.

- Swing will call actionPerformed (line 7) on every timer tick. action-Performed updates the positions of the snake and the apple. If the game is over, it displays a dialog and resets the game. Finally, it triggers a repaint with (.repaint this).

- Swing calls keyPressed (line 16) in response to keyboard input. key-Pressed calls update-direction to change the snake's direction. (If the keyboard input was not an arrow key, the dirs function returns nil and update-direction does nothing.)

- The game panel ignores keyReleased and keyTyped.

The game function creates a new game:

```
Line 1    (defn game []
   -        (let [snake (ref (create-snake))
   -              apple (ref (create-apple))
   -              frame (JFrame. "Snake")
   5              panel (game-panel frame snake apple)
   -              timer (Timer. turn-millis panel)]
   -          (doto panel
   -            (.setFocusable true)
   -            (.addKeyListener panel))
   10          (doto frame
   -            (.add panel)
   -            (.pack)
   -            (.setVisible true))
   -          (.start timer)
   15          [snake, apple, timer]))
```

On line 2, game creates all the necessary game objects: the mutable model objects snake and apple, and the UI components frame, panel, and timer. Lines 7 and 10 perform boilerplate initialization of the panel and frame. Line 14 starts the game by kicking off the timer.

Line 15 returns a vector with the snake, apple, and time. This is for convenience when testing at the REPL: you can use these objects to move the snake and apple or to start and stop the game.

Go ahead and play the game again; you have earned it. To start the game, use the snake library at the REPL, and run game. If you have entered the code yourself, you can use the library name you picked (examples.reader in the instructions); otherwise, you can use the completed sample at examples.snake:

```
(use 'examples.snake)

(game)
⇒   [#<Ref clojure.lang.Ref@6ea27cbe>
     #<Ref clojure.lang.Ref@6dabd6b0>
     #<Timer javax.swing.Timer@32f60451>]
```

The game window may appear behind your REPL window. If this happens, use your local operating-system fu to locate the game window.

There are many possible improvements to the Snake game. If the snake reaches the edge of the screen, perhaps it should turn to avoid disappearing from view. Or (tough love) maybe you just lose the game! Make the Snake your own by improving it to suit your personal style.

Snakes Without Refs

We chose to implement the snake game's mutable model using refs so that we could coordinate the updates to the snake and the apple. Other approaches are also valid.

For example, you could combine the snake and apple state into a single game object. With only one object, coordination is no longer required, and you can use an atom instead.

The file examples/atom-snake.clj demonstrates this approach. Functions like update-positions become part of the functional model and return a new game object with updated state:

examples/atom_snake.clj
```
(defn update-positions [{snake :snake, apple :apple, :as game}]
  (if (eats? snake apple)
    (merge game {:apple (create-apple) :snake (move snake :grow)})
    (merge game {:snake (move snake)}))))
```

Notice how destructuring makes it easy to get at the internals of the game: both snake and apple are bound by the argument list.

The actual mutable updates are now all atom swap!s. I found these to be simple enough to leave them in the UI function game-panel, as this excerpt shows:

```
(actionPerformed [e]
  (swap! game update-positions)
  (when (lose? (@game :snake))
    (swap! game reset-game)
    (JOptionPane/showMessageDialog frame "You lose!")))
```

There are other possibilities as well. Chris Houser's fork of the book's sample code[2] demonstrates using an agent that Thread/sleeps instead of a Swing timer, as well as using a new agent per game turn to update the game's state.

Lancet's runonce system does not lend itself to a wide variety of approaches, like the snake game does. We will need to think carefully about a build system's concurrency semantics in order to choose the right concurrency API.

---

2. http://github.com/Chouser/programming-clojure

6.7 Making Lancet Targets Run Only Once

So far, you have worked on making Lancet able to invoke existing Ant tasks. Now it is time to think about how to implement a Lancet *target*, that is, a function that runs only once per build. Because we will build targets on top of functions, *any Clojure function can become a target.*

Targets are what makes Lancet dependency-based. Calling a target is the same as saying "I depend on this target." Each target should execute only once, no matter how many times it is called. In other words:

1. The first caller of any target should execute the target.

2. All subsequent callers of a target should wait for the first caller to finish and then move on without calling the target again.

In this chapter, you have seen Clojure's concurrency library: refs, atoms, agents, and vars. Another possibility is to dip down into Java and use the locking or atomic capabilities in Java itself. Let's now consider each of these in turn to find the best approach for implementing targets.

- Refs provide coordinated, synchronous updates. At first glance, this looks like a good fit for targets. But Clojure transactions must be side effect free. Build tasks certainly have side effects, and retrying might be expensive or even incorrect, so rule out refs.

- Atoms cannot do the job alone. They provide no coordination and hence no way to wait for the first caller of a task to finish. We will use an atom to remember the return value of each target after it is called.

- Agents *almost* work. Every target could have an agent, and you could send-off the work of the target. Subsequent callers could await the completion of any targets they need. However, you cannot await one agent while in another agent. This prevents possible deadlocks and enforces the idea that agents are *not* a coordination mechanism. Rule out agents.

- Vars would unnecessarily limit Lancet to running on a single thread. Rule out vars.

Another possibility is good old-fashioned locking. It is perfectly fine to use locks in Clojure, if that is what your design calls for. Lancet needs to make coordinated, synchronous updates to impure functions, and this is a job for locks.

At the REPL, create a function named create-runonce. This function will take an ordinary function and return a new function that will run only once.

lancet/step_3_repl.clj

```
Line 1   (defn create-runonce [function]
     2     (let [sentinel (Object.)
     3           result (atom sentinel)]
     4       (fn [& args]
     5         (locking sentinel
     6           (if (= @result sentinel)
     7             (reset! result (function))
     8             @result)))))
```

create-runonce works as follows:

- Line 2 creates a sentinel object. Whenever you see the sentinel value, you know that the target function has not yet run. The sentinel is a simple Java object so that it will never compare as equal to anything else.

- The result atom (line 3) remembers the return value from calling a target. It is initially set to sentinel, which means that the target has not run yet.

- Line 5 locks the sentinel. This guarantees that only one thread at a time can execute the code that follows.

- If the result is sentinel, then this is the first caller. Line 7 calls the function and reset!s the result.

- If the result is not sentinel, then this is not the first caller, so there is nothing to do but return the value of result.

Create a function named println-once that runs println only once, using create-runonce:

```
(def println-once
  (create-runonce #(println "there can be only one!")))
⇒     #'user/println-once
```

Now for the moment of truth. Call println-once twice.

```
> (println-once "there can be only one!")
| there can be only one!
⇒     nil

user=> (println-once "there can be only one!")
⇒     nil
```

Now that you have the core code working, let's make it more usable. It would be nice to have a simple predicate to see whether a target has run. For testing, it would also be useful to be able to reset a target so that it will run again. Create a runonce function that returns three values:

- A has-run? predicate
- A reset-fn
- The runonce function itself

lancet/step_3_complete.clj

```
Line 1  (defn runonce
   -      "Create a function that will only run once. All other invocations
   -      return the first calculated value. The function can have side effects.
   -      Returns a [has-run-predicate, reset-fn, once-fn]"
   5      [function]
   -      (let [sentinel (Object.)
   -            result (atom sentinel)
   -            reset-fn (fn [] (reset! result sentinel) nil)
   -            has-run? #(not= @result sentinel)]
  10        [has-run?
   -         reset-fn
   -         (fn [& args]
   -           (locking sentinel
   -             (if (= @result sentinel)
  15               (reset! result (function))
   -               @result)))]))
```

This is the same as the previous create-runonce, with two additions. reset-fn (line 8) simply sets the result back to sentinel, as if the target had never run. The has-run? predicate returns true if the result is not sentinel.

Notice that runonce encapsulates its implementation details. The sentinel and result objects are created in a local let and can never be accessed directly outside the function. Instead, you access them only through their "API," the three functions returned by runonce. This is similar to using a private field in an OO language but is more flexible and more granular.

runonce creates a complete, albeit minimal, dependency system that can work with *any Clojure function*. The current feature set includes the following:

- Run-once semantics for any function
- A predicate to check a runonce function's status
- A reset function for testing runonces

All that, and the entire codebase is less than two dozen lines.

Lancet Step 3: runonce

lancet/step_3.clj

```
(defn runonce
 "Create a function that will only run once. All other invocations
 return the first calculated value. The function can have side effects.
 Returns a [has-run-predicate, reset-fn, once-fn]"
 [function]
 (let [sentinel (Object.)
       result (atom sentinel)
       reset-fn (fn [] (reset! result sentinel))
       has-run? #(not= @result sentinel)]
   [has-run?
    reset-fn
    (fn [& args]
      (locking sentinel
        (if (= @result sentinel)
          (reset! result (function))
          @result)))]))
```

6.8 Wrapping Up

Clojure's concurrency model is the most innovative part of the language. The combination of software transactional memory, agents, atoms, and dynamic binding that you have seen in this chapter gives Clojure powerful abstractions for all sorts of concurrent systems. It also makes Clojure one of the few languages suited to the coming generation of multicore computer hardware.

But there's still more. Clojure's macro implementation is easy to learn and use correctly for common tasks and yet powerful enough for the harder macro-related tasks. In the next chapter, you will see how Clojure is bringing macros to mainstream programming.

Chapter 7

Macros

Macros give Clojure great power. With most programming techniques, you build features *within* the language. When you write macros, it is more accurate to say that you are "adding features to" the language. This is a powerful and dangerous ability, so you should follow the rules in Section 7.1, *When to Use Macros*, at least until you have enough experience to decide for yourself when to bend the rules. Section 7.2, *Writing a Control Flow Macro*, on the next page jump-starts that experience, walking you through adding a new feature to Clojure.

While powerful, macros are not always simple. Clojure works to make macros as simple as is feasible by including conveniences to solve many common problems that occur when writing macros. Section 7.3, *Making Macros Simpler*, on page 198 explains these problems and shows how Clojure mitigates them.

Macros are so different from other programming idioms that you may struggle knowing when to use them. There is no better guide than the shared experience of the community, so Section 7.4, *Taxonomy of Macros*, on page 204 introduces a taxonomy of Clojure macros, based on the macros in Clojure and clojure-contrib.

Finally, the chapter concludes with Lancet. Using macros, you will turn Lancet from a clunky API into an elegant DSL.

7.1 When to Use Macros

Macro Club has two rules, plus one exception.

The first rule of Macro Club is Don't Write Macros. Macros are complex, and they require you to think carefully about the interplay of macro expansion time and compile time. If you can write it as a function, think twice before using a macro.

The second rule of Macro Club is Write Macros If That Is The Only Way to Encapsulate a Pattern. All programming languages provide some way to encapsulate patterns, but without macros these mechanisms are incomplete. In most languages, you sense that incompleteness whenever you say "My life would be easier if only my language had feature X." In Clojure, you just implement feature X using a macro.

The exception to the rule is that *you can write any macro that makes life easier for your callers when compared with an equivalent function.* But to understand this exception, you need some practice writing macros and comparing them to functions. So, let's get started with an example.

7.2 Writing a Control Flow Macro

Clojure provides the if special form as part of the language:

```
(if (= 1 1) (println "yep, math still works today"))
| yep, math still works today
```

Some languages have an unless, which is (almost) the opposite of if. unless performs a test and then executes its body only if the test is logically false.

Clojure doesn't have unless, but it does have an equivalent macro called when-not. For the sake of having a simple example to start with, let's pretend that when-not doesn't exist and create an implementation of unless. To follow the rules of Macro Club, begin by trying to write unless as a function:

examples/macros.clj

```
; This is doomed to fail...
(defn unless [expr form]
  (if expr nil form))
```

Check that unless correctly evaluates its form when its test expr is false:

```
(unless false (println "this should print"))
| this should print
```

Things appear fine so far. But let's be diligent and test the true case too:

```
(unless true (println "this should not print"))
| this should not print
```

Clearly something has gone wrong. The problem is that Clojure evaluates all the arguments before passing them to a function, so the println is called before unless *ever sees it*. In fact, both calls to unless earlier call println too soon, before entering the unless function. To see this, add a println inside unless:

```
(defn unless [expr form]
  (println "About to test...")
  (if expr nil form))
```

Now you can clearly see that function arguments are always evaluated before passing them to unless:

```
(unless false (println "this should print"))
| this should print
| About to test...

(unless true (println "this should not print"))
| this should not print
| About to test...
```

Macros solve this problem, because they do not evaluate their arguments immediately. Instead, you get to choose when (and if!) the arguments to a macro are evaluated.

When Clojure encounters a macro, it processes it in two steps. First, it expands (executes) the macro and substitutes the result back into the program. This is called *macro expansion time*. Then it continues with the normal *compile time*.

To write unless, you need to write Clojure code to perform the following translation at macro expansion time:

```
(unless expr form) -> (if expr nil form)
```

Then, you need to tell Clojure that your code is a macro by using defmacro, which looks almost like defn:

```
(defmacro name doc-string? attr-map? [params*] body)
```

Because Clojure code is just Clojure data, you already have all the tools you need to write unless. Write the unless macro using list to build the if expression:

```
(defmacro unless [expr form]
  (list 'if expr nil form))
```

The body of unless executes at macro expansion time, producing an if form for compilation. If you enter this expression at the REPL:

```
(unless false (println "this should print"))
```

then Clojure will (invisibly to you) expand the unless form into:

```
(if false nil (println "this should print"))
```

Then, Clojure compiles and executes the expanded if form. Verify that unless works correctly for both true and false:

```
(unless false (println "this should print"))
| this should print
```
⇒   nil

```
(unless true (println "this should not print"))
```
⇒   nil

Congratulations, you have written your first macro. unless may seem pretty simple, but consider this: what you have just done is *impossible* in most languages. In languages without macros, special forms get in the way.

Special Forms, Design Patterns, and Macros

Clojure has no special syntax for code. Code is composed of data structures. This is true for normal functions but also for special forms and macros.

Consider a language with more syntactic variety, such as Java.[1] In Java, the most flexible mechanism for writing code is the instance method. Imagine that you are writing a Java program. If you discover a recurring pattern in some instance methods, you have the entire Java language at your disposal to encapsulate that recurring pattern.

Good so far. But Java also has lots of "special forms" (although they are not normally called by that name). Unlike Clojure special forms, which are just Clojure data, each Java special form has its own syntax. For example, if is a special form in Java. If you discover a recurring pattern of usage involving **if**, there is *no way to encapsulate* that pattern. You cannot create an **unless**, so you are stuck simulating **unless** with an idiomatic usage of **if**:

```
if (!something) ...
```

This may seem like a relatively minor problem. Java programmers can certainly learn to mentally make the translation from if (!foo) to unless

---

1.   I am not trying to beat up on Java in particular; it is just easier to talk about a specific language, and Java is well known.

(foo). But the problem is not just with **if**: *every distinct syntactic form* in the language inhibits your ability to encapsulate recurring patterns involving that form.

As another example, Java **new** is a special form. Polymorphism is not available for **new**, so you must simulate polymorphism, for example with idiomatic usage of a class method:

```
Widget w = WidgetFactory.makeWidget(...)
```

This idiom is a little bulkier. It introduces a whole new class, WidgetFactory. This class is meaningless in the problem domain and exists only to work around the constructor special form. Unlike the unless idiom, the "polymorphic instantiation" idiom is complicated enough that there is more than one way to implement a solution. Thus, the idiom should more properly be called a *design pattern*.

The Wikipedia defines a design pattern[2] to be a "general reusable solution to a commonly occurring problem in software design." It goes on to state that a "design pattern is not a finished design that can be transformed *directly* (emphasis added) into code."

That is where macros fit in. Macros provide a layer of *indirection* so that you can *automate the common parts of any recurring pattern*. Macros and code-as-data work together, enabling you to reprogram your language on the fly to encapsulate patterns.

Of course, this argument does not go entirely in one direction. Many people would argue that having a bunch of special syntactic forms makes a programming language easier to learn or read. I do not agree, but even if I did, I would be willing to trade syntactic variety for a powerful macro system. Once you get used to code as data, the ability to automate design patterns is a huge payoff.

Expanding Macros

When you created the unless macro, you quoted the symbol if:

```
(defmacro unless [expr form]
  (list 'if expr nil form))
```

---

2. http://en.wikipedia.org/wiki/Design_pattern_(computer_science)

But you did not quote any other symbols. To understand why, you need to think carefully about what happens at macro expansion time:

- By quoting 'if, you prevent Clojure from directly evaluating if at macro expansion time. Instead, evaluation strips off the quote, leaving if to be compiled.

- You do not want to quote expr and form, because they are macro arguments. Clojure will substitute them without evaluation at macro expansion time.

- You do not need to quote nil, since nil evaluates to itself.

Thinking about what needs to be quoted can get complicated quickly. Fortunately, you do not have to do this work in your head. Clojure includes diagnostic functions so that you can test macro expansions at the REPL.

The function macroexpand-1 will show you what happens at macro expansion time:

```
(macroexpand-1 form)
```

Use macroexpand-1 to prove that unless expands to a sensible if expression:

```
(macroexpand-1 '(unless false (println "this should print")))
```
⇒   (if false nil (println "this should print"))

Macros are complicated beasts, and I cannot overstate the importance of testing them with macroexpand-1. Let's go back and try some incorrect versions of unless. Here is one that incorrectly quotes the expr:

```
(defmacro bad-unless [expr form]
  (list 'if 'expr nil form))
```

When you expand bad-unless, you will see that it generates the symbol expr, instead of the actual test expression:

```
(macroexpand-1 '(bad-unless false (println "this should print")))
```
⇒   (if expr nil (println "this should print"))

If you try to actually use the bad-unless macro, Clojure will complain that it cannot resolve the symbol expr:

```
(bad-unless false (println "this should print"))
```
⇒   java.lang.Exception: Unable to resolve symbol: expr in this context

Sometimes macros expand into other macros. When this happens, Clojure will continue to expand all macros, until only normal code remains.

For example, the .. macro expands recursively, producing a dot operator call, wrapped in another .. to handle any arguments that remain.
You can see this with the following macro expansion:

```
(macroexpand-1 '(.. arm getHand getFinger))
⇒    (clojure.core/.. (. arm getHand) getFinger)
```

If you want to see .. expanded all the way, use macroexpand:

```
(macroexpand form)
```

If you macroexpand a call to .., it will recursively expand until only dot
operators remain:

```
(macroexpand '(.. arm getHand getFinger))
⇒    (. (. arm getHand) getFinger)
```

(It is not a problem that arm, getHand, and getFinger do not exist. You
are only expanding them, not attempting to compile and execute them.)

Another recursive macro is and. If you call and with more than two
arguments, it will expand to include another call to and, with one less
argument:

```
(macroexpand '(and 1 2 3))
⇒   (let* [and__2863 1]
       (if and__2863 (clojure.core/and 2 3) and__2863))
```

This time, macroexpand does *not* expand all the way. macroexpand
works only against the top level of the form you give it. Since the expansion of and creates a new and nested inside the form, macroexpand does
not expand it.

when and when-not

Your unless macro could be improved slightly to execute multiple forms,
avoiding this error:

```
(unless false (println "this") (println "and also this"))
⇒    java.lang.IllegalArgumentException: \
Wrong number of args passed to: macros$unless
```

Think about how you would write the improved unless. You would need
to capture a variable argument list and stick a do in front of it so that
every form executes. Clojure provides exactly this behavior in its when
and when-not macros:

```
(when test & body)
```

```
(when-not test & body)
```

when-not is the improved unless you are looking for:

```
(when-not false (println "this") (println "and also this"))
| this
| and also this
⇒   nil
```

Given your practice writing unless, you should now have no trouble reading the source for when-not:

```
; from Clojure core
(defmacro when-not [test & body]
  (list 'if test nil (cons 'do body)))
```

And, of course, you can use macroexpand-1 to see how when-not works:

```
(macroexpand-1 '(when-not false (print "1") (print "2")))
⇒   (if false nil (do (print "1") (print "2")))
```

when is the opposite of when-not and executes its forms only when its test is true. Note that when differs from if in two ways:

- if allows an else clause, and when does not. This reflects English usage, because nobody says "when … else."

- Since when does not have to use its second argument as an else clause, it is free to take a variable argument list and execute all the arguments inside a do.

You don't really need an unless macro. Just use Clojure's when-not. Always check to see whether somebody else has written the macro you need.

7.3 Making Macros Simpler

The unless macro is a great simple example, but most macros are more complex. In this section, we will build a set of increasingly complex macros, introducing Clojure features as we go. For your reference, the features introduced in this section are summarized in Figure 7.1, on page 200.

First, let's build a replica of Clojure's .. macro. We'll call it chain, since it chains a series of method calls. Here are some sample expansions of chain:

Macro Call	Expansion
(chain arm getHand)	(. arm getHand)
(chain arm getHand getFinger)	(. (. arm getHand) getFinger)

Begin by implementing the simple case where the chain calls only one method. The macro needs only to make a simple list:

examples/macros/chain_1.clj

```
; chain reimplements Clojure's .. macro
(defmacro chain [x form]
  (list '. x form))
```

chain needs to support any number of arguments, so the rest of the implementation should define a recursion. The list manipulation becomes more complex, since you need to build two lists and concat them together:

examples/macros/chain_2.clj

```
(defmacro chain
  ([x form] (list '. x form))
  ([x form & more] (concat (list 'chain (list '. x form)) more)))
```

Test chain using macroexpand to make sure it generates the correct expansions:

```
(macroexpand '(chain arm getHand))
```
⇒
```
    (. arm getHand)
```

```
(macroexpand '(chain arm getHand getFinger))
```
⇒
```
    (. (. arm getHand) getFinger)
```

The chain macro works fine as written, but it is difficult to read the expression that handles more than one argument:

```
(concat (list 'chain (list '. x form)) more)))
```

The definition of chain oscillates between macro code and the body to be generated. The intermingling of the two makes the entire thing hard to read. And this is just a baby of a form, only one line in length. As macro forms grow more complex, assembly functions such as list and concat quickly obscure the meaning of the macro.

One solution to this kind of problem is a templating language. If macros were created from templates, you could take a "fill in the blanks" approach to creating them. The definition of chain might look like this:

```
; hypothetical templating language
(defmacro chain
  ([x form] (. ${x} ${form}))
  ([x form & more] (chain (. ${x} ${form}) ${more})))
```

In this hypothetical templating language, the ${} lets you substitute arguments into the macro expansion.

Form	Description
foo#	Auto-gensym: Inside a syntax quoted section, create a unique name prefixed with foo.
(gensym prefix?)	Create a unique name, with optional prefix.
(macroexpand form)	Expand form with macroexpand-1 repeatedly until the returned form is no longer a macro.
(macroexpand-1 form)	Show how Clojure will expand form.
(list-frag? ~@form list-frag?)	Splicing unquote: Use inside a syntax-quote to splice an unquoted list into a template.
`form	Syntax quote: Quote form, but allow internal unquoting so that form acts a template. Symbols inside form are resolved to help prevent inadvertent symbol capture.
~form	Unquote: Use inside a syntax-quote to substitute an unquoted value.

Figure 7.1: CLOJURE SUPPORT FOR MACRO WRITERS

Notice how much easier the definition is to read and how it clearly shows what the expansion will look like.

Syntax Quote, Unquote, and Splicing Unquote

Clojure macros support templating without introducing a separate language. The *syntax quote* character, which is a backquote (`), works almost like normal quoting. But inside a syntax quoted list, the *unquote character* (~, a tilde) turns quoting off again. The overall effect is templates that look like this:

examples/macros/chain_3.clj
```
(defmacro chain [x form]
  `(. ~x ~form))
```

Test that this new version of chain can correctly generate a single method call:

```
(macroexpand '(chain arm getHand))
⇒    (. arm getHand)
```

Unfortunately, the syntax quote/unquote approach will not quite work
for the multiple-argument variant of chain:

examples/macros/chain_4.clj

```
; Does not quite work
(defmacro chain
  ([x form] `(. ~x ~form))
  ([x form & more] `(chain (. ~x ~form) ~more)))
```

When you expand this chain, the parentheses aren't quite right:

```
(macroexpand '(chain arm getHand getFinger))
```
⇒   `(. (. arm getHand) (getFinger))`

The last argument to chain is a list of more arguments. When you drop
more into the macro "template," it has parentheses because it is a list.
But you don't want these parentheses; you want more to be *spliced* into
the list. This comes up often enough that there is a reader macro for it:
splicing unquote (~@). Rewrite chain using splicing unquote to splice in
more:

examples/macros/chain_5.clj

```
(defmacro chain
  ([x form] `(. ~x ~form))
  ([x form & more] `(chain (. ~x ~form) ~@more)))
```

Now, the expansion should be spot on:

```
(macroexpand '(chain arm getHand getFinger))
```
⇒   `(. (. arm getHand) getFinger)`

Many macros follow the pattern of chain, aka Clojure ..:

1. Begin the macro body with a syntax quote (`) to treat the entire
   thing as a template.

2. Insert individual arguments with an unquote (~).

3. Splice in more arguments with splicing unquote (~@).

The macros we have built so far have been simple enough to avoid
creating any bindings with let or binding. Let's create such a macro next.

Creating Names in a Macro

Clojure has a time macro that times an expression, writing the elapsed
time to the console:

```
(time (str "a" "b"))
| "Elapsed time: 0.06 msecs"
```
⇒   `"ab"`

Let's build a variant of time called bench, designed to collect data across many runs. Instead of writing to the console, bench will return a map that includes both the return value of the original expression and the elapsed time.

The best way to begin writing a macro is to write its desired expansion by hand. bench should expand like this:

```
; (bench (str "a" "b"))
;   should expand to
(let [start (System/nanoTime)
      result (str "a" "b")]
  {:result result :elapsed (- (System/nanoTime) start)})
```

⇒   {:elapsed 61000, :result "ab"}

The let binds start to the start time and then executes the expression to be benched, binding it to result. Finally, the form returns a map including the result and the elapsed time since start.

With the expansion in hand, you can now work backwards and write the macro to generate the expansion. Using the technique from the previous section, try writing bench using syntax quoting and unquoting:

examples/macros/bench_1.clj

```
; This won't work
(defmacro bench [expr]
  `(let [start (System/nanoTime)
         result ~expr]
     {:result result :elapsed (- (System/nanoTime) start)}))
```

If you try to call this version of bench, Clojure will complain:

```
(bench (str "a" "b"))
```
⇒   java.lang.Exception: Can't let qualified name: examples.macros/start

Clojure is accusing you of trying to let a qualified name, which is illegal. Calling macroexpand-1 confirms the problem:

```
(macroexpand-1 '(bench (str "a" "b")))
```
⇒   (clojure.core/let [examples.macros/start (System/nanoTime)
                      examples.macros/result (str "a" "b")]
        {:elapsed (clojure.core/- (System/nanoTime) examples.macros/start)
         :result examples.macros/result})

When a syntax-quoted form encounters a symbol, it resolves the symbol to a fully qualified name. At the moment, this seems like an irritant, because you *want* to create local names, specifically start and result. But Clojure's approach protects you from a nasty macro bug called *symbol capture*.

What would happen if macro expansion *did* allow the unqualified symbols start and result, then bench was later used in a scope where those names were already bound to something else? The macro would *capture* the names and bind them to different values, with bizarre results. If bench captured its symbols, it would appear to work fine most of the time. Adding one and two would give you three:

```
(let [a 1 b 2]
  (bench (+ a b)))
⇒    {:result 3, :elapsed 39000}
```

...until the unlucky day that you picked a local name like start, which collided with a name inside bench:

```
(let [start 1 end 2]
  (bench (+ start end)))
⇒    {:result 1228277342451783002, :elapsed 39000}
```

bench captures the symbol start and binds it to (System/nanoTime). All of a sudden, one plus two seems to equal 1228277342451783002.

Clojure's insistence on resolving names in macros helps protect you from symbol capture, but you still don't have a working bench. You need some way to introduce local names, ideally *unique* ones that cannot collide with any names used by the caller.

Clojure provides a reader form for creating unique local names. Inside a syntax-quoted form, you can append an octothorpe (#) to an unqualified name, and Clojure will create an autogenerated symbol, or *autogensym*: a symbol based on the name plus an underscore and a unique ID. Try it at the REPL:

```
'foo#
foo__1004
```

With automatically generated symbols at your disposal, it is easy to implement bench correctly:

```
(defmacro bench [expr]
  `(let [start# (System/nanoTime)
         result# ~expr]
     {:result result# :elapsed (- (System/nanoTime) start#)}))
```

And test it at the REPL:

```
(bench (str "a" "b"))
⇒    {:elapsed 63000, :result "ab"}
```

Clojure makes it easy to generate unique names, but if you are determined, you can still force symbol capture. The sample code for the book includes an evil-bench that shows a combination of syntax quoting, quoting, and unquoting that leads to symbol capture. Don't use symbol capture unless you have a thorough understanding of macros.

7.4 Taxonomy of Macros

Now that you have written several macros, we can restate the Rules of Macro Club with more supporting detail.

The first rule of Macro Club is Don't Write Macros. Macros are complex. If the preceding sections did not convince you of this, the Lancet example at the end of the chapter is more complex still, and a few of the macros in Clojure itself are extremely complex. (If none of the macros in Clojure seems complex to you, my company is hiring.[3])

The second rule of Macro Club is Write Macros If That Is the Only Way to Encapsulate a Pattern. As you have seen, the patterns that resist encapsulation tend to arise around special forms, which are irregularities in a language. So, rule 2 can also be called the Special Form Rule.

Special forms have special powers that you, the programmer, do not have:

- Special forms provide the most basic flow control structures, such as if and recur. All flow control macros must eventually call a special form.

- Special forms provide direct access to Java. Whenever you call Java from Clojure, you are going through at least one special form, such as the dot or new.

- Names are created and bound through special forms, whether defining a var with def, creating a lexical binding with let, or creating a dynamic binding with binding.

As powerful as they are, special forms are not functions. They cannot do some things that functions can do. You cannot apply a special form, store a special form in a var, or use a special form as a filter with the sequence library. In short, special forms are not first-class citizens of the language.

The specialness of special forms could be a major problem and lead to repetitive, unmaintainable patterns in your code. But macros neatly

---

3. http://thinkrelevance.com

Justification	Category	Examples
Special form	Conditional evaluation	when, when-not, and, or, comment
Special form	Defining vars	defn, defmacro, defmulti, defstruct, declare
Special form	Java interop	.., doto, import-static
Caller convenience	Postponing evaluation	lazy-cat, lazy-seq, delay
Caller convenience	Wrapping evaluation	with-open, dosync, without-str, time, assert
Caller convenience	Avoiding a lambda	(Same as for "Wrapping evaluation")

Figure 7.2: TAXONOMY OF CLOJURE MACROS

solve the problem, because you can use macros to generate special forms. In a practical sense, *all language features are first-class features at macro expansion time.*

Macros that generate special forms are often the most difficult to write but also the most rewarding. As if by magic, such macros seem to *add new features to the language.*

The exception to the Macro Club rules is caller convenience: *you can write any macro that makes life easier for your callers when compared with an equivalent function.* Because macros do not evaluate their arguments, callers can pass raw code to a macro, instead of wrapping the code in an anonymous function. Or, callers can pass unescaped names, instead of quoted symbols or strings.

I reviewed the macros in Clojure and clojure-contrib, and almost all of them follow the rules of Macro Club. Also, they fit into one or more of the categories shown in Figure 7.2.

Let's examine each of the categories in turn.

Conditional Evaluation

Because macros do not immediately evaluate their arguments, they can be used to create custom control structures. You have already seen this with the unless example on Section 7.2, *Writing a Control Flow Macro*, on page 192.

Macros that do conditional evaluation tend to be fairly simple to read and write. They follow a common form: evaluate some argument (the condition). Then, based on that evaluation, pick which other arguments to evaluate, if any. A good example is Clojure's and:

```
Line 1  (defmacro and
     2    ([] true)
     3    ([x] x)
     4    ([x & rest]
     5      `(let [and# ~x]
     6        (if and# (and ~@rest) and#)))))
```

and is defined recursively. The zero- and one-argument bodies set up the base cases:

- For no arguments, return true.

- For one argument, return that argument.

For two or more arguments, and uses the first argument as its condition, evaluating it on line 5. Then, if the condition is true, and proceeds to evaluate the remaining arguments by recursively anding the rest (line 6).

and must be a macro, in order to short-circuit evaluation after the first nontrue value is encountered. Unsurprisingly, and has a close cousin macro, or. Their signatures are the same:

```
(and & exprs)
```

```
(or & exprs)
```

The difference is that and stops on the first logical false, while or stops on the first logical true:

```
(and 1 0 nil false)
```
⇒   nil

```
(or 1 0 nil false)
```
⇒   1

The all-time short-circuit evaluation champion is the comment macro:

```
(comment & exprs)
```

comment never evaluates *any* of its arguments and is sometimes used at the end of a source code file to demonstrate usage of an API. For example, the Clojure inspector library ends with the following comment, demonstrating the use of the inspector:

```
(comment

(load-file "src/inspector.clj")
(refer 'inspector)
(inspect-tree {:a 1 :b 2 :c [1 2 3 {:d 4 :e 5 :f [6 7 8]}]})
(inspect-table [[1 2 3][4 5 6][7 8 9][10 11 12]])

)
```

Notice the lack of indentation. This would be nonstandard in most Clojure code but is useful in comment, whose purpose is to draw attention to its body.

Creating Vars

Clojure vars are created by the def special form. Anything else that creates a var must eventually call def. So, for example, defn, defmacro, and defmulti are all themselves macros.

To demonstrate writing macros that create vars, we will look at two macros that are also part of Clojure: defstruct and declare.

Clojure provides a low-level function for creating structs called create-struct:

```
(create-struct & key-symbols)
```

Use create-struct to create a person struct:

```
(def person (create-struct :first-name :last-name))
    #'user/person
```

create-struct works, but it is visually noisy. Given that you often want to immediately def a new struct, you will typically call defstruct, which combines def and create-struct in a single operation:

```
(defstruct name & key-symbols)
```

defstruct is a simple macro, and it is already part of Clojure:

```
(defmacro defstruct
  [name & keys]
  `(def ~name (create-struct ~@keys)))
```

This macro looks so simple that you may be tempted to try to write it as a function. You won't be able to, because def is a special form. You must generate def at macro time; you cannot make "dynamic" calls to def at runtime.

defstruct makes a single line easier to read, but some macros can also condense many lines down into a single form. Consider the problem of forward declarations. You are writing a program that needs forward references to vars a, b, c, and d. You can call def with no arguments to define the var names without an initial binding:

```
(def a)
(def b)
(def c)
(def d)
```

But this is tedious and wastes a lot of vertical space. The declare macro takes a variable list of names and defs each name for you:

```
(declare & names)
```

Now you can declare all the names in a single compact form:

```
(declare a b c d)
```
⇒   #'user/d

The implementation of declare is built into Clojure:

```
(defmacro declare
  [& names] `(do ~@(map #(list 'def %) names)))
```

Let's analyze declare from the inside out. The anonymous function #(list 'def %) is responsible for generating a single def. You can test this form alone at the REPL:

```
(#(list 'def %) 'a)
```
⇒   (def a)

The map invokes the inner function once for each symbol passed in. Again, you can test this form at the REPL:

```
(map #(list 'def %) '[a b c d])
```
⇒   ((def a) (def b) (def c) (def d))

Finally, the leading do makes the entire expansion into a single legal Clojure form:

```
'(do ~@(map #(list 'def %) '[a b c d]))
```
⇒   (do (def a) (def b) (def c) (def d))

Substituting '[a b c d] in the previous form is the manual equivalent of testing the entire macro with macroexpand-1:

```
(macroexpand-1 '(declare a b c d))
```
⇒   (do (def a) (def b) (def c) (def d))

Many of the most interesting parts of Clojure are macros that expand into special forms involving def. We have explored a few here, but you can read the source of any of them. Most of them live at src/clj/clojure/ core.clj in the Clojure source distribution.

Java Interop

Clojure programs call into Java via the . (dot), new, and set! special forms. However, idiomatic Clojure code often uses macros such as .. (threaded member access) and doto to simplify forms that call Java.

You (or anyone else) can extend how Clojure calls Java by writing a macro. Consider the following scenario. You are writing code that uses several of the constants in java.lang.Math:

```
Math/PI
```
⇒   3.141592653589793

```
(Math/pow 10 3)
```
⇒   1000.0

In a longer segment of code, the Math/ prefix would quickly become distracting, so it would be nice if you could say simply PI and pow. Clojure doesn't provide any direct way to do this, but you could define a bunch of vars by hand:

```
(def PI Math/PI)
```
⇒   #'user/PI

```
(defn pow [b e] (Math/pow b e))
```
⇒   #'user/pow

Stuart Sierra has automated the boilerplate with the import-static macro:

```
(clojure.contrib.import-static/import-static class & members)
```

import-static imports static members of a Java class as names in the local namespace. Use import-static to import the members you want from Math.

```
(use '[clojure.contrib.import-static :only (import-static)])
(import-static java.lang.Math PI pow)
```
⇒   nil

```
PI
```
⇒   3.141592653589793

```
(pow 10 3)
```
⇒   1000.0

Besides import-static, clojure-contrib includes several other macros that simplify Java interop tasks:

- javalog/with-logger binds a logger for execution of a set of forms.

- error-kit[4] provides a set of macros augmenting Java-style exception handling with *continues*, which are like Common Lisp restarts.

Postponing Evaluation

Most sequences in Clojure are lazy. When you are building a lazy sequence, you often want to combine several forms whose evaluation is postponed until the sequence is forced. Since evaluation is not immediate, a macro is required.

You have already seen such a macro in Section 4.3, *Lazy and Infinite Sequences*, on page 105: lazy-seq. Another example is delay:

```
(delay & exprs)
```

When you create a delay, it holds on to its exprs and does nothing with them until it is forced to. Try creating a delay that simulates a long calculation by sleeping:

```
(def slow-calc (delay (Thread/sleep 5000) "done!"))
```
⇒   `#'user/slow-calc`

To actually execute the delay, you must force it:

```
(force x)
```

Try forcing your slow-calc a few times:

```
(force slow-calc)
```
⇒   `"done!"`

```
(force slow-calc)
```
⇒   `"done!"`

The first time you force a delay, it executes its expressions and caches the result. Subsequent forces simply return the cached value.

The macros that implement lazy and delayed evaluation all call Java code in clojure.jar. In your own code, you should not call such Java APIs directly. Treat the lazy/delayed evaluation macros as the public API, and the Java classes as implementation detail that is subject to change.

---

4. error-kit is under active development. See the announcement http://tinyurl.com/error-kit-announcement for intro documentation.

Wrapping Evaluation

Many macros wrap the evaluation of a set of forms, adding some special semantics before and/or after the forms are evaluated. You have already seen several examples of this kind of macro:

- time starts a timer, evaluates forms, and then reports how long they took to execute.
- let and binding establish bindings, evaluate some forms, and then tear down the bindings.
- with-open takes an open file (or other resource), executes some forms, and then makes sure the resource is closed in a **finally** block.
- dosync executes forms within a transaction.

Another example of a wrapper macro is with-out-str:

```
(with-out-str & exprs)
```

with-out-str temporarily binds *out* to a new StringWriter, evaluates its exprs, and then returns the string written to *out*. with-out-str makes it easy to use print and println to build strings on the fly:

```
(with-out-str (print "hello, ") (print "world"))
⇒    "hello, world"
```

The implementation of with-out-str has a simple structure that can act as a template for writing similar macros:

```
Line 1  (defmacro with-out-str
     2    [& body]
     3    `(let [s# (new java.io.StringWriter)]
     4       (binding [*out* s#]
     5         ~@body
     6         (str s#))))
```

Wrapper macros usually take a variable number of arguments (line 2), which are the forms to be evaluated. They then proceed in three steps:

1. *Setup:* Create some special context for evaluation, introducing bindings with let (line 3) and bindings (line 4) as necessary.
2. *Evaluation:* Evaluate the forms (line 5). Since there are typically a variable number of forms, insert them via a splicing unquote ~@.
3. *Teardown:* Reset the execution context to normal, and return a value as appropriate (line 6)

When writing a wrapper macro, always ask yourself whether you need a **finally** block to implement the teardown step correctly. For with-out-str, the answer is no, because both let and binding take care of their own cleanup. If, however, you are setting some global or thread-local state via a Java API, you will need a **finally** block to reset this state.

This talk of mutable state leads to another observation. Any code whose behavior changes when executed inside a wrapper macro is obviously *not* a pure function. print and println behave differently based on the value of *out* and so are not pure functions. Macros that set a binding, such as with-out-str, do so to alter the behavior of an impure function somewhere.

Not all wrappers change the behavior of the functions they wrap. You have already seen time, which simply times a function's execution. Another example is assert:

```
(assert expr)
```

assert tests an expression and raises an exception if it is not logically true:

```
(assert (= 1 1))
```
⇒ nil

```
(assert (= 1 2))
```
⇒ java.lang.Exception: Assert failed: (= 1 2)

Macros like assert and time violate the first rule of Macro Club in order to avoid unnecessary lambdas.

Avoiding Lambdas

For historical reasons, anonymous functions are often called *lambdas*. Sometimes a macro can be replaced by a function call, with the arguments wrapped in a lambda. For example, the bench macro from Section 7.3, *Syntax Quote, Unquote, and Splicing Unquote*, on page 200 does not need to be a macro. You can write it as a function:

```
(defn bench-fn [f]
  (let [start (System/nanoTime)
        result (f)]
    {:result result :elapsed (- (System/nanoTime) start)}))
```

However, if you want to call bench-fn, you must pass it a function that wraps the form you want to execute. The following code shows the difference:

```
; macro
(bench (+ 1 2))
```
⇒ {:elapsed 44000, :result 3}

```
; function
(bench-fn (fn [] (+ 1 2)))
```
⇒
```
    {:elapsed 53000, :result 3}
```

For things like bench, macros and anonymous functions are near substitutes. Both prevent immediate execution of a form. However, the anonymous function approach requires more work on the part of the caller, so it is OK to break the first rule and write a macro instead of a function.

Another reason to prefer a macro for bench is that bench-fn is not a perfect substitute; it adds the overhead of an anonymous function call at runtime. Since bench's purpose is to time things, you should avoid this overhead.

Now that you have seen how and where macros are used, let's use them to convert Lancet into a DSL.

7.5 Making a Lancet DSL

In previous chapters, you have given Lancet the ability to call Ant tasks and the ability to define targets (functions with run-once semantics). With these abilities alone, you could use Lancet to write build scripts.

However, calling Lancet is clunky, and using it feels more like calling an API than writing a build script. In this section, you will convert Lancet into a DSL that is cleaner and simpler than Ant.

Two macros will make this possible:

- A deftarget macro for defining targets
- A define-ant-task macro that creates easy-to-use Ant tasks

The code in this section depends on lancet.step-2-complete (Section 4.6, *Lancet Step 2: Setting Properties*, on page 125) and lancet.step-3-complete (Section 6.7, *Making Lancet Targets Run Only Once*, on page 187). You can use these libraries via the following:

lancet/step_4_repl.clj

```
(use 'lancet.step-2-complete 'lancet.step-3-complete)
```

Creating Lancet Targets

In Section 6.7, *Making Lancet Targets Run Only Once*, on page 187, you created a runonce function:

```
(runonce f) -> [has-run-fn reset-fn once-fn]
```

In this section, you will make runonce easy to use by creating a deftarget
macro that automates creating Lancet targets with runonce:

```
(deftarget fname docstring & forms)
```

First, let's review how runonce works. Given any function f, runonce will
return a vector with the following:

- A has-run-fn predicate that will tell whether once-fn has run

- A reset-fn function that will reset once-fn's status

- A once-fn that will perform the original function f exactly once

deftarget needs to store the once-fn under the name fname, but where
should it put the helper functions has-run-fn and reset-fn? Since these
helper functions are linked to the function itself, metadata seems a
reasonable place to put them.

As usual, let's approach the macro backwards by first writing the code
that the macro should expand to. The expanded macro will need to call
runonce, binding the results to some temporary name. Then it should
create a new def, pointing to the once-fn, and with metadata pointing
to the helper functions. Create a function named boo that prints boo!
once:

```
; (deftarget boo "doc" (println "boo!"))
;    should expand to
(let [[has-run-fn reset-fn once-fn] (runonce #(println "boo!"))]
  (def #^{:has-run-fn has-run-fn :reset-fn reset-fn :doc "doc"}
       boo once-fn))
⇒    #'user/boo
```

The let uses destructuring to bind runonce's return vector directly into
the three names has-run-fn, reset-fn, and once-fn. Then the def places
has-run-fn and reset-fn under metadata keys and defs boo to once-fn.

Test that boo was defined correctly. It should print only once:

```
(boo)
| boo!
⇒    nil

(boo)
⇒    nil
```

Also, the var boo should have metadata under the keys :has-run-fn and
:reset-fn:

```
(meta #'boo)
⇒    {:name boo,
```

```
 :has-run-fn #<long mangled name>,
 :reset-fn #<long mangled name>,
 ... etc. ...
```

Callers will not want to poke around in metadata to query or set a function's run status. Let's build some helpers that can call has-run-fn and reset-fn on a particular function. First, create a has-run? that takes a var, extracts the has-run-fn from its metadata, and calls it:

lancet/step_4_repl.clj

```
(defn has-run? [v]
  ((:has-run-fn (meta v))))
```

Notice the doubled parentheses. The inner parentheses call :has-run-fn to look up the function, and the outer parentheses call the function itself. Use has-run? to check that boo has already run:

(has-run? #'boo)
⇒   true

Because has-run? is written as a function, you have to remember to pass the var #'boo. If you try to pass the symbol boo, has-run? will check the metadata on the function itself, instead of the var. Since the function has no metadata, this will lead to a NullPointerException:

(has-run? boo)
⇒   java.lang.NullPointerException

has-run? would be easier to remember and use if callers could just pass boo. To make this work, you need to prevent Clojure from evaluating boo before calling has-run?. The solution is another macro. Rewrite has-run? as a macro:

lancet/step_4_repl.clj

```
(defmacro has-run? [f]
  `((:has-run-fn (meta (var ~f)))))
```

Now you should be able to test has-run? with boo:

(has-run? boo)
⇒   true

has-run? is an example that *could* be written as a function but is worth rewriting as a macro for the convenience of the caller. Go ahead and write reset along similar lines:

lancet/step_4_repl.clj

```
(defmacro reset [f]
  `((:reset-fn (meta (var ~f)))))
```

Using reset, you can reset the run status of boo to false:

```
(reset boo)
```
⇒   `nil`

```
(has-run? boo)
```
⇒   `false`

Now that the helper macros are in place, you can return to the main task: defining deftarget. In a source-code editor, begin with the hand-coded expansion that a deftarget should generate:

```
(let [[has-run-fn reset-fn once-fn] (runonce #(println "boo!"))]
  (def #^{:has-run-fn has-run-fn :reset-fn reset-fn :doc "doc"}
      boo once-fn))
```

Next, wrap the expansion in the proposed signature for deftarget:

```
(defmacro deftarget [sym doc & forms]
  (let [[has-run-fn reset-fn once-fn]
        (runonce #(println "boo!"))]
    (def #^{:has-run-fn has-run-fn
            :reset-fn reset-fn
            :doc "doc"}
        boo once-fn)))
```

You are going to implement this macro as a template, so syntax-quote the expansion, and plug in the arguments in the appropriate places:

```
(defmacro deftarget [sym doc & forms]
  `(let [[has-run-fn reset-fn once-fn] (runonce (fn [] ~@forms))]
     (def #^{:has-run-fn has-run-fn :reset-fn reset-fn :doc ~doc}
         ~sym once-fn)))
```

Notice that when you substituted in ~@forms, you also converted from the reader macro form #(...) to the more explicit (fn [] ...). You should generally avoid reader macros in macro expansions, since reader macros are evaluated at read time, before macro expansion begins.

You'll have a similar problem with the metadata reader macro #^, which applies its metadata at read time. That's too early, since you want the metadata applied to the def at compile time, after the macro has expanded. So, convert the reader macro to an equivalent functional form:

`lancet/deftarget_1.clj`

```
(defmacro deftarget [sym doc & forms]
  `(let [[has-run-fn reset-fn once-fn] (runonce (fn [] ~@forms))]
     (def ~(with-meta sym {:has-run-fn has-run-fn
                           :reset-fn reset-fn
                           :doc doc})
           once-fn)))
```

Now you have something that you can try to load at the REPL. Your load command will differ from the following one depending on how you named the file:

```
(use :reload 'lancet.deftarget-1)
```
⇒   java.lang.Exception: Unable to resolve symbol: has-run-fn in this context

This is a problem you have seen before. You need to let unique local names, so append a # to all the names that you let inside the macro:

```
(defmacro deftarget [sym doc & forms]
  '(let [[has-run-fn# reset-fn# once-fn#] (runonce (fn [] ~@forms))]
     (def ~(with-meta sym {:has-run-fn has-run-fn# :reset-fn reset-fn# :doc doc})
       once-fn#)))
```

Unfortunately, the automatic symbols will not work this time:

```
(use :reload 'lancet.deftarget-1)
```
⇒   java.lang.Exception: Unable to resolve symbol: has-run-fn in this context

The problem is the unquoting of the with-meta form. Symbols generated by appending the # are valid only within a syntax-quoted form. If you turn quoting back off, you cannot use them. So, now you have to generate some unique symbols yourself. Clojure provides gensym for this purpose:

```
(gensym prefix?)
```

You can call gensym with a prefix or let Clojure use its default prefix G__:

```
(gensym)
```
⇒   G__137

```
(gensym "has-run-fn__")
```
⇒   has-run-fn__145

You'll need to replace has-run-fn and reset-fn with gensyms, since they're used outside the syntax quote. once-fn# can continue to use Clojure's auto-gensym, since it is not needed outside of the syntax quote. Update deftarget to let the symbols it needs before expanding the template:

```
lancet/step_4_repl.clj
```
```
(defmacro deftarget [sym doc & forms]
  (let [has-run-fn (gensym "hr-") reset-fn (gensym "rf-")]
    `(let [[~has-run-fn ~reset-fn once-fn#] (runonce (fn [] ~@forms))]
       (def ~(with-meta
               sym
               {:doc doc :has-run-fn has-run-fn :reset-fn reset-fn})
         once-fn#))))
```

Now you have a deftarget ready to use. Test it first with macroexpand-1. You can bind the special variable *print-meta* and call the prn function to print the macro expansion with metadata included:

```
(binding [*print-meta* true]
  (prn (macroexpand-1
  '(deftarget foo "docstr" (println "hello")))))
| (clojure.core/let
|   [[hr-506 rf-507 once-fn__143]
|    (lancet.step-3-complete/runonce
|      (clojure.core/fn [] #^{:line 13} (println "hello")))]
|   (def #^{:has-run-fn hr-506, :reset-fn rf-507, :doc "docstr"}
|        foo once-fn__143))
```

Now, try using deftarget to define a runonce function. Make sure that the function itself and the has-run? and reset functions work as expected.

```
(deftarget foo "demo function"
  (println "There can be only one!"))
⇒    #'user/foo

(foo)
| There can be only one!
⇒    nil

(has-run? foo)
⇒    true

(reset foo)
⇒    nil

(has-run? foo)
⇒    false
```

Writing deftarget was quite a bit more complex than the other macros you have written so far. But the benefits are large. The trio of deftarget, has-run?, and reset feel like part of a Lancet language, not a Clojure API.

You might find it helpful to compare deftarget to an object-oriented design. Notice that the deftarget design creates no new classes. Instead, it uses Clojure's small, powerful set of abstractions: functions, metadata, agents, and macros. However, deftarget has some of the key benefits associated with object-oriented design:

- *Encapsulation:* The agent that tracks whether a function has run is not exposed directly.
- *Reuse:* You can deftarget any function, and a deftarget function can be used anywhere a normal function would be used.

We now need one more set of macros to make Lancet complete.

Defining Ant Tasks for Lancet

Using the code in Section 4.6, *Lancet Step 2: Setting Properties*, on page 125, you can instantiate and execute Ant tasks as follows:

```
(def echo
  (instantiate-task ant-project "echo" {:message "hello"}))
```
⇒
```
    #'user/echo
```

```
(.execute echo)
|   [echo] hello
```
⇒
```
    nil
```

In this section, your goal is to simplify that syntax to the bare essentials:

```
(echo {:message "hello"})
|   [echo] hello
```
⇒
```
    nil
```

To do this, you will create two macros:

- define-ant-task will create a function named after an Ant task. The function will create and execute an Ant task.

- define-all-ant-tasks will reflect against the Ant project to get the complete list of available tasks and call define-ant-task once for each of them.

Let's build define-ant-task first. As always, begin with what you want the expanded macro to look like. To wrap an Ant task in a function, you could do something like this:

```
; (define-ant-task ant-echo echo)
;    should expand to
(defn ant-echo [props]
  (let [task (instantiate-task ant-project "echo" props)]
    (.execute task)
    task))
```

This expansion shows two things that are not strictly necessary but will be useful later:

1. define-ant-task will take two arguments: the name of the function to create followed by the name of the Ant task. Ninety percent of the time these names will be the same, but occasionally the function name will be different to avoid collision with a name in clojure.core.

2. define-ant-task will return the created task. This is rarely used in Lancet itself but will be useful in the unit tests.

Writing define-ant-task is fairly simple. The only parts that need to vary from one call to the next are the names of the function and underlying Ant task. Create the define-ant-task macro thusly:

`lancet/step_4_repl.clj`

```
(defmacro define-ant-task [clj-name ant-name]
  `(defn ~clj-name [props#]
     (let [task# (instantiate-task ant-project ~(name ant-name) props#)]
       (.execute task#)
       task#)))
```

Test define-ant-task by creating a mkdir task and then calling mkdir:

```
(define-ant-task mkdir mkdir)
```
⇒
```
    #'user/mkdir
```

```
(mkdir {:dir (java.io.File. "foo")})
|   [mkdir] Created dir: /Book/code/lancet/foo
```
⇒
```
    #<Mkdir org.apache.tools.ant.taskdefs.Mkdir@26e0696c>
```

You're almost there. Now you just need to reflect against your ant-project to get all available task names. The getTaskDefinitions method returns a Java Hashtable mapping task names to implementation classes. You need only the names, so you can call Java's keySet method on the hash. Create a helper function called task-names that returns the task names as a Clojure seq of symbols:

`lancet/step_4_repl.clj`

```
(defn task-names []
  (map symbol (sort (.. ant-project getTaskDefinitions keySet))))
```

Call task-names, and you should get a long seq of names:

```
(task-names)
```
⇒
```
    (ant antcall antstructure apply apt available
     ... many more ...)
```

Now you are ready to write define-ant-tasks. You need to map all the task names to a call to define-ant-task and splice the entire thing after a do so that the macro expands into a legal Clojure form.

Since this macro is a one-liner, let's live dangerously and implement it directly without writing an expansion first:

`lancet/step_4_repl.clj`

```
(defmacro define-all-ant-tasks []
  `(do ~@(map (fn [n] `(define-ant-task ~n ~n)) (task-names))))
```

Use macroexpand-1 to check that the expansion works correctly:

```
(macroexpand-1 '(define-all-ant-tasks))
```
⇒   (do (user/define-ant-task fail fail)
          (user/define-ant-task tar tar)
                ... many more ...)

Everything is looking fine. But when you try to generate all the tasks in task-names, you fail:

```
(define-all-ant-tasks)
```
⇒   java.lang.Exception: Name conflict,
      can't def import because namespace: user
      refers to:#'clojure.core/import

The problem here is unrelated to macros. Some Ant task names, like import, collide with Clojure names. To work around this, create a safe-ant-name function that prepends ant- to any name that already exists in the current namespace:

lancet/step_4_repl.clj

```
(defn safe-ant-name [n]
  (if (resolve n) (symbol (str "ant-" n)) n))
```

safe-ant-name attempts to resolve a name in the current namespace. If the name resolves, it is a collision and needs to have ant- prepended.

Now, redefine define-ant-tasks to call safe-ant-name on the first argument to define-ant-task:

lancet/step_4_repl.clj

```
(defmacro define-all-ant-tasks []
  `(do ~@(map (fn [n] `(define-ant-task ~(safe-ant-name n) ~n)) (task-names))))
```

Now you should be able to define all the Ant tasks you have available:

```
(define-all-ant-tasks)
```
⇒   #'user/sleep

The return value of define-all-ant-tasks is the last task defined, which was sleep on my machine. Go ahead and test sleep for a few seconds:

```
(sleep {:seconds 5})
... time passes ...
```
⇒   #<Sleep org.apache.tools.ant.taskdefs.Sleep@625b057b>

Lancet is now a minimal but complete build language. You can define dependency relationships by creating runonce functions. These can in turn call any Ant task *or* any Clojure function. The Lancet language is more concise than Ant and more regular. Best of all, you do not have to jump through any hoops to extend it. You just write Clojure code.

The completed code for this chapter is in Section 7.5, *Lancet Step 4: DSL*. It is fewer than fifty lines, but more than half of those lines are macros. This is definitely the most complex code in the book, but bear two things in mind:

1. The macro code is a thin wrapper over the rest of Lancet. Most of Lancet is quite simple, and the complex parts are cleanly separated from the rest.

2. The macros justify their complexity by doing a *huge* amount of work. Without macros, you might end up writing an XML-based language, like Ant. Instead of fifty lines of infrastructure code, you would have *thousands* of lines, plus an additional tax on every new task. Or you could define your own custom language grammar and then write or generate a parser for it. When compared with these options, a little bit of heavy lifting with macros is a reasonable alternative.

Lancet Step 4: DSL

`lancet/step_4_complete.clj`

```clojure
(ns lancet.step-4-complete
  (:use [clojure.contrib.except :only (throw-if)]
        lancet.step-2-complete lancet.step-3-complete))

(defmacro has-run? [f]
  `((:has-run-fn (meta (var ~f)))))

(defmacro reset [f]
  `((:reset-fn (meta (var ~f)))))

(defmacro deftarget [sym doc & forms]
  (let [has-run-fn (gensym "hr-") reset-fn (gensym "rf-")]
    `(let [[~has-run-fn ~reset-fn once-fn#] (runonce (fn [] ~@forms))]
       (def ~(with-meta
               sym
               {:doc doc :has-run-fn has-run-fn :reset-fn reset-fn})
         once-fn#))))

(defmacro define-ant-task [clj-name ant-name]
  `(defn ~clj-name [props#]
     (let [task#
           (instantiate-task ant-project ~(name ant-name) props#)]
       (.execute task#)
       task#)))

(defn task-names []
  (map symbol (sort (.. ant-project getTaskDefinitions keySet))))
```

```
(defn safe-ant-name [n]
  (if (resolve n) (symbol (str "ant-" n)) n))

(defmacro define-all-ant-tasks []
  `(do ~@(map (fn [n] `(define-ant-task ~(safe-ant-name n) ~n))
              (task-names))))

(define-all-ant-tasks)
```

7.6 Wrapping Up

Clojure macros let you automate patterns in your code. Because they transform source code at macro expansion time, you can use macros to abstract away *any* kind of pattern in your code. You are not limited to working within Clojure. With macros, you can *extend* Clojure into your problem domain.

Internally, Clojure uses macros to implement many of its most powerful features. One of these features is multimethods, to which we turn next.

Chapter 8

Multimethods

Clojure multimethods provide a flexible way to associate a function with a set of inputs. This is similar to Java polymorphism but more general. When you call a Java method, Java selects a specific implementation to execute by examining the *type* of a *single object*. When you call a Clojure multimethod, Clojure selects a specific implementation to execute by examining the result of *any function you choose*, applied to *all* the function's arguments.

In this chapter, you will develop a thirst for multimethods by first living without them. Then you will build an increasingly complex series of multimethod implementations. First, you will use multimethods to simulate polymorphism. Then, you will use multimethods to implement various ad hoc taxonomies.

Multimethods in Clojure are used much less often than polymorphism in object-oriented languages. But where they are used, they are often the key feature in the code. Section 8.5, *When Should I Use Multimethods?*, on page 236 explores how multimethods are used in several open source Clojure projects and offers guidelines for when to use them in your own programs.

At the end of the chapter, you will use multimethods to add a new feature to Lancet: customizable type coercions for use when creating Ant tasks.

If you are reading the book in chapter order, then once you have completed this chapter, you will have seen all the key features of the Clojure language.

8.1 Living Without Multimethods

The best way to appreciate multimethods is to spend a few minutes living without them. So let's do that. Clojure can already print anything with print/println. But pretend for a moment that these functions do not exist and that you need to build a generic print mechanism. To get started, create a my-print function that can print a string to the standard output stream *out*:

examples/life_without_multi.clj

```
(defn my-print [ob]
  (.write *out* ob))
```

Next, create a my-println that simply calls my-print and then adds a line feed:

examples/life_without_multi.clj

```
(defn my-println [ob]
  (my-print ob)
  (.write *out* "\n"))
```

The line feed makes my-println's output easier to read when testing at the REPL. For the remainder of this section, you will make changes to my-print and test them by calling my-println. Test that my-println works with strings:

```
(my-println "hello")
| hello
```
⇒   nil

That is nice, but my-println does not work quite so well with nonstrings such as nil:

```
(my-println nil)
```
⇒   java.lang.NullPointerException

That's not a big deal, though. Just use cond to add special-case handling for nil:

examples/life_without_multi.clj

```
(defn my-print [ob]
  (cond
    (nil? ob) (.write *out* "nil")
    (string? ob) (.write *out* ob)))
```

With the conditional in place, you can print nil with no trouble:

```
(my-println nil)
| nil
```
⇒   nil

Of course, there are still all kinds of types that my-println cannot deal with. If you try to print a vector, neither of the cond clauses will match, and the program will print nothing at all:

```
(my-println [1 2 3])
   nil
```
⇒

By now you know the drill. Just add another cond clause for the vector case. The implementation here is a little more complex, so you might want to separate the actual printing into a helper function, such as my-print-vector:

examples/life_without_multi.clj

```
(use '[clojure.contrib.str-utils :only (str-join)])
(defn my-print-vector [ob]
  (.write *out*"[")
  (.write *out* (str-join " " ob))
  (.write *out* "]"))

(defn my-print [ob]
  (cond
    (vector? ob) (my-print-vector ob)
    (nil? ob) (.write *out* "nil")
    (string? ob) (.write *out* ob)))
```

Make sure that you can now print a vector:

```
(my-println [1 2 3])
| [1 2 3]
   nil
```
⇒

my-println now supports three types: strings, vectors, and nil. And you have a road map for new types: just add new clauses to the cond in my-println. But it is a crummy road map, because it conflates two things: the decision process for selecting an implementation and the specific implementation detail.

You can improve the situation somewhat by pulling out helper functions like my-print-vector. However, then you have to make two separate changes every time you want to a add new feature to my-println:

- Create a new type-specific helper function.

- Modify the existing my-println to add a new cond invoking the feature-specific helper.

What you really want is a way to add new features to the system by adding new code in a single place, without having to modify any existing code. The solution, of course, is multimethods.

8.2 Defining Multimethods

To define a multimethod, use defmulti:

```
(defmulti name dispatch-fn)
```

name is the name of the new multimethod, and Clojure will invoke dispatch-fn against the method arguments to select one particular method (implementation) of the multimethod.

Consider my-print from the previous section. It takes a single argument, the thing to be printed, and you want to select a specific implementation based on the type of that argument. So, dispatch-fn needs to be a function of one argument that returns the type of that argument. Clojure has a built-in function matching this description, namely, class. Use class to create a multimethod called my-print:

```
examples/multimethods.clj
(defmulti my-print class)
```

At this point, you have provided a description of how the multimethod will select a specific method but no actual specific methods. Unsurprisingly, attempts to call my-print will fail:

```
(my-println "foo")
⇒    java.lang.IllegalArgumentException: \
            No method for dispatch value
```

To add a specific method implementation to my-println, use defmethod:

```
(defmethod name dispatch-val & fn-tail)
```

name is the name of the multimethod to which an implementation belongs. Clojure matches the result of defmulti's dispatch function with dispatch-val to select a method, and fn-tail contains arguments and body forms just like a normal function.

Create a my-print implementation that matches on strings:

```
examples/multimethods.clj
(defmethod my-print String [s]
  (.write *out* s))
```

Now, call my-println with a string argument:

```
(my-println "stu")
| stu
⇒    nil
```

Next, create a my-print that matches on nil:

```
(defmethod my-print nil [s]
  (.write *out* "nil"))
```

Notice that you have solved the problem raised in the previous section. Instead of being joined in a big cond, each implementation of my-println is separate. Methods of a multimethod can live anywhere in your source, and you can add new ones any time, without having to touch the original code.

Dispatch Is Inheritance-Aware

Multimethod dispatch knows about Java inheritance. To see this, create a my-print that handles Number by simply printing a number's toString representation:

```
(defmethod my-print Number [n]
  (.write *out* (.toString n)))
```

Test the Number implementation with an integer:

```
(my-println 42)
| 42
⇒   nil
```

42 is an Integer, not a Number. Multimethod dispatch is smart enough to know that an integer is a number and match anyway. Internally, dispatch uses the isa? function:

```
(isa? child parent)
```

isa? knows about Java inheritance, so it knows that an Integer is a Number:

```
(isa? Integer Number)
⇒   true
```

isa? is not limited to inheritance. Its behavior can be extended dynamically at runtime, as you will see later in Section 8.4, *Creating Ad Hoc Taxonomies*, on page 232.

Multimethod Defaults

It would be nice if my-print could have a fallback representation that you could use for any type you have not specifically defined. You can use :default as a dispatch value to handle any methods that do not match anything more specific. Using :default, create a my-println that prints the Java toString value of objects, wrapped in #<>:

```
examples/multimethods.clj
```

```
(defmethod my-print :default [s]
  (.write *out* "#<")
  (.write *out* (.toString s))
  (.write *out* ">"))
```

Now test that my-println can print any old random thing, using the default method:

```
(my-println (java.sql.Date. 0))
```
⇒   `#<1969-12-31>`

```
(my-println (java.util.Random.))
```
⇒   `#<java.util.Random@1c398896>`

In the unlikely event that :default already has some specific meaning in your domain, you can create a multimethod using this alternate signature:

```
(defmulti name dispatch-fn :default default-value)
```

The default-value lets you specify your own default. Maybe you would like to call it :everything-else:

```
examples/multimethods/default.clj
```

```
(defmulti my-print class :default :everything-else)
(defmethod my-print String [s]
  (.write *out* s))
(defmethod my-print :everything-else [_]
  (.write *out* "Not implemented yet..."))
```

Any dispatch value that does not otherwise match will now match against :everything-else.

Dispatching a multimethod on the type of the first argument, as you have done with my-print, is by far the most common kind of dispatch. In many object-oriented languages, in fact, it is the *only* kind of dynamic dispatch, and it goes by the name *polymorphism*.

Clojure's dispatch is much more general. Let's add a few complexities to my-print and move beyond what is possible with plain ol' polymorphism.

8.3 Moving Beyond Simple Dispatch

Clojure's print function prints various "sequencey" things as lists. If you wanted my-print to do something similar, you could add a method that dispatched on a collection interface high in the Java inheritance hierarchy, such as Collection:

```
examples/multimethods.clj
```
```
(use '[clojure.contrib.str-utils :only (str-join)])
(defmethod my-print java.util.Collection [c]
  (.write *out* "(")
  (.write *out* (str-join " " c))
  (.write *out* ")"))
```

Now, try various sequences to see that they get a nice print representation:

```
(my-println (take 6 (cycle [1 2 3])))
| (1 2 3 1 2 3)
⇒   nil
```

```
(my-println [1 2 3])
| (1 2 3)
⇒   nil
```

Perfectionist that you are, you cannot stand that vectors print with rounded braces, unlike their literal square-brace syntax. So, add yet another my-print method, this time to handle vectors. Vectors all implement a IPersistentVector, so this should work:

```
examples/multimethods.clj
```
```
(defmethod my-print clojure.lang.IPersistentVector [c]
  (.write *out* "[")
  (.write *out* (str-join " " c))
  (.write *out* "]"))
```

But it doesn't work. Instead, printing vectors now throws an exception:

```
(my-println [1 2 3])
⇒   java.lang.IllegalArgumentException: Multiple methods match
    dispatch value: class clojure.lang.LazilyPersistentVector ->
    interface clojure.lang.IPersistentVector and
    interface java.util.Collection,
    and neither is preferred
```

The problem is that two dispatch values now match for vectors: Collection and IPersistentVector. Many languages constrain method dispatch to make sure these conflicts never happen, such as by forbidding multiple inheritance. Clojure takes a different approach. You can create conflicts, and you can resolve them with prefer-method:

```
(prefer-method multi-name loved-dispatch dissed-dispatch)
```

When you call prefer-method for a multimethod, you tell it to prefer the loved-dispatch value over the dissed-dispatch value whenever there is a conflict. Since you want the vector version of my-print to trump the collection version, tell the multimethod what you want:

examples/multimethods.clj

```
(prefer-method
 my-print clojure.lang.IPersistentVector java.util.Collection)
```

Now, you should be able to route both vectors and other sequences to the correct method implementation:

```
(my-println (take 6 (cycle [1 2 3])))
| (1 2 3 1 2 3)
     nil
```
⇒

```
(my-println [1 2 3])
| [1 2 3]
     nil
```
⇒

Many languages create complex rules, or arbitrary limitations, in order to resolve ambiguities in their systems for dispatching functions. Clojure allows a much simpler approach: Just don't worry about it! If there is an ambiguity, use prefer-method to resolve it.

8.4 Creating Ad Hoc Taxonomies

Multimethods let you create ad hoc taxonomies, which can be helpful when you discover type relationships that are not explicitly declared as such.

For example, consider a financial application that deals with checking and savings accounts. Define a Clojure struct for an account, using a tag to distinguish the two. Place the code in the namespace examples.multimethods.account. To do this, you will need to create a file named examples/multimethods/account.clj on your classpath[1] and then enter the following code:

examples/multimethods/account.clj

```
(ns examples.multimethods.account)

(defstruct account :id :tag :balance)
```

Now, you are going to create two different checking accounts, tagged as ::Checking and ::Savings. The capital names are a Clojure convention

---

1. Note that the example code for the book includes a completed version of this example, already on the classpath. To work through the example yourself, simply move or rename the completed example to get it out of the way.

to show the keywords are acting as types. The doubled :: causes the keywords to resolve in the current namespace. To see the namespace resolution happen, compare entering :Checking and ::Checking at the REPL:

```
:Checking
```
⇒
```
    :Checking
```

```
::Checking
```
⇒
```
    :user/Checking
```

Placing keywords in a namespace helps prevent name collisions with other people's code. When you want to use ::Savings or ::Checking from another namespace, you will need to fully qualify them:

```
(struct account 1 ::examples.multimethods.account/Savings 100M)
```
⇒
```
    {:id 1, :tag :examples.multimethods.account/Savings,
     :balance 100M}
```

Full names get tedious quickly, so you can use alias to specify a shorter alias for a long namespace name:

```
(alias short-name-symbol namespace-symbol)
```

Use alias to create the short name acc:

```
(alias 'acc 'examples.multimethods.account)
```
⇒
```
    nil
```

Now that the acc alias is available, create two top-level test objects, a savings account and a checking account:

```
(def test-savings (struct account 1 ::acc/Savings 100M))
```
⇒
```
    #'user/test-savings
```
```
(def test-checking (struct account 2 ::acc/Checking 250M))
```
⇒
```
    #'user/test-checking
```

Note that the trailing M creates a BigDecimal literal and does not mean you have millions of dollars.

The interest rate for checking accounts is 0 and for savings accounts is 5 percent. Create a multimethod interest-rate that dispatches based on :tag, like so:

examples/multimethods/account.clj

```
(defmulti interest-rate :tag)
(defmethod interest-rate ::acc/Checking [_] 0M)
(defmethod interest-rate ::acc/Savings [_] 0.05M)
```

Check your test-savings and test-checking to make sure that interest-rate works as expected.

```
(interest-rate test-savings)
⇒   0.05M

(interest-rate test-checking)
⇒   0M
```

Accounts have an annual service charge, with rules as follows:

- Normal checking accounts pay a $25 service charge.
- Normal savings accounts pay a $10 service charge.
- Premium accounts have no fee.
- Checking accounts with a balance of $5,000 or more are premium.
- Savings accounts with a balance of $1,000 or more are premium.

In a realistic example, the rules would be more complex. Premium status would be driven by average balance over time, and there would probably be other ways to qualify. But the previous rules are complex enough to demonstrate the point.

You could implement service-charge with a bunch of conditional logic, but premium feels like a type, even though there is no explicit premium tag on an account. Create an account-level multimethod that returns ::Premium or ::Basic:

examples/multimethods/account.clj

```
(defmulti account-level :tag)
(defmethod account-level ::acc/Checking [acct]
  (if (>= (:balance acct) 5000) ::acc/Premium ::acc/Basic))
(defmethod account-level ::acc/Savings [acct]
  (if (>= (:balance acct) 1000) ::acc/Premium ::acc/Basic))
```

Test account-level to make sure that checking and savings accounts require different balance levels to reach ::Premium status:

```
(account-level (struct account 1 ::acc/Savings 2000M))
⇒    :examples.multimethods.account/Premium
(account-level (struct account 1 ::acc/Checking 2000M))
⇒    :examples.multimethods.account/Basic
```

Now you might be tempted to implement service-charge using account-level as a dispatch function:

examples/multimethods/service_charge_1.clj

```
; bad approach
(defmulti service-charge account-level)
(defmethod service-charge ::Basic [acct]
  (if (= (:tag acct) ::Checking) 25 10))
(defmethod service-charge ::Premium [_] 0)
```

The conditional logic in service-charge for ::Basic is exactly the kind of type-driven conditional that multimethods should help us avoid. The problem here is that you are already dispatching by account-level, and now you need to be dispatching by :tag as well. No problem—you can dispatch on *both*. Write a service-charge whose dispatch function calls both account-level and :tag, returning the results in a vector:

examples/multimethods/service_charge_2.clj

```
(defmulti service-charge (fn [acct] [(account-level acct) (:tag acct)]))
(defmethod service-charge [::acc/Basic ::acc/Checking]   [_] 25)
(defmethod service-charge [::acc/Basic ::acc/Savings]    [_] 10)
(defmethod service-charge [::acc/Premium ::acc/Checking] [_] 0)
(defmethod service-charge [::acc/Premium ::acc/Savings]  [_] 0)
```

This version of service-charge dispatches against two different taxonomies: the :tag intrinsic to an account and the externally defined account-level. Try a few accounts to verify that service-charge works as expected:

```
(service-charge {:tag ::acc/Checking :balance 1000})
```
⇒   25

```
(service-charge {:tag ::acc/Savings :balance 1000})
```
⇒   0

Notice that the previous tests did not even bother to create a "real" account for testing. Structs like account are simply maps that are optimized for storing particular fields, but nothing stops you from using a plain old map if you find it more convenient.

Adding Inheritance to Ad Hoc Types

There is one further improvement you can make to service-charge. Since all premium accounts have the same service charge, it feels redundant to have to define two separate service-charge methods for ::Savings and ::Checking accounts. It would be nice to have a parent type ::Account, so you could define a multimethod that matches ::Premium for any kind of ::Account. Clojure lets you define arbitrary parent/child relationships with derive:

```
(derive child parent)
```

Using derive, you can specify that both ::Savings and ::Checking are kinds of ::Account:

examples/multimethods/service_charge_3.clj

```
(derive ::acc/Savings ::acc/Account)
(derive ::acc/Checking ::acc/Account)
```

When you start to use derive, isa? comes into its own. In addition to understanding Java inheritance, isa? knows all about derived relationships:

```
(isa? ::acc/Savings ::acc/Account)
```
⇒
```
    true
```

Now that Clojure knows that Savings and Checking are Accounts, you can define a service-charge using a single method to handle ::Premium:

examples/multimethods/service_charge_3.clj

```
(defmulti service-charge (fn [acct] [(account-level acct) (:tag acct)]))
(defmethod service-charge [::acc/Basic ::acc/Checking]   [_] 25)
(defmethod service-charge [::acc/Basic ::acc/Savings]    [_] 10)
(defmethod service-charge [::acc/Premium ::acc/Account]  [_] 0)
```

At first glance, you may think that derive and isa? simply duplicate functionality that is already available to Clojure via Java inheritance. This is not the case. Java inheritance relationships are forever fixed at the moment you define a class. derived relationships can be created when you need them and can be *applied to existing objects without their knowledge or consent.* So, when you discover a useful relationship between existing objects, you can derive that relationship without touching the original objects' source code and without creating tiresome "wrapper" classes.

If the number of different ways you might define a multimethod has your head spinning, don't worry. In practice, most Clojure code uses multimethods sparingly. Let's take a look at some open source Clojure code to get a better idea of how multimethods are used.

8.5   When Should I Use Multimethods?

Multimethods are extremely flexible, and with that flexibility comes choices. How should you choose when to use multimethods, as opposed to some other technique? I approached this question from two directions, asking the following:

- Where do Clojure projects use multimethods?

- Where do Clojure projects *eschew* multimethods?

Let's begin with the first question, by reviewing multimethod use. The multimethod use in several open source Clojure projects is summarized in Figure 8.1, on the facing page.

Project	LoC	Dispatch By Class	Dispatch By Ad Hoc Type	Total
Clojure	5056	4	3	7
Clojure-contrib	3585	2	1	3
Compojure	1255	0	0	0
Webjure	850	0	0	0

Figure 8.1: MULTIMETHOD USE IN CLOJURE PROJECTS

The most striking thing is that multimethods are *rare*—about one per 1,000 lines of code in the projects sampled. So, don't worry that you are missing something important if you build a Clojure application with few, or no, multimethods. A Clojure program that defines no multimethods is not nearly as odd as an object-oriented program with no polymorphism.

Many multimethods dispatch on class. Dispatch-by-class is the easiest kind of dispatch to understand and implement. We already covered it in detail with the my-print example, so I will say no more about it here.

Clojure multimethods that dispatch on something other than class are so rare that we can discuss them individually. In the projects listed in the table, only the Clojure inspector and the clojure-contrib test-is libraries use unusual dispatch functions.

The Inspector

Clojure's inspector library uses Swing to create simple views of data. You can use it to get a tree view of your system properties:

```
(use '[clojure.inspector :only (inspect inspect-tree)])
(inspect-tree (System/getProperties))
```
⇒   #<JFrame ...>

inspect-tree returns (and displays) a JFrame with a tree view of anything that is treeish. So, you could also pass a nested map to inspect-tree:

```
(inspect-tree {:clojure {:creator "Rich" :runs-on-jvm true}})
```
⇒   #<JFrame ...>

Treeish things are made up of nodes that can answer two questions:

- Who are my children?

- Am I a leaf node?

The treeish concepts of "tree," "node," and "leaf" all sound like candidates for classes or interfaces in an object-oriented design. But the inspector does not work this way. Instead, it adds a "treeish" type system in an ad hoc way to existing types, using a dispatch function named collection-tag:

```
; from Clojure's clojure/inspector.clj
(defn collection-tag [x]
  (cond
    (instance? java.util.Map$Entry x) :entry
    (instance? clojure.lang.IPersistentMap x) :map
    (instance? java.util.Map x) :map
    (instance? clojure.lang.Sequential x) :seq
    :else :atom))
```

collection-tag returns one of the keywords :entry, :map, :seq, or :atom. These act as the type system for the treeish world. The collection-tag function is then used to dispatch three different multimethods that select specific implementations based on the treeish type system.

```
(defmulti is-leaf collection-tag)
(defmulti get-child
  (fn [parent index] (collection-tag parent)))
(defmulti get-child-count collection-tag)
; method implementations elided for brevity
```

The treeish type system is added around the existing Java type system. Existing objects do not have to *do* anything to become treeish; the inspector library does it for them. Treeish demonstrates a powerful style of reuse. You can discover new type relationships in existing code and take advantage of these relationships simply, without having to modify the original code.

test-is

The test-is library in clojure-contrib lets you write several different kinds of assertions using the is macro. You can assert that arbitrary functions are true. For example, 10 is not a string:

```
(use :reload '[clojure.contrib.test-is :only (is)])
(is (string? 10))

FAIL in  (:12)
expected: (string? 10)
  actual: (not (string? 10))
⇒    false
```

Although you can use an arbitrary function, is knows about a few specific functions and provides more detailed error messages. For example, you can check that a string is not an instance? of Collection:

```
(is (instance? java.util.Collection "foo"))
```

```
FAIL in  (:15)
expected: (instance? java.util.Collection "foo")
  actual: java.lang.String
⇒    false
```

is also knows about =. Verify that power does not equal wisdom.

```
(is (= "power" "wisdom"))
⇒    java.lang.AssertionError:
     "power" is "power" but should be "wisdom"
```

Internally, is uses a multimethod named assert-expr, which dispatches not on the type but the actual *identity* of its first argument:

```
(defmulti assert-expr (fn [form message] (first form)))
```

Since the first argument is a symbol representing what function to check, this amounts to yet another ad hoc type system. This time, there are three types: =, instance?, and everything else.

The various assert-expr methods add specific error messages associated with different functions you might call from is. Because multimethods are open ended, you can add your own assert-expr methods with improved error messages for other functions you frequently pass to is.

Counterexamples

As you saw in Section 8.4, *Creating Ad Hoc Taxonomies*, on page 232, you can often use multimethods to hoist branches that are based on type out of the main flow of your functions. To find counterexamples where multimethods should not be used, I looked through Clojure's core to find type branches that had *not* been hoisted to multimethods.

A simple example is Clojure's class, which is a null-safe wrapper for the underlying Java getClass. Minus comments and metadata, class is as follows:

```
(defn class [x]
  (if (nil? x) x (. x (getClass))))
```

You could write your own version of class as a multimethod by dispatching on identity:

examples/multimethods.clj

```
(defmulti my-class identity)
(defmethod my-class nil [_] nil)
(defmethod my-class :default [x] (.getClass x))
```

Any nil-check could be rewritten this way. But I find the original class function easier to read than the multimethod version. This is a nice "exception that proves the rule." Even though class branches on type, the branching version is easier to read.

Use the following general rules when deciding whether to create a function or a multimethod:

- If a function branches based on a type, or multiple types, consider a multimethod.

- Types are whatever you discover them to be. They do not have to be explicit Java classes or data tags.

- You should be able to interpret the dispatch value of a defmethod without having to refer to the defmulti.

- Do not use multimethods merely to handle optional arguments or recursion.

When in doubt, try writing the function in both styles, and pick the one that seems more readable.

As luck would have it, the Lancet sample application needs a multimethod—and not just a boring single dispatch either. Lancet needs an oddball function that dispatches on the class of two different arguments. Let's go build it.

8.6 Adding Type Coercions to Lancet

In Section 3.5, *Adding Ant Projects and Tasks to Lancet*, on page 85, I glossed over an irritant in Lancet's Ant integration. When you create an Ant task, you have to know the types of any properties used to configure the task. For example, the dir property of mkdir is not a String:

```
(.setDir mkdir-task "sample-dir")
⇒    java.lang.ClassCastException
```

Instead, you have to know that the dir property is a File:

```
(.setDir mkdir-task (java.io.File. "sample-dir"))
⇒    nil
```

If you spend time trying out various other Ant tasks in Lancet, you will see that the problem is serious. Furthermore, Ant does *not* have this problem, even though Ant task properties usually begin their life as strings in an XML document. Ant must know how to convert strings into other types on demand. Lancet will need to do something similar.

Let's create a generic coercion system for Lancet. To coerce an argument from one type to another, you need to know two things: the type of the source and the type of the destination. Create a coerce multimethod that dispatches on a destination *class* and a source *instance*:

`lancet/step_5_repl.clj`

```
(defmulti coerce
  (fn [dest-class src-inst] [dest-class (class src-inst)]))
```

The destination is listed first for consistency with Clojure functions like cast.

Now, you can write a coerce method that coerces Strings to Files:

`lancet/step_5_repl.clj`

```
(defmethod coerce [java.io.File String] [_ str]
  (java.io.File. str))
```

This is very clean. With almost no noise, it says to the reader: "in order to make a File from a String, you must call the File constructor." Make sure that it works:

```
(coerce java.io.File "foo")
⇒    #<File foo>
```

Not every coercion will be so simple. For example, Ant has its own notion of truth. The strings "on", "yes", and "true" are all true, regardless of case. Create a coercion that enforces this:

`lancet/step_5_repl.clj`

```
(defmethod coerce [Boolean/TYPE String] [_ str]
  (contains? #{"on" "yes" "true"} (.toLowerCase str)))
```

Make sure that it works:

```
(coerce Boolean/TYPE "no")
⇒    false

(coerce Boolean/TYPE "yes")
⇒    true
```

```
(coerce Boolean/TYPE "TRUE")
```
⇒   true

Even though the last defmethod looks Ant-specific, the mechanism is general. Different applications can mix and match coercions to suit their needs. If truth works a little differently in the valley, no problem:

```
(defmethod coerce [Boolean/TYPE String] [_ str]
  (contains? #{"totally" "way"} (.toLowerCase str)))
```

You are going to want to pass all Ant property setters through the coercion mechanism, so as a last step create a default coercion. This coercion simply verifies that the type is already compatible with the destination by calling Clojure's cast:

> lancet/step_5_repl.clj

```
(defmethod coerce :default [dest-cls obj] (cast dest-cls obj))
```

Make sure this works by trying a few sensible and insensible coercions:

```
(coerce Comparable "hello")
```
⇒   "hello"

```
(coerce java.io.File (java.util.Random.))
```
⇒   java.lang.ClassCastException

Now let's add coercion support to Lancet's set-property. You will need to start with the code from Section 4.6, *Lancet Step 2: Setting Properties*, on page 125. In that code, set-properties is defined as follows:

> lancet/snippets.clj

```
Line 1  (use '[clojure.contrib.except :only (throw-if)])
     2  (defn set-property! [inst prop value]
     3    (let [pd (property-descriptor inst prop)]
     4      (throw-if (nil? pd) (str "No such property " prop))
     5      (.invoke (.getWriteMethod pd) inst (into-array [value]))))
```

On line 5, you need to coerce the value before invoking the property write method. coerce expects a destination class, but Lancet currently provides a property-writing Method. You can get the destination class from that Method with a little Java reflection:

> lancet/step_5_repl.clj

```
(defn get-property-class [write-method]
  (first (.getParameterTypes write-method)))
```

Next, enhance set-property! to use coerce.

The expression that calls invoke is getting fairly complex, so introduce a let of write-method and dest-class to make set-property more readable:

`lancet/step_5_repl.clj`

```
(defn set-property! [inst prop value]
  (let [pd (property-descriptor inst prop)]
    (throw-if (nil? pd) (str "No such property " prop))
    (let [write-method (.getWriteMethod pd)
          dest-class (get-property-class write-method)]
      (.invoke
       write-method inst (into-array [(coerce dest-class value)])))))
```

You can test the coercions by instantiating Ant tasks and passing in plain old strings. For example, create a mkdir task, and pass in dir as a string.

```
(def mkfoo
 (instantiate-task ant-project "mkdir" {:dir "foo"}))
-> #'user/mkfoo

(.execute mkfoo)
     [mkdir] Created dir:/lancet-test/foo
```

The completed code for this section is listed in Section 8.6, *Lancet Step 5: Type Coercions*. As you explore Ant, you may find other coercions, but Ant task integration is now almost complete. Lancet's Ant integration can now do the following:

- Create any Ant task

- Set arbitrary Java properties

- Define common coercions for property setters

The codebase size for Ant task integration is about fifty lines.

Lancet Step 5: Type Coercions

`lancet/step_5_complete.clj`

```
(ns lancet.step-5-complete
    (:use clojure.contrib.except)
    (:import (java.beans Introspector)))

(defmulti coerce
  (fn [dest-class src-inst] [dest-class (class src-inst)]))

(defmethod coerce [java.io.File String] [_ str]
  (java.io.File. str))
```

```clojure
(defmethod coerce [Boolean/TYPE String] [_ str]
  (contains? #{"on" "yes" "true"} (.toLowerCase str)))

(defmethod coerce :default [dest-cls obj] (cast dest-cls obj))

(def
 #^{:doc "Dummy ant project to keep Ant tasks happy"}
 ant-project
 (let [proj (org.apache.tools.ant.Project.)
       logger (org.apache.tools.ant.NoBannerLogger.)]
   (doto logger
     (.setMessageOutputLevel org.apache.tools.ant.Project/MSG_INFO)
     (.setOutputPrintStream System/out)
     (.setErrorPrintStream System/err))
   (doto proj
     (.init)
     (.addBuildListener logger))))

(defn property-descriptor [inst prop-name]
  (first
    (filter #(= (name prop-name) (.getName %))
            (.getPropertyDescriptors
              (Introspector/getBeanInfo (class inst))))))

(defn get-property-class [write-method]
  (first (.getParameterTypes write-method)))

(defn set-property! [inst prop value]
  (let [pd (property-descriptor inst prop)]
    (throw-if (nil? pd) (str "No such property " prop))
    (let [write-method (.getWriteMethod pd)
          dest-class (get-property-class write-method)]
      (.invoke
        write-method inst (into-array [(coerce dest-class value)])))))

(defn set-properties! [inst prop-map]
  (doseq [[k v] prop-map] (set-property! inst k v)))

(defn instantiate-task [project name props]
  (let [task (.createTask project name)]
    (throw-if (nil? task) (str "No task named " name))
    (doto task
      (.init)
      (.setProject project)
      (set-properties! props))))
```

8.7 Wrapping Up

Multimethods support arbitrary dispatch. Usually multimethods work based on type relationships. Sometimes these types are formal, as in Java classes. Other times they are informal and ad hoc and emerge from the properties of objects in the system.

With multimethods under your belt, you now know the core of Clojure, and it is time to build some more substantial examples using third-party libraries.

Chapter 9
Clojure in the Wild

Now that you have learned the basics of the Clojure language, it is time for you to begin using Clojure in your own projects. But as you run out the door to start work on your killer Clojure app, you realize that you do not yet know how to use Clojure for everyday programming tasks:

- How do I write unit tests for my Clojure code?

- How do I access relational data from Clojure?

- How do I build a simple web application in Clojure?

These questions do not have a simple answer because there are *so many choices*. With Clojure, you have access to the entire world of Java APIs for data access, XML, GUI development, web development, testing, graphics, and more. In addition, idiomatic Clojure libraries are beginning to appear.

There are so many choices, and innovation is proceeding so swiftly, that I will not attempt to cover all the possible choices. Instead, I will simply open Pandora's box and show you a few *possible* answers to the earlier questions. In this chapter, you will learn how to do the following:

- Build unit tests with the test-is library

- Access relational data with JDBC and Clojure's sql library

- Create web applications with the Compojure framework

These examples demonstrate Clojure's value in a wide variety of settings and should whet your appetite for the exciting world of Clojure development.

9.1 Automating Tests

Clojure makes it easy to test your code in the REPL. But for any nontrivial codebase, manual testing at the REPL is not enough. You should also have a set of *self-validating* tests. Self-validating tests report success or failure, so you do not have to interpret results manually by reading off values at the REPL. This section introduces two testing libraries: the test function in the Clojure core and clojure.contrib.test-is.

Test with :test

Clojure attaches tests to functions with :test metadata. To see :test in action, consider the index-of-any function introduced in Section 2.6, *Where's My for Loop?*, on page 50. The Java version includes the following examples in the method comment:

```
StringUtils.indexOfAny(null, *)              = -1
StringUtils.indexOfAny("", *)                = -1
StringUtils.indexOfAny(*, null)              = -1
StringUtils.indexOfAny(*, [])                = -1
StringUtils.indexOfAny("zzabyycdxx",['z','a']) = 0
StringUtils.indexOfAny("zzabyycdxx",['b','y']) = 3
StringUtils.indexOfAny("aba", ['z'])         = -1
```

In Clojure, you can add these tests as metadata on the index-of-any function:

```
examples/index_of_any.clj
(defn index-filter [pred coll]
  (when pred (for [[idx elt] (indexed coll) :when (pred elt)] idx)))

(defn
  #^{:test (fn []
            (assert (nil? (index-of-any #{\a} nil)))
            (assert (nil? (index-of-any #{\a} "")))
            (assert (nil? (index-of-any nil "foo")))
            (assert (nil? (index-of-any #{} "foo")))
            (assert (zero? (index-of-any #{\z \a} "zzabyycdxx")))
            (assert (= 3 (index-of-any #{\b \y} "zzabyycdxx")))
            (assert (nil? (index-of-any #{\z} "aba"))))}
  index-of-any
  [pred coll]
  (first (index-filter pred coll)))
```

The :test metadata key takes as its value a test function. In the previous example, the test function exercises index-of-any, using (assert expr) to test that various exprs are true.

You can run the tests from the REPL using the test function:

```
(test a-var)
```

test looks up the test function in a-var's :test metadata and runs the test. Note that test takes a var, not a symbol. Try testing index-of-any:

```
(test #'index-of-any)
```
⇒   :ok

To see what happens when a test fails, create a test with an assertion that is not true:

examples/exploring.clj
```
(defn
  #^{:test (fn []
             (assert (nil? (busted))))}
  busted [] "busted")
```

```
(test #'busted)
```
⇒   java.lang.Exception: Assert failed: (nil? (busted))

:test is simple and easy to use, and it keeps your tests as close as possible to the code they test. However, most developers are accustomed to frameworks that keep tests separate from code. Clojure-contrib provides this via the test-is library.

Test with test-is

Stuart Sierra's test-is library lets you write tests with the deftest macro:

```
(clojure.contrib.test-is/deftest testname & forms)
```

The test forms make assertions via the is macro:

```
(clojure.contrib.test-is/is form message?)
```

form is any predicate, and message is an optional error message. You could begin testing index-of-any thusly:

examples/test/index_of_any.clj
```
(ns examples.test.index-of-any
    (:use examples.index-of-any clojure.contrib.test-is))

(deftest test-index-of-any-with-nil-args
  (is (nil? (index-of-any #{\a} nil)))
  (is (nil? (index-of-any nil "foo"))))

(deftest test-index-of-any-with-empty-args
  (is (nil? (index-of-any #{\a} "")))
  (is (nil? (index-of-any #{} "foo"))))
```

```
(deftest test-index-of-any-with-match
  (is (zero? (index-of-any #{\z \a} "zzabyycdxx")))
  (is (= 3 (index-of-any #{\b \y} "zzabyycdxx"))))

(deftest test-index-of-any-without-match
  (is (nil? (index-of-any #{\z} "aba"))))
```

In the previous section's :test example, the test function contained seven assertions. Here, those seven assertions are divided into four different tests. This is a matter of taste. Since deftest gives you the chance to create more than one test for the same function, it encourages you to group smaller sets of assertions under meaningful test names.

You can run all tests in a group of namespaces with run-tests:

```
(clojure.contrib.test-is/run-tests & namespaces)
```

If you do not specify any namespaces, run-tests will default to the current namespace. Assuming you entered the index-of-any tests at the REPL, you could run them with this:

```
(run-tests)
Testing user

Ran 4 tests 7 assertions.
0 failures, 0 exceptions.
```

To see a test fail, create a test with a failing assertion:

examples/test/fail.clj

```
(deftest test-that-demonstrates-failure
  (is (= 5 (+ 2 2))))

Testing user

FAIL in (test-that-demonstrates-failure) (NO_SOURCE_FILE:5)
expected: (= 5 (+ 2 2))
  actual: (not= 5 4)

Ran 1 tests containing 1 assertions.
1 failures, 0 errors.
```

Unlike assert, is can also take an optional error message. When a test fails, is appends the optional error message after the generic error message:

examples/test/fail.clj

```
(deftest test-that-demonstrates-error-message
  (is (= 3 Math/PI) "PI is an integer!?"))
```

```
Testing user

FAIL in (test-that-demonstrates-error-message) (NO_SOURCE_FILE:2)
PI is an integer!?
expected: (= 3 Math/PI)
  actual: (not= 3 3.141592653589793)
```

The is macro can, of course, also be used inside a :test function.

It is particularly important that tests cover less-used paths through code, such as error handling. To this end, you can use the (is (thrown?)) form to test that an exception occurred:

examples/test/exploring.clj

```
(deftest test-divide-by-zero
  (is (thrown? ArithmeticException (/ 5 0))))
```

thrown? is an example of a custom assert expression. You can add your own assert expressions to test-is; see the source code for the assert-expr multimethod for details.

The example code for this book is tested using test-is. The tests demonstrate several features that are not covered here; see the examples/test and lancet/test directories for more examples using test-is.

Test However You Want

Clojure's test capabilities are lightweight and easy to use. What if you want something that integrates with an existing build system and runs on your continuous integration box?

If you have an existing Java infrastructure, another answer is "Test with whatever framework you already use." Clojure code is Java code.

All Clojure sequences implement Java collection interfaces. All Clojure functions implement Callable and Runnable. So, you can write your tests with any Java-compatible test framework: JUnit, TestNG, or even EasyB or JTestR. Good luck, and please consider open sourcing any reusable pieces you invent along the way.

Next, let's take a look at how Clojure can access relational data.

9.2 Data Access

Stephen C. Gilardi's clojure.contrib.sql provides convenience wrappers for accessing a database using Java Database Connectivity (JDBC).[1] You do not need any prior experience with JDBC to work through the examples in this section. However, sql is a thin wrapper, and on a real project you would need to learn JDBC.

The example in this section is a database of code snippets. To store the snippets, you will use the HSQLDB database. You will need to add lib/hsqldb.jar to your classpath when launching Clojure. (The REPL launch scripts bin/repl.sh and bin\repl.bat include lib/hsqldb.jar for you.)

The entry point for sql is the with-connection macro:

```
(clojure.contrib.sql/with-connection db-spec & body)
```

The db-spec contains connection information, which is then passed to JDBC's DriverManager. The body is a set of forms. with-connection will open a JDBC Connection, execute the forms in body, and then close the connection.

Define a db var to hold the database connection specification, which you will need throughout this example:

examples/snippet.clj

```
; replace "snippet-db" with a full path!
(def db {:classname "org.hsqldb.jdbcDriver"
         :subprotocol "hsqldb"
         :subname "file:snippet-db"})
```

The :subname tells HSQLDB to store the database in filenames based on snippet-db. Make sure you change the name snippet-db to a valid full path on your local filesystem so that various examples in this chapter will all access the same database.

Now you are ready to create the snippets table. The create-table function creates a table:

```
(clojure.contrib.sql/create-table name & column-specs)
```

The name names the table, and a column-spec is an array describing a column in the table. Create a function named create-snippets that

---

1. For years, JDBC was officially a trademark, not an acronym. As of this writing, both Sun and Wikipedia have bowed to common sense and acknowledge that it stands for Java Database Connectivity.

creates a snippets table with a primary key id, a string body, and a datetime created_at:

`examples/snippet.clj`

```
(use 'clojure.contrib.sql)
(defn create-snippets []
  (create-table :snippets
    [:id :int "IDENTITY" "PRIMARY KEY"]
    [:body :varchar "NOT NULL"]
    [:created_at :datetime]))
```

Try to create the snippets table from the REPL:

(create-snippets)
⇒ java.lang.Exception: no current database connection

This is where with-connection comes into play. In order to create the table, call create-snippets from within with-connection, specifying db as your database:

(with-connection db (create-snippets))
⇒ (0)

The return value of (0) indicates success. Failure would cause an exception, which you can see by trying to create the same table again:

(with-connection db (create-snippets))
⇒ java.lang.Exception: transaction rolled back: failed batch

Calling create-snippets a second time fails because the table already exists.

Now you are ready to add some rows to the snippets table. The insert-values function adds rows:

`(clojure.contrib.sql/insert-values table column-names & values)`

column-names is a vector of column names, and each value is a vector of column values.

Create an insert-snippets function that adds a few sample snippets, specifying a body and setting the created_at to the current time.

`examples/snippet.clj`

```
(defn now [] (java.sql.Timestamp. (.getTime (java.util.Date.))))
(defn insert-snippets []
  (let [timestamp (now)]
    (seq
      (insert-values :snippets
        [:body :created_at]
        ["(println :boo)" timestamp]
        ["(defn foo [] 1)" timestamp]))))
```

The now function gets the current time in a JDBC-friendly format. The let calls now only once, guaranteeing that both records have the same created_at value.

The entire insert-values call is wrapped in a seq to convert the return value (a Java array of insertion counts) into a REPL-friendly Clojure sequence. Insert the records:

```
(with-connection db (insert-snippets))
⇒    (1 1)
```

The (1 1) indicates that insert-snippets issued two SQL statements, each of which successfully updated one row.

Now that you have some rows in the table, you are ready to issue a query. The with-query-results macro issues some sql and then executes the forms in body with results bound to a sequence of the results:

```
(with-query-results results sql & body)
```

Use with-query-results to create a print-snippets function that simply prints all the snippets:

examples/snippet.clj

```
(defn print-snippets []
  (with-query-results res ["select * from snippets"]
    (println res)))
```

Use print-snippets to print the contents of the snippets table:

```
(with-connection db (print-snippets))
| ({:id 0, :body (println :boo),
|    :created_at #<Timestamp 2009-01-03 11:40:19.985>}
|   {:id 1, :body (defn foo [] 1),
|    :created_at #<Timestamp 2009-01-03 11:40:19.985>})
```

What if you wanted to hold on to the snippets, such as to use them as the model to back some kind of user interface? with-query-results returns the last form in its body, so you might expect to write select-snippets like this:

examples/snippet.clj

```
; Broken!
(defn select-snippets []
  (with-query-results res ["select * from snippets"] res))
```

But it won't work:

```
(with-connection db (select-snippets))
⇒    java.sql.SQLException: No data is available
```

The problem is ordering of execution. select-snippets returns a lazy sequence over the JDBC ResultSet. But JDBC results can *themselves* be lazy. So, neither Clojure nor JDBC realizes the result set inside with-connection. By the time the REPL tries to print the snippets, both the connection and the ResultSet are closed.

To get access to the snippets outside of a database connection, realize them with a doall. This will spin through the results, caching them in the Clojure sequence. The connection and result set can then safely close, freeing precious database resources. Everyone is happy:

examples/snippet.clj
```
(defn select-snippets []
  (with-connection db
    (with-query-results res ["select * from snippets"] (doall res))))
```

Verify that the improved select-snippets works:

(select-snippets)
```
⇒  ({:id 0, :body (println :boo),
     :created_at #<Timestamp 2009-01-03 11:40:19.985>}
    {:id 1, :body (defn foo [] 1),
     :created_at #<Timestamp 2009-01-03 11:40:19.985>})
```

The idiom of realizing a result set is common enough to deserve its own function. Create a sql-query function that runs a query and then realizes its result set with doall:

examples/snippet.clj
```
(defn sql-query [q]
  (with-query-results res q (doall res)))
```

Verify that sql-query works by selecting the body of all snippets:

(with-connection db (sql-query ["select body from snippets"]))
```
⇒  ({:body "(println :boo)"} {:body "(defn foo [] 1)"})
```

You now have almost everything you need for the data layer of a simple code snippet application. The one remaining detail is a function that can insert a new snippet *and return the ID of the new snippet*. This code is HSQLDB-specific, and I will spare you the exploration required. Implement the last-created-id method as follows:

examples/snippet.clj
```
(defn last-created-id
  "Extract the last created id. Must be called in a transaction
   that performed an insert. Expects HSQLDB return structure of
   the form [{:@p0 id}]."
  []
  (first (vals (first (sql-query ["CALL IDENTITY()"])))))
```

To use last-created-id, place it at the end of a transaction that inserts a snippet. sql provides the transaction macro for this purpose:

```
(clojure.contrib.sql/transaction & body)
```

Use transaction, plus your previously defined now and last-created-id functions, to implement insert-snippet:

examples/snippet.clj

```
(defn insert-snippet [body]
  (with-connection db
    (transaction
      (insert-values :snippets
        [:body :created_at]
        [body (now)])
      (last-created-id))))
```

If you call insert-snippet multiple times, you will see the returned ID increase:

```
(insert-snippet "(+ 1 1)")
```
⇒   4

```
(insert-snippet "(ref true)")
```
⇒   5

You now have a minimal library for adding and reviewing snippets.

Other Library Options

If you are accustomed to using a persistence framework such as Hibernate,[2] iBATIS,[3] or ActiveRecord,[4] then sql will probably seem very low-level. That's because it is. If you want a higher-level tool, you have two options:

- Use a Java framework such a Hibernate or iBatis from Clojure.
- Use one of the emerging Clojure-specific persistence libraries.

The Java frameworks are well-documented elsewhere. Be careful in choosing one of these frameworks for a Clojure app. Most of them will bring *a lot* of Java flavor with them. In particular, they will tend to use Java classes to represent database tables, instead of simple maps. They will also bring in XML and/or Java annotations for configuration. None of these are idiomatic Clojure.

---

2. http://www.hibernate.org/
3. http://ibatis.apache.org/
4. http://ar.rubyonrails.com/

The pure-Clojure persistence frameworks are in pre-beta development at the time of this writing. You may want to look some of the following:

clj-record

clj-record[5] is John D. Hume's port of ActiveRecord to Clojure. It currently supports a subset of ActiveRecord's relationships and validations. Here's an example from the unit tests:

```
(ns clj-record.test.model.manufacturer
  (:require [clj-record.core :as cljrec]))

(cljrec/init-model
  (has-many products)
  (validates name "empty!" #(not (empty? %)))
  (validates name "starts with whitespace!" #(not (re-find #"^\s" %)))
  (validates name "ends with whitespace!" #(not (re-find #"\s$" %)))
  (validates grade "negative!" #(or (nil? %) (>= % 0))))
```

clojureql

clojureql[6] is Lau B. Jensen and Meikel Brandmeyer's Clojure DSL for SQL. This example is from demo.clj:

```
(execute
 (sql
  (query [id name] developers.employees
         (and (> id 5)
              (< id 8)))))
⇒  {:name Jack D., :id 6}
   {:name Mike, :id 7}
```

Clojure is a very good fit for SQL, providing the expressiveness of SQL embedded in the full Clojure language.

9.3 Web Development

James Reeves' Compojure[7] is a Clojure web framework inspired by Ruby's Sinatra.[8] Here we will use Compojure and the Jetty web server to build a user interface for creating and viewing code snippets.

Compojure has a number of JAR dependencies. The sample code for the book includes recent versions of these JARs, and the launch scripts bin/snippet.sh (*nix) and bin/snippet.bat (Windows) will launch Clojure

---

5. http://github.com/duelinmarkers/clj-record
6. http://github.com/Lau-of-DK/clojureql
7. http://github.com/weavejester/compojure
8. http://sinatra.rubyforge.org/

with all the necessary JAR files on the classpath. Try running the appropriate launch script from the root directory of the sample code:

```
bin/snippet.sh
TODO: implement reader/snippet_server.clj!
user=>
```

Notice that the launch script gives you a REPL so that you can try things interactively. As you work through this section, add your code to the file reader/snippet_server.clj. For your first change, remove the line that prints the TODO message. To test your change, reload the file at the REPL with this:

```
(use :reload 'reader.snippet-server)
```
⇒   nil

Your next task is to create some simple routes with defroutes:

```
(compojure/defroutes name doc & routes)
```

A route routes HTTP requests to a Clojure form and looks like this:

```
(HTTP-VERB url-pattern body)
```

A handler can do something as simple as returning a string:

```
(GET "/hello" "<h1>Hello!</h1>")
```

Or a handler can call arbitrary code, possibly passing along information from the request:

```
(GET "/:id" (show-snippet (params :id)))
```

Most servlets will want a catchall handler for invalid requests. Compojure provides page-not-found:

```
(compojure/page-not-found)
```

By default, page-not-found will set the HTTP status code to 404 and return a file located at public/404.html.

Using defroutes, add code to reader/snippet_server.clj to create two routes for the snippet-app. The app should return pong for a GET of /ping and a 404 for anything else.

```
examples/server/step_1.clj
```
```
(use 'compojure)
(defroutes snippet-app
  "Create and view snippets."
  (GET "/ping" "pong")

  (ANY "*"
    (page-not-found)))
```

ANY matches all HTTP verbs, and * matches all URLs. Compojure checks handlers in the order they are declared, so it is important for the catchall handler to come last.

Now, you can run your snippet-app with run-server:

```
(compojure/run-server options? & paths-and-servlets)
```

The options specify things such as the :port number, and the paths-and-servlets is a sequence alternating between paths and the servlets that serve them. Use run-server to run a server on port 8080, handling all paths:

```
examples/server/step_1.clj
```

```
(run-server {:port 8080}
  "/*" (servlet snippet-app))
```

You should see a console message from Jetty:

```
| 2009-05-01 INFO:  Logging to STDERR ...
| 2009-05-01 INFO:  jetty-6.1.14
| 2009-05-01 INFO:  Started SocketConnector@0.0.0.0:8080
⇒   nil
```

While the server is running, its log traffic will be interleaved with your REPL input and output. I find this convenient, because everything is in one place. If the server log traffic obscures your REPL prompt, simply hit ⎡Enter⎤, and you will get a new prompt.

Test the server using the browser of your choice. http://localhost:8080/ping should return pong, and any other name should return Page Not Found.

Building HTML

Now that you have a simple servlet in place, let's build an HTML form for entering a new snippet and some HTML for displaying a snippet. The text-area function builds an HTML textarea:

```
(compojure/text-area options? name value?)
```

Compojure converts the options map into attributes on the textarea tag. The most important attributes, name and value, have their own dedicated parameters. Other Compojure HTML functions duplicate this idiom, exposing the most important attributes as explicit parameters but always providing the options for less frequently used attributes.

It is trivial to test Compojure's HTML functions, because they simply emit a tree of vectors and maps that correspond to the eventual HTML.

Try calling text-area from the REPL:

```
(use 'compojure)
(text-area "body")
⇒   [:textarea {:id "body", :name "body"} nil]
```

Compojure's html function will convert this internal representation into actual HTML:

```
(compojure/html & trees)
```

To see the actual HTML of your textarea, simply println its html:

```
(println (html (text-area "body")))
<textarea id="body" name="body"></textarea>
```

To create a form for users to input snippets, you will need two more Compojure helpers: form-to and submit-button:

```
(compojure/form-to handler & body)
```

```
(compojure/submit-button options? & text)
```

The handler is a vector containing an HTTP verb and a URL, which will be the target of the form. The body forms build the internals of the form. submit-button is a trivial helper, with a signature analogous to text-area's.

Create a new-snippet function in reader/snippet_server.clj that creates a new snippet form. Since snippets are the primary purpose of the application, new-snippet can post back to the root URL of the app:

examples/server/step_2.clj

```
(defn new-snippet []
  (html
    (form-to [:post "/"]
      (text-area {:rows 20 :cols 73} "body")
      [:br]
      (submit-button "Save"))))
```

Notice that you can safely mix helper functions like text-area and submit-button with plain old vectors like [:br]. This is made possible by Compojure's intermediate tree-of-vectors representation.

Test new-snippet at the REPL:

```
(use :reload 'reader.snippet-server)
(println (new-snippet))
| <form action="/" method="POST">
|   <textarea cols="73" id="body" name="body" rows="20"></textarea>
|   <br />
|   <input type="submit" value="Save" />
| </form>
⇒   nil
```

Next, create a show-snippet function that shows an existing snippet. show-snippet should call out to the select-snippet function described in Section 9.2, *Data Access*, on page 252 and then show the body and created-at fields of the snippet, each in their own div. Since the body is code, also wrap it in a pre/code pair:

examples/server/step_2.clj

```
(defn show-snippet [id]
  (let [snippet (select-snippet id)]
    (html
      [:div [:pre [:code (:body snippet)]]]
      [:div (:created_at snippet)])))
```

You do not need any new helper functions for show-snippet, because the div, pre, and code tags are just plain old HTML.

Test show-snippet by creating a new snippet and then showing it:

```
(use :reload 'reader.snippet-server 'examples.snippet)
(insert-snippet "hello")
```
⇒
```
   5
```

```
(println (show-snippet 5))
| <div>
|   <pre>
|     <code>hello</code>
|   </pre>
| </div>
| <div>
|   2009-01-04 12:47:08.193
| </div>
```
⇒
```
   nil
```

As you can see, Compojure's HTML library is easy to use. Better yet, it is cleanly separated from the other parts of Compojure and can be tested at the REPL without going through the entire web stack.

Posts and Redirects

The last helper function you need to write is something that creates new snippets. create-snippet will be a little different from new-snippet and show-snippet, because it will not return HTML. Instead, after an HTTP POST, it will *redirect* the caller to a different URL. Compojure provides redirect-to for this purpose:

```
(compojure/redirect-to location)
```

Create a function named create-snippet that takes the body of a new snippet and calls insert-snippet to add it to the database. create-snippet should redirect to the ID of the new snippet if insert-snippet succeeds and redirect to the top-level URL if insert-snippet fails:

examples/server/step_2.clj

```
(defn create-snippet [body]
  (if-let [id (insert-snippet body)]
    (redirect-to (str "/" id))
    (redirect-to "/")))
```

Test create-snippet from the REPL:

```
(create-snippet "this is too easy")
⇒   [302 {"Location" "/6"}]
```

Instead of returning an HTML string, redirect-to returns a vector with an HTTP status code, plus a map of data that is used to set the response header.

Now that you have created the "action functions" for creating and displaying snippets, you need to associate them with your servlet. Add the following handlers to your snippet-servlet definition:

examples/server/step_2.clj

```
(GET "/"
   (new-snippet))

(GET "/:id"
   (show-snippet (params :id)))

(POST "/"
   (create-snippet (:body params)))
```

Make sure you add these handlers before the catchall ANY handler. On every request, params is bound to a map of the query parameters, so (:body params) extracts the body posted by the user. Also, (params :id) returns the part of the URL that matches the :id in /:id. Restart the snippet REPL and try creating a few snippets!

Finishing Touches

To put a little polish on the snippet application, let's add a few nice-to-haves: layout and code highlighting.

Across a web application, pages often share a common layout: Java-Scripts, style sheets, wrapper divs, and so on. Snippet pages should have the following common layout elements:

- The title should be placed in a title element in the header and in an h2 in the body.

- The header should include Dan Webb's code-highlighter.js,[9] plus Clojure-specific highlighting rules in clojure.js.[10] These files are included in the public/javascripts directory of the sample code.
- The header should also include code-highlighter.css from the public/stylesheets directory so that you can see colors for the styles that code-highlighter.js adds to code.

Compojure's include-js and include-css functions will create the appropriate HTML for including JavaScript and CSS files:

```
(compojure/include-js & scripts)
```

```
(compojure/include-css & scripts)
```

Create a layout function that takes a title and some body forms and lays out a page with the common features described earlier:

```
examples/server/step_3.clj
(defn layout [title & body]
  (html
    [:head
      [:title title]
      (include-js "/public/javascripts/code-highlighter.js"
                  "/public/javascripts/clojure.js")
      (include-css "/public/stylesheets/code-highlighter.css")]
    [:body
      [:h2 title]
      body]))
```

Again, Compojure's design makes it trivial to test layout from the REPL:

```
(println (layout "Sample Title" "Sample Page"))
| <head>
|   <title>Sample Title</title>
|   <script src="/public/javascripts/code-highlighter.js"
|           type="text/javascript"></script>
|   <script src="/public/javascripts/clojure.js"
|           type="text/javascript"></script>
|   <link href="/public/stylesheets/code-highlighter.css" rel="stylesheet"
|         type="text/css" />
| </head>
| <body>
|   <h2>Sample Title</h2>
|   Sample Page
| </body>
⇒   nil
```

---

9. http://svn.danwebb.net/external/CodeHighlighter/

10. I could have sworn I got this file from http://groups.google.com.sg/group/clojure/files, but it is not there any longer.

Update new-snippet to use the custom layout instead of the generic html
to build the page:

examples/server/step_3.clj

```
(defn new-snippet []
  (layout "Create a Snippet"
    (form-to [:post "/"]
      (text-area {:rows 20 :cols 73} "body")
      [:br]
      (submit-button "Save"))))
```

Update show-snippet in similar fashion. Also, change the :code keyword
to :code.clojure:

examples/server/step_3.clj

```
(defn show-snippet [id]
  (layout (str "Snippet " id)
    (let [snippet (select-snippet id)]
      (html
        [:div [:pre [:code.clojure (:body snippet)]]]
        [:div (:created_at snippet)]))))
```

:code.clojure is a bit of syntactic sugar for adding class attributes to an
HTML element. You can test this at the REPL:

```
(println (html [:code.clojure]))
| <code class="clojure" />
    nil
```
⇒

The highlighter of the snippet application uses the CSS class to select
language-specific highlighting rules.

There is one last change you need to make: actually serving the Java-
Script and CSS files. Compojure provides the serve-file function for serving static files:

```
(compojure/serve-file root? path)
```

If root is not specified, then files are served relative to the public directory. Not coincidentally, I placed the JavaScript and CSS files in public. Add the following handler just before the catchall handler in your
servlet definition:

examples/server/step_3.clj

```
(GET "/public/*"
  (or (serve-file (params :*)) :next))
```

The (params :*) extracts the filename from the URL pattern /public/*.
(Yes, :* is a legal keyword.)

What happens if a file is not found? serve-file returns nil. The or form then returns :next, which directs Compojure to continue searching for a matching handler. The catchall handler will then report that the page was not found.

Make sure that you have the most recent version of your reader.snippet-server loaded and try creating some snippets. You should now see titles on every page, and the snippets should have syntax coloring.

The completed code for the snippet server is in the file code/examples/server/complete.clj.

You can run the completed example with the following commands. On Windows:

```
bin\snippet-solution.bat
```

On *nix:

```
bin/snippet-solution.sh
```

Weighing in at less than 50 lines, the snippet server provides the entire Controller and View layers for the snippet application.

9.4 Farewell

Congratulations. You have come a long way in a short time. You have learned the many ideas that combine to make Clojure great: Lisp, Java, functional programming, and explicit concurrency. And in this chapter, you have seen a brief sample of how the Clojure community is using Clojure for a variety of tasks: automated testing, data access, and web development.

We have only scratched the surface of Clojure's great potential, and I hope you will take the next step and become an active part of the Clojure community. Join the mailing list.[11] Hang out on IRC.[12] The Clojure community is friendly and welcoming, and we would love to hear from you.

---

11. http://groups.google.com/group/clojure
12. #clojure

Editor Support

Editor support for Clojure is evolving rapidly, so some of the information here may be out-of-date by the time you read this. Check the archives of the mailing list[1] for recent announcements.

Clojure code is concise and expressive. As a result, editor support is not quite as important as for some other languages. However, you will want an editor than can at least indent code correctly and can match parentheses.

While writing the book, I used Emacs plus Jeffrey Chu's clojure-mode, available at http://github.com/jochu/clojure-mode. Emacs support for Clojure is quite good, but if you are not already an Emacs user, you might prefer to start with an editor you are familiar with from among these:

Editor	Project Name	Project URL
Eclipse	clojure-dev[2]	http://code.google.com/p/clojure-dev/
Emacs	clojure-mode	http://github.com/jochu/clojure-mode
IntelliJ IDEA	La Clojure	http://plugins.intellij.net/plugin/?id=4050
jEdit	jedit modes	http://github.com/djspiewak/jedit-modes/tree/master/
NetBeans	enclojure	http://enclojure.org
TextMate	clojure-tmbundle	http://github.com/nullstyle/clojure-tmbundle
Vim	Gorilla	http://kotka.de/projects/clojure/gorilla.html
Vim	VimClojure	http://kotka.de/projects/clojure/vimclojure.html

Bill Clementson has written a quick overview that includes setting up Clojure, Emacs support, and debugging with JSwat.[3]

---

1. http://groups.google.com/group/clojure
2. http://code.google.com/p/clojure-dev/
3. http://bc.tech.coop/blog/081023.html

Appendix B

Bibliography

[Goe06]   Brian Goetz. *Java Concurrency in Practice*. Addison-Wesley, Reading, MA, 2006.

[Hof99]   Douglas R. Hofstadter. *Gödel, Escher, Bach: An Eternal Golden Braid*. Basic Books, New York, 20th anniv edition, 1999.

[McC06]   Steve McConnell. *Software Estimation: Demystifying the Black Art*. Microsoft Press, Redmond, WA, 2006.

Index